Family Estrangement

MW00997641

Family estrangement is larger than conflict and more complicated than betrayal. It is entwined in contradictory beliefs, values, behaviours and goals and is the result of at least one member of the family considering reconciliation impossible and/or undesirable. The cessation of familial relations, whether that involves rejection or deciding to leave, can be an inordinately traumatising experience. Whilst data suggests that around 1 in 12 people are estranged from at least one family member this topic is rarely discussed or researched.

Based on the author's in-depth research and exploration of the topic of estrangement, *Family Estrangement: A Matter of Perspective* captures the unique lived experiences of both estrangee and estranger. Offering multiple perspectives drawn from academic and popular literature as well as case studies, the book contextualises its chapters within current theoretical understandings of family relationships and estrangement, including Loss and Grief theories, Attachment Theory and Bowen Family Systems Theory. Practice sections provide estranged readers and professionals with a structured approach to exploring the various aspects of estrangement within a family and to help them identify resilience, strengths and strategies which individuals may harness as they attempt to live with estrangement.

Written with the aim to provide guidance in understanding estrangement in context, this book is suitable for estranged family members and all professionals who encounter and work with people affected by estrangement, including social workers, counsellors, psychologists, allied health professionals, doctors, nurses and legal professions.

Kylie Agllias is a social work researcher, educator and Honorary Conjoint Lecturer at the University of Newcastle, Australia. She is particularly interested in qualitative research that investigates sensitive issues and highlights the lived experience of vulnerable populations.

Family Estrangement

A matter of perspective

Kylie Agllias

Routledge
Taylor & Francis Group

LONDON AND NEW YORK

First published 2017
by Routledge
2 Park Square, Milton Park, Abingdon, Oxon OX14 4RN

and by Routledge
711 Third Avenue, New York, NY 10017

Routledge is an imprint of the Taylor & Francis Group, an informa business

British Library Cataloguing-in-Publication Data
A catalogue record for this book is available from the British Library

Library of Congress Cataloging in Publication Data
Names: Agllias, Kylie, author.
Title: Family estrangement : a matter of perspective / Kylie Agllias.
Description: Milton Park, Abingdon, Oxon ; New York, NY : Routledge, 2016. |
Includes bibliographical references and index.
Identifiers: LCCN 2016003139| ISBN 9781472458582 (hbk) |
ISBN 9781472458612 (pbk) | ISBN 9781315581910 (ebk)
Subjects: LCSH: Families--Psychological aspects. | Interpersonal conflict. |
Alienation (Social psychology)
Classification: LCC HQ697 .A35 2016 | DDC 302.5/44–dc23
LC record available at http://lccn.loc.gov/2016003139

ISBN: 978-1-4724-5858-2 (hbk)
ISBN: 978-1-4724-5861-2 (pbk)
ISBN: 978-1-315-58191-0 (ebk)

Typeset in Sabon and Humanist 777
by Florence Production Ltd, Stoodleigh, Devon, UK

Contents

Figures

Tables

Acknowledgements

I would like to acknowledge the research participants who faithfully and generously contributed their time, knowledge and experience to broadening social understandings about family estrangement. Without their courage, this book would not be possible. I would also like to acknowledge and thank my thoughtful and insightful critical readers: Jill Gibbons, Karen Barrett, Kara Agllias, Leigh Williams and Patricia Williams. I would like to thank Anne Patricia, for her never-ending enthusiasm and confidence in this project. I would like to thank Kara, Paige, Tyson, Nic, David and Xav for the energy and inspiration they bring to my life. Finally, I would like to acknowledge Jim for his encouragement and the space to write this book, as well as the critical conversations and personal insights along the way. Thank you for your enduring love.

About the author

Kylie Agllias (BSW, PhD) is a social work researcher and educator. Employed as a social work lecturer at the University of Newcastle (NSW, Australia) from 2004 until 2014, she currently occupies a conjoint lecturer position at the same institution. Kylie's interest in family estrangement was formalised through her doctoral research (2007–2011), and further developed through two associated studies in 2012 and 2013. She has published widely in the area of family estrangement with a book chapter, encyclopedia entry, blogs for Psychology Today, and a number of articles in journals such as *Affilia*, *Australian Social Work*, *Families in Society* and *Qualitative Health Research*. She has been disseminating information about family estrangement through professional workshops, presentations to interest groups, public lectures and media interviews since 2007. Kylie is particularly interested in qualitative research that investigates sensitive issues and highlights the lived experience of vulnerable populations. She is the author of a number of book chapters and articles in areas such as: feminism and women's issues (including poverty, criminal justice, drugs and alcohol); social work pedagogy and the undergraduate experience; social work in Australasia; unemployment; refugee families; and research methodology.

Chapter 1   **Breaking the silence**

Just that moment – it's like aha, the penny dropped. Up to that point I'd been making decisions that took me further and further away from the family. . . . Decision by decision by decision we just got further and further away.

(Brenda)

Being rejected by family, or deciding to leave, can be one of the most traumatic experiences in a person's life. While many people experience estrangement from family members, this is rarely discussed in the social and policy context or prioritised in family research. Stories of estrangement are increasingly reported in the media, particularly when the estrangement story has a tragic, celebrity or newsworthy element. In the domestic sphere, estrangement self-help groups and forums are rapidly forming online to meet a demand for support that seems unaddressed by human services. However, these sources are not often positioned to represent the multiple perspectives inherent in estrangement. Instead, adult children are maligned for estranging an older parent, or parents shamed for casting out a child, and other relationship types, such as sibling to sibling, are usually overlooked altogether. A balanced perspective about the causes and experiences of estrangement is hard to find. In fact, some people who have joined estrangement forums have reported being vilified for offering a different perspective, as if being *estranged* again by the people purporting to support them.

Family estrangement is larger than 'conflict', more complicated than 'betrayal': it is entwined in perception, conflicting beliefs, values, behaviours and goals. In some cases, estrangement is initiated as a survival mechanism – the estranger believes estrangement is their only chance of moving forward from hurt (and maybe abuse). Regardless, both parties are often left with unfinished business, a pain that originates from a fundamental need for attachment and an ongoing fear that seems to settle close to the heart of self-doubt. Even those people who do not experience a significant or primary grief response to the estrangement are likely to experience associated or secondary psychological and practical losses due to the relationship dissolution. Family estrangement is often shrouded in secrecy and shame, with many hiding their estrangement from others and limiting their social life in the process.

In this spirit, this book does not aim to provide universal answers to the cause, prevention or cure of estrangement, because to do so would be misleading and

1

disrespectful to the experience of each estranged individual and family. It offers multiple perspectives about an historically complex and under-researched phenomenon. It is founded on my eight-year investigation of family estrangement, including the findings from two in-depth qualitative phenomenological research studies with 25 older parents who were estranged from at least one adult child, and 26 adult children who were estranged from at least one parent, as well as a mixed method survey with 27 social workers who had worked with estranged clients towards the end of life. It should be noted that the studies with the older parents and adult children were primarily aimed at investigating the parent and child dynamic. Participants in these two studies referred to 81 estrangements that were current at the time of the first in depth interview (ranging from one month to 43 years in duration). They also discussed 12 estrangements that had been reconciled. However, considerable additional data was also collected and analysed in relation to intergenerational estrangements between siblings, cousins, aunts, uncles, grandparents and grandchildren.

By taking a phenomenological approach to research and the ongoing exploration of estrangement, I have attempted to capture the unique and important perspectives or lived experiences of the estrangee and the estranger without situating one as more honourable than the other. I examine estrangement without judging the parties involved, or their decisions about remaining estranged, or attempting to reconcile: estrangement is a very personal, unique and extremely complex situation to navigate, let alone evaluate from an outsider perspective. While readers might be more interested in chapters pertaining to their own experience or therapeutic work, the remaining chapters can offer additional and useful insights into the development of estrangement and learning to live with it. It is hoped that these chapters bring new perspectives to dominant estrangement narratives.

This book also draws from informal conversations I have had with numerous estranged individuals and families who have provided a wealth of additional insight into their often confusing and distressing experiences. These interactions were initiated by estranged people from around the world who contacted me because they were often desperate to understand the phenomenon they were experiencing and wished to share their story with someone who they thought might listen without judgement or who might be able to shed some light on the situation. I have also gained considerable insight into the estrangement experience from the professionals and community members who have attended my educational workshops, public lectures and conference papers for the past 6 years.

Finally, the book critically reviews knowledge from academic and popular literature to provide *guidance* in understanding estrangement in context. It provides my commentary on the current ideas, theories and research pertaining to family estrangement, giving priority to the voices of those who have first-hand experience through examples and relevant quotations. It examines the contributors to family estrangement, the intergenerational effects of family estrangement, the experience of being estranged and estranging another, thoughts about living well with estrangement, as well as forgiveness and reconciliation. Finally, it attempts to contribute, in some small way, to 'breaking the silence' about family estrangement.

Confidentiality

The voices in this book are particularly important. They bring depth, nuance and lived experience to the theoretical constructs and research findings depicted. These voices belong to 78 research participants who agreed to share their personal or professional stories. Each participant has been allocated a pseudonym to protect their identity, but their words are directly quoted and their stories are fundamental to understanding estrangement.

Who is this book for?

The book is written for individuals and families experiencing family estrangement and the practitioners who work with them, taking into account that a number of practitioners may be experiencing estrangement themselves. Practitioners are defined as all the professional people who encounter and work with people affected by estrangement, from frontline services to longer-term therapeutic work (including counsellors, social workers, family therapists, psychologists, allied health professionals, doctors, nurses and legal professionals). It is important to acknowledge, however, that family or joint therapeutic interventions are not covered in this book, because work in this field could constitute a separate edition. The book is focused on the adult experience of estrangement, but acknowledges estrangements that have developed or been inherited during childhood. Each chapter provides a theoretical and research-based coverage of the particular topic, and there is a section at the end of many chapters where critical questions and exercises are posed. These can be used privately to increase personal and family insight, within the therapeutic context, or to further professional development through critical reflection. There are links to additional resources in the final chapter. The exercises and resources have not been separated into client and practitioner categories. My experience suggests that many individuals and families experiencing estrangement are often highly motivated and prolific readers of a range of estrangement related material, whereas practitioners often need to dip in and out of estrangement literature according to the issues their clients and caseloads present. Therefore the book is designed to be read from cover to cover as well as for directed and specific purposes. It should be noted that the book focuses primarily on the individual experience of family estrangement and practise encounters with the individual.

What about abuse?

Emotional, physical, sexual, financial and online abuse may contribute directly and indirectly to the development and continuation of family estrangement. Like estrangement, abuse is an issue that society often minimises, overlooks and refrains from exploring in any depth. Therefore, it is important to acknowledge this and clarify my position early in this book. I clearly take the position that abuse is not acceptable. I strongly adhere to the belief that estrangement from a perpetrator of abuse is a legitimate and often essential way to promote health and healing for survivors. There are times when reconciliation is *not* appropriate. There are other instances where survivors of abuse find some form of reconciliation or forgiveness important to their health and healing. The very personal decision to estrange or attempt some form of reconciliation is one that should always be respected.

The human race encompasses abusive parents; abusive children; abusive spouses; abusive siblings; abusive cousins, aunts and uncles. There are abusive grandparents, abusive grandchildren and abusive adoptive and step-family members. In some instances abuse is at the core of estrangement; estrangement might be used as an act of abuse, or people might estrange to escape abuse. In other instances abuse from a third party might result in estrangement. For example, a woman in a domestically violent marital relationship might be prevented from seeing her adult children or elderly parents through a range of manipulative and abusive tactics enacted by her spouse. This book fully acknowledges that in some instances, estrangement is caused by one cruel, selfish and abusive person. However, in most cases it is much more complex, where abuse is intricately entwined with family secrets, denials and corrosive practices that undermine relationships throughout the generations, and it is important to consider the effect of abuse beyond the individual and examine intergenerational effects (particularly the potential for future abuse and estrangement).

Defining family

In this book, the concept of *family* incorporates and extends components like kinship and affinity. Based on Bedford and Blieszner's (1997) definition, family members may be biological (or blood relatives) or they may have become a part of the family through adoption, marriage or social designation, and this includes de facto or common law relationships between heterosexual, homosexual and mixed orientation couples. Members may continue to be referred to as *family* after death and irrespective of levels of contact, affective involvement or contact (Bedford & Blieszner, 1997). Family has an ever evolving history including a past, present and future (Floyd *et al.*, 2006).

Defining family estrangement

The term *estrangement* originates from two Latin terms; *extraneare*, which means 'treat as a stranger', and *extraneus*, which means 'not belonging to the family' (Oxford Dictionaries, 2014). Despite an ever increasing assumed knowledge and usage of the terms *estrangement* and *family estrangement*, there does not appear to be a common definition. In the media, blogs and chat rooms, *family estrangement* tends to primarily signify a lack of physical contact. Authors of clinical books and literature tend not to define the term specifically – with the exception of Bowen, as discussed in Chapter 2 – and it is often used alongside and in tandem with phrases and concepts such as 'family rifts', 'family conflict' and 'cutoff'. While self-definition of, and identification with, family estrangement is warranted and important in clinical practice, it makes any discussion of estrangement limited.

To this end, I define family estrangement as: the condition of being physically and or emotionally distanced from one or more family members, either by choice or at the request or decision of the other. It is generally enacted to reduce implicit or explicit conflict, anxiety or tension between the parties. It is characterised by a lack of trust and emotional intimacy, disparate values, and a belief that resolution is highly unlikely, unnecessary or impossible. It involves some level of dissatisfaction by at least one party. However, it is important to note that *dissatisfaction* does not necessarily mean that the dissatisfied party wants to reconcile. Rather dissatisfaction usually relates to unmet relational expectations that elicit some level of negative emotion. Estrangement tends to be an ongoing relational process, rather than a one-off event. There are two primary types of estrangement referred to in this book in order to provide clarity throughout the discussion: (i) *physical estrangement*, and (ii) *emotional estrangement*. Many people experience *cyclical estrangement*, where they move between physical and emotional estrangement.

According to the aforementioned definition of family estrangement, a *distant relationship* differs from an *estranged relationship*. A distant relationship is one where family members might drift apart or stop contact for months, years or decades, but are quite happy to interact if their paths cross (at a family reunion for example). This type of situation is much more likely to occur between more genetically or structurally removed relatives, when families are large and there are a number of relationship partners to choose from, or when circumstances such as migration or imprisonment create barriers to contact and communication. In these situations, it is highly unlikely that family members consider themselves to be estranged. They still regard the other person as *family*: generally, they have not experienced overt or covert conflict and there is no lingering hurt or disagreement. Both parties have similar expectations for the relationship and neither is unduly dissatisfied with the relationship or the other person's behaviour.

Before proceeding to a deeper discussion about the types of family estrangement, it is important to clarify the relationship between family estrangement and parental alienation. Family estrangement is often confused or used interchangeably with the concept of parental alienation that occurs in childhood. *Parental alienation* is often used distinctly from the term *estrangement* in custody and therapeutic contexts as an important way to distinguish between a child's illegitimate or legitimate separation from a parent. For instance, parental alienation is considered to be the child's distancing from a parent due to the intentional alienating acts, tactics and manipulation of the other parent, whereas estrangement is considered to be the distancing from a parent at the instigation of that parent or child. In this book, parental alienation is recognised as *one* of the many instigators of, or contributors to, the broader concept of adult family estrangement. Parental alienation may commence in childhood and continue into adulthood or it might be a factor in the development of family estrangement in adulthood. Research indicates that parental alienation is a genuine phenomenon (Baker, 2006; Baker & Chambers, 2011). Family estrangement research indicates that *alienating tactics* are used – more broadly and outside of a specific diagnosis of parental alienation – in a number of families where family estrangement occurs in adulthood (Agllias, 2015a, 2015b). Parental alienation will be discussed further in Chapter 2, alongside the concept of third party alienation.

Physical estrangement

She just came home one day, walked through the house, took all her clothes, and said 'I won't be back' and went, and I haven't seen her since. She was 15, she'd be in her late 50s [now].

(Virginia)

A *physical estrangement* is evident when physical contact is stopped or dramatically reduced. Exchanges of affection or support are usually non-existent or rejected by one party, although some people report a limited or one-way exchange. In these instances, one party might continue to send birthday cards or gifts despite receiving a limited response or no response at all, or there might be a strictly limited interaction. For example, a daughter might send photos of grandchildren to her estranged mother every 6 months, and the mother might reply with thanks, but no further contact is offered or pursued. Most often gestures of contact and support are rebuffed by the person who initiated the estrangement, and gifts are disposed of or returned. Physical estrangement is often maintained or reinforced by one or both parties deliberately eliminating some or all sources of contact (e.g. changing phone numbers, moving residence, refraining from disclosing information on public Internet forums), or it might result from the inaction associated with long-term physical estrangement (e.g. parties not informing each other when they change address).

Physical estrangement is often instigated by one person during a heated argument or conflict. In these instances, one party usually storms off after making accusations of wrongdoing, declaring that they will never speak again. In other instances, physical estrangement is announced in a letter, email, text or through a third party. Letters and emails often document a list of historic annoyances and complaints against the other person. Phrases like 'you'll never see us again' or 'you're dead to me' are often used. Letters can be particularly important to the sender because they allow them to say things that they often feel too powerless to say in person; however, they can be extremely detrimental to the continuation of the relationship because their physical existence means that the words cannot be forgotten. They can be read, re-read and preserved even after death.

In some instances, physical estrangement might occur without an announcement. One party might simply stop contact after a conflict or event (e.g. a family get-together or parental divorce). The person who estranges offers no explanation for their departure, often assuming or suggesting that the other party 'knows what they've done wrong'. Most people in physical estrangements have experienced emotional estrangement – and maybe cyclical estrangement – before making a decision to cease contact altogether. It should be noted that physical estrangements often appear to result from the smallest or silliest of issues, but in actuality these are mostly 'last straw' events where years or decades of annoyances culminate in what *appears* to be a serious overreaction in the moment.

Emotional estrangement

> *The more it went on, the less they wanted to see of me . . . and I'd say, 'Can we call in?' And we'd call in, and it was sort of okay, you know, sort of – she was pretty cool.*
>
> (Carol)

An *emotional estrangement* is evident when parties have limited, uncomfortable and emotionally absent or strained contact, and where exchanges of support are usually perfunctory or obligatory. So family members will have some contact and they might meet for important events such as birthdays, Christmases and weddings, but these meetings are often described as stressful and strained. People regularly describe significant anticipatory stress leading up to the interaction, searching for excuses to avoid the interaction, and *walking on eggshells* during it. Family members tend to exhibit a false politeness when they do meet – although this might break down into curtness, rudeness or passive-aggressive gestures as the interaction continues – and they will tend to avoid any topics of conversation that might evoke strong emotions or lead to overt disagreement or conflict. It is difficult to tell when an emotional estrangement commences; some people will say it has always existed in their relationship. However, as time passes, people in emotional estrangements tend to lessen contact or place increasingly strict boundaries around compulsory interactions (e.g. emotionally estranged siblings might both attend their cousin's wedding, but one might ask to be seated at a separate table).

Cyclical estrangement

Sometimes I would just think, I just can't be bothered with this, it's just too hard. I would just keep myself to myself, and that might go on for a few months. Then I would feel guilty [and go back]. This last time she really overstepped the mark and that's why I just thought, oh god, I can't be bothered with you.

(Linda)

Estrangement is often cyclical in nature. Cyclical estrangement is evident when the relationship fluctuates between physical estrangement, emotional estrangement and/or periods of reconciliation across a number of cycles (and often decades). (It is important to note that the term *reconciliation* in this book refers to a continuum of relational states from the resumption of contact without acknowledgment of previous conflict or dissatisfaction, to the acknowledgement and resolution of previous issues). In these instances, emotional or physical distance appears to be used to recover from a difficult relationship, to gather strength before re-evaluating the potential value of the relationship and regrouping. Most people in long-term physical estrangements have experienced cycles of estrangement before making a decision to cease contact altogether.

Other types of estrangement

There are five other types of estrangement that are referred to and discussed further in this book: *absent estrangement, mutually disengaged estrangement, inherited estrangement, secondary estrangement* and *self-protective estrangement*. These estrangements are defined by the way they develop, and can take either a physical or emotional form. *Absent estrangements* develop from parental absence in childhood and continue into, or are re-established in the child's adult years. *Mutually disengaged estrangements* occur when relationships tend to disappear over time, when shared experiences are minimal or non-existent. While often dissatisfied with the situation, neither party appears to have the desire to continue the relationship. *Inherited estrangements* are when estrangements are passed from one generation to the next. For example, if a grandfather estranges his daughter, the estrangement is often inherited by – or passed down to – his daughter's children. *Secondary estrangements* develop from a primary estrangement, when a third party takes sides with one of the estranged pair, or they may be drawn or enticed into an estrangement by one of the parties. *Self-protective estrangements* are enacted by an estranged person who tries to protect their privacy or safety from the second party by cutting off a third person (who might pass on information).

7

Defining the parties

There are a number of issues in defining the parties in the estrangement dynamic, particularly in relation to terms that do not pathologise or blame individuals for being estranged from or estranging a family member. However, in order to discuss estrangement with some clarity, different parties need to be named. The following terms have been chosen for ease of reading, and with all due respect.

Estrangee

A person who has been physically or emotionally estranged, disowned, or cut off by a family member or members. An estrangee does not choose the relationship dissolution.

Estranger

A person who chooses to dissolve a family relationship, or emotionally distance themselves from a family member or members. They may declare this position to the other party, stop contact without an announcement or use emotional withdrawal to maintain distance.

Estranged person

A person who has no, or limited, emotional and or physical interactions with one or more family members, regardless of how this developed, and feels in some way dissatisfied with this arrangement. This can be an estrangee or an estranger.

It is important to note that people often switch between being an estrangee and an estranger – in the same relationship and different relationships – across time. People refer to periods when they were the estranger and others where they were the estrangee. They will often discuss conflicting estrangement actions and positions, seemingly unaware of the contradiction. This seems particularly so when estrangees have been separated from a relative for a long period of time, and they make the decision not to attempt reconciliation. While this decision is rarely communicated to the estranger – because the estranger is no longer contactable or receptive to contact – the estrangee might define this decision (or psychological commitment) as 'estranging' the other. They might start telling others that they 'estranged' the other person. For example, one estrangee who had not been contacted by her children for decades announced that she was finally 'estranging them all'. This appeared to mean that she was no longer available to them, should they return.

Estrangement: A rare occurrence?

Many people believe that their estrangement is in some way atypical or rare. However, research shows that family estrangement is a common event across the lifespan, with various measures and typologies suggesting rates of between 4 and 27 per cent in different populations (Silverstein & Bengston, 1997; Szydlik, 2008; Van Gaalen & Dykstra, 2006). A study of Australian palliative care social workers found that they worked with an average of four estranged clients per month (Agllias, 2013a). A recent survey of 2,083 residents in the United Kingdom appears to offer the most accurate current measure of physical family estrangement (IpsosMORI, 2014). In this study, researchers found that 8 per cent of respondents aged over 15 years were physically estranged from at least one family member.

The UK study (IpsosMORI, 2014) showed that estrangement crossed all socio-economic boundaries; gender, age, income, education, employment, parental status and social grade. However, it is highly probable that the survey provides a conservative estimate of the prevalence of family estrangement because it does not account for emotional estrangement, estrangements across the lifetime or homeless people and those living in residential facilities. Finally, the survey does not identify how many people the respondent was estranged from, and estrangement often has flow-on effects, where one estrangement can lead to secondary or associated estrangements. Surprisingly, results concluded that 73 per cent of respondents were *not aware* of an estranged person in their family, friendship group or workplace and 84 per cent of estranged respondents said that they were unaware of others experiencing family estrangement (including their family, friends and colleagues). The results of this survey highlight the commonality of estrangement but they also add weight to findings from other studies that portray estrangement as an often isolating experience, where many people hide, minimise or disguise their estranged status from others (Agllias, 2011, 2013b, 2014; Jerrome, 1994).

Upcoming chapters

Chapter 2: How did we get here?

Estrangement often appears to occur as the result of an insignificant event – an unwanted comment, a missed birthday call or odd look – but in reality it is most likely the result of years and sometimes decades of misunderstandings, secrets, hurt and feelings of betrayal. It is regularly entwined with a number of traumatic events and stressful conditions such as divorce, poverty, mental illness, drug and alcohol use and domestic violence. These complexities are discussed in terms of current theoretical understandings, such as Attachment Theory, family stress pile-up, third party alienation and Bowen Family Systems Theory. A practice section encourages the mapping of intergenerational estrangements and taking an inventory of personal and familial life stressors in order to view estrangement in its broader context.

Chapter 3: Losing a loved one

Being cast aside by one's own family can be a devastating experience which many describe as a traumatic and life-changing event. Research shows that many estranged people have 'little or no idea' why they were cast aside. This chapter explores the initial and longer-term responses to *physical estrangement* for those who do not choose the dissolution of the relationship. It is underpinned by the notion of ambiguous loss and disenfranchised grief. It describes the issues of powerlessness that result from refusal of contact. It examines society's ideal constructions of 'family' and how these pressures can lead to guilt, shame and social withdrawal. It discusses triggers for pain and the notion of 'unfinished business'. Finally, a practice section encourages the use of critical questions to assess the current estrangement status and identify existing resilience, strengths and strategies that might be harnessed as people learn to live with estrangement.

Chapter 4: Deciding to leave family

Deciding to *physically estrange* from a family member is most often a significant and painful decision. Refusing contact is usually only enacted as a last resort, in an attempt to restore health and a sense of self, after a series of distancing or conflictual events. The person who initiates estrangement is often seen as the 'wrongdoer' or 'villian' in the situation, and sometimes viewed as unaffected. However, this chapter explores the experience of choosing estrangement, including loss and grief responses, missing *a family* – and the emotional, physical and financial losses that accrue without family – as well as the longer-term distrust that can manifest in other relationships. It describes the renewed sense of freedom, healing and self-growth many experience and contrasts this with the considerable emotional energy required to maintain the estrangement. Finally, a practice section encourages the use of critical questions to assess the current estrangement status and identify existing resilience, strengths and strategies that might be harnessed as people learn to live with estrangement.

Chapter 5: When there are few shared experiences

This chapter examines estrangements characterised by few shared experiences. This includes instances where family members are still in contact but there are few shared or enjoyable experiences due to *emotional estrangement*. It examines *mutually disengaged estrangement*, where the relationship seems to have simply disappeared. Family members cannot remember who made the last phone call or sent the last email, and no one seems inclined to make the next move. It also examines the *absent estrangement*, where estrangement has developed from parental absence in childhood and has continued into, or been re-established in the child's adulthood. The chapter discusses the potentially complicated losses associated with these types of estrangements, including prolonged feelings of injustice, ambiguity, ambivalence and disenfranchisement. Finally, a practice section encourages the use of critical questions to assess the current estrangement status – including the practices and processes being employed to maintain emotional distancing – and identify existing resilience, strengths and strategies that might be harnessed as people learn to live with estrangement.

Chapter 6: The intergenerational consequences of estrangement

Family estrangement extends beyond two individuals. It often draws a third person, or indeed a whole family, into the fray. This chapter discusses inherited estrangements, secondary estrangements and estrangements that are enacted as a form of self-protection, as well as exploring some theoretical underpinnings of the intergenerational transmission of estrangement. It examines the importance of intergenerational connections and the potential relational losses associated with estrangement, as well as the potentially risky ways that some families attempt to recreate a sense of family and place after estrangement. Finally, a practice section encourages a critical evaluation of the impact of estrangement on the intergenerational family.

Chapter 7: Learning, living, growing

This chapter builds on the notion that estrangement constitutes a significant intra-personal and interpersonal journey. It draws from research that indicates that learning to 'live with estrangement' is based on acceptance of the things that cannot be changed and a realistic evaluation of the estrangement situation. This chapter offers practical suggestions for 'learning, living and growing' despite estrangement or until reconciliation is possible, including recommendations for practitioners. It draws on trauma and resilience understandings about the importance of community and reconnection for healing. Finally, a practice section encourages the evaluation of progress and the development of a personalised estrangement plan for long-term health and wellbeing.

Chapter 8: Forgiveness and reconciliation

This chapter challenges conventional ideas of forgiveness and reconciliation, which are often situated in notions of the perfect family, unconditional love, trust, safety and 'happily ever after'. It suggests that the *normal family* is a site of contention, where love and happiness often entwine with jealousy, misunderstanding, favouritism and injustice. Hence a realistic evaluation of the possibility of reconciliation and readiness for reconciliation is encouraged, and suggestions made for maintaining relationships after reconciliation. A brief discussion on self-reconciliation builds on the concepts introduced in Chapter 5 for people who are unable or unwilling to reconcile. The chapter concludes with a practice section that encourages reflection on readiness for reconciliation and details some key resources for estranged family members and the practitioners who work with them.

Chapter 2   **How did we get here?**

He had sent me a letter to say I was a big disappointment, I embarrassed him at his wedding and my mother was there and my daughter was there, my sister was there and honestly they don't know what he's talking about.

(Trish)

The estrangement experience usually involves significant questioning and rumination, with some people becoming fixated upon finding an answer. Estranged family members regularly ask questions like 'What went wrong?' and 'What *caused* this?' They are likely to mull over a number of personalised hypotheses: 'I reckon divorce has to have something to do with it, but maybe her bipolar made her this way', as well as more universal ones: 'This generation is so dismissive of their parents', or 'The war generation were never emotionally connected to their kids'. In reality, most estranged people *know* that there is no definitive answer to their question, but an answer appears to be the only possible cure to the pain that engulfs them. Sometimes an obsessive occupation with causation serves as a legitimate way for an estranged person to avoid a full engagement with a painful grieving process. However, there is no empirical evidence about the cause or causes of family estrangement. This chapter draws on a limited body of knowledge about, the *likely* and *possible contributors* to, family estrangement, but it is important to recognise that singular explanations are too simplistic to offer the answers to such a complex phenomenon. The chapter draws from available research, including individual studies of specific groups where estrangement has been reported (e.g. homeless men or lesbian women); qualitative studies specifically asking about the development of estrangement; and theories about estrangement. Some of these studies focus on *attributions* for family estrangement, or the ways that estranged individuals explain the development of estrangement. Again, it is important to understand that these studies do not offer clear evidence about the factors that cause estrangement, rather they offer insights into factors that possibly contribute. The chapter concludes with a practice section that encourages the reader or client to begin to situate their estrangement in context, through an examination of the intergenerational family and intergenerational and interpersonal stressors.

Conflict in the intergenerational family

Intergenerational relationships are usually the most significant and enduring bonds that occur across the lifespan. Research shows that modern intergenerational families remain a prime site for reciprocal exchanges of emotional and instrumental support, and family members provide particularly important roles in awkward and emergency situations (Bengston & Oyama, 2007; Dykstra & Fokkema, 2011; Neyer & Lang, 2003). However, there are challenges inherent in long and intimate relationships, and adults are more likely to experience conflict with, and feel ambivalent towards, family members than non-kin (Fingerman et al., 2004). Some theorise that ambivalence – holding negative and positive emotions simultaneously – is more likely to occur in relationships 'of indefinite duration, in relationships based in authority and in situations where relationship partners occupy different positions in the social structure' (Merton & Barber cited in Pillemer & Suitor, 2002, p. 603).

Intergenerational conflicts might also be exacerbated by the emergence of four-generational living families, where family members are required to balance historical family experiences and expectations with socially scripted ideals about family roles and responsibilities, alongside individual and nuclear family needs and goals at any given time. Research suggests that four-generation lineages may offer more contacts and exchanges, but this may not coincide with stronger affectional bonds, and may be related to more family-related stress (Sun & Matthews, 2012). Indeed, conflict and ambivalence appear natural to, and frequent in, intergenerational and interpersonal relationships (Roloff & Waite Miller, 2006; Szydlik, 2008). Generally, research shows that it is mostly undesirable and difficult to terminate and replace family relationships, compared to purely voluntary relationships with friends and acquaintances (Fingerman et al., 2004; Krause & Rook, 2003), and most conflicts are resolved in some way or another. When family conflict occurs, members make decisions about their response, including confronting the person, ignoring the issue, finding indirect methods of resolution, avoiding the person physically or psychologically or ceasing contact altogether. Many intergenerational conflicts may be 'put aside' in order to keep the peace, avoid confrontation, protect feelings and maintain emotional and functional supports (Beaton et al., 2003), but some will contribute to the development of family estrangement. In fact, estrangement often appears to result from months or years of tension and conflict about family issues which members refuse to speak about, deny or merely resign themselves to. Some theorists suggest that estrangement is created across time and throughout the generations (Bowen, 1982; Titelman, 2003b). Conflict and tension might culminate in a single, often minor, and sometimes unrelated incident, resulting in estrangement, or family members might gradually withdraw emotionally from each other.

Estrangement: Complex stressors and perception

An increasing number of studies also suggest that estrangement evolves across time (Agllias, 2008, 2011, 2014; Robinson, 2011; Scharp, 2014). It is a complex socio-politically and historically situated phenomenon that is regularly entwined with intergenerational stressors, such as traumatic events, divorce, poverty, mental illness, drug and alcohol use and domestic violence. It is highly possible that these stressors – and particularly when stressors culminate dramatically in certain periods during the family life cycle – make families vulnerable to estrangement. For example, stressors such as domestic violence or parental ill health often affect the capacity to parent, which can in turn affect attachment or the protection of children from abuse. The ripple effects of such stressors might be felt across generations and they will also intersect with secondary vulnerabilities experienced by individuals in the family system (such as a child who is bullied at school, or a parent who is highly reactive to criticism). In some instances these stressors will culminate in family estrangement. Stressors can be viewed as having a direct or an indirect impact on the development of estrangement.

The effect of stressors can also be viewed through the lens of *perceived relational evaluation*. For example, family functioning is often based on the assumption that members will look after each other's welfare without immediate reward, and the level of emotional intimacy will sustain disagreement and inequity for a much longer period than in non-familial relationships. However, people have limited resources to dedicate to their relationships and this is particularly so in times of excessive stress. During these periods, they may need to make relational evaluations in order to decide which relationships they will invest in and which ones they will disregard (Sprecher, 1992). Relational evaluation is the extent to which a person perceives that a relational partner values them. Generally, a low relational evaluation is the perception that one is less valued by a relational partner than desired or expected (MacDonald *et al.*, 2005). People will make *low relational evaluations* and might avoid or reject relationships when they *perceive* one or more of the following:

1. Danger – that the person might physically or emotionally harm them, or fail to protect them or their loved ones from harm.
2. Low worth – that the person has little to offer or contribute to their goals, lifestyle or wellbeing.
3. Exploitation – that the person might take advantage or take more than they give in return. This is a perception of fairness.
4. Rejection – that the person does not like and accept them, and potentially threatens their desire to belong to the family or group (Leary *et al.*, 2001).

Of course, perception is heightened when a person has had a previous experience of danger, limited support, exploitation or rejection. Interestingly, 'even when one's relational value is positive (and the person is still somewhat accepted), a decline in perceived relational value compared to some previous time – relational devaluation – is typically hurtful and traumatic' (Leary, 2005, p. 41). For example, if a father is attending to lengthy and distressing divorce proceedings, he might have less time for his adolescent son. The son might perceive the father as contributing less than previously or he might perceive his preoccupation as *rejection*. If parentification – where the son is expected to take on adult roles to compensate for the father's absence – occurs during this period, the son might also perceive *exploitation*. The important thing here is *perception*. While the father might be doing everything in his power to maintain a safe and happy home for his son, the son's perception – or relational evaluation – will be core to the likelihood of future estrangement.

Perception is influenced by a number of factors beyond what is happening to the person in the moment, including: past experiences and expectations of the other person; the perceptions, opinions or influences of other parties; patterns of thinking; emotional reactivity; emotional state; motivations; values; and culture. Let's take the example of two adult sisters (Julie and Anne). Anne's adolescent evaluation of Julie as potentially *dangerous and rejecting* developed from an incident when she perceived that her sister did not protect her from bullying at school (a situation also highly charged with, and influenced by, Anne's emotional responses at the time). Despite a primarily collegial relationship in adulthood, this perception and relational evaluation is reactivated and confirmed when Anne hears – from a third party – that Julie has not invited her children to their cousin's birthday event. This event falls a few weeks after the death of Anne's mother-in-law, a woman she has viewed as *a mother*, and at a time when Anne's desire for family closeness and support is particularly heightened. Anne's previous perceptions of family secrecy, and her current values about openness and transparency, are also challenged by this scenario. However, if we look at the other side of this situation, it is highly unlikely that 12-year-old Julie had the power, understanding or capacity to prevent Anne's childhood bullying. Julie might have sound reasons for holding her son's birthday party as a 'school friends only event' (including a notion that she was supporting Anne's grieving by lessening her parental obligations and giving her some space). Regardless of the reality, motivations and intentions behind Julie's actions, Anne's *perception* of these events will inform her immediate response and is likely to influence future perceptions if left unspoken, unchallenged or unexamined.

As the previous section illustrates, the development and eventuality of estrangement is influenced by a number of factors, from the biological to the social, historical and political. As a consequence, a range of theories and research findings are reviewed throughout this chapter, but it is important not to consider these as singular or causal explanations. Rather, they illuminate a 'complex interplay of situational factors' that might initiate and increase the likelihood of developing into the unique and nuanced experience of family estrangement.

Togetherness and differentiation

I've got to nurture people, you know what I mean? So maybe I suffocated her, but she wanted me to.

(Dianne)

Family therapists have regularly suggested that it is important for family members to achieve a balance between togetherness and separateness (related concepts include enmeshment and disengagement) (Barrera *et al.*, 2011; Daniels, 1990; Kabat, 1998; Minuchin, 1974). Balanced relationships will involve emotional mutuality, emotional reciprocity and the accommodation of difference or diversity, which effectively forms a basis for continued psychological growth (Bowen, 1982; Kabat, 1998). However, excessive emotional dependence (togetherness) may threaten a person's ability to separate and function independently, may heighten awareness to any sign of potential rejection, and may make the relationship more susceptible to estrangement, while disengagement (separateness) can contribute to a range of physical and emotional vulnerabilities in the isolated individual, as discussed throughout the following chapters (ibid.).

Dr Murray Bowen (1913–1990) developed the most definitive and well-cited theoretical work relevant to understanding family estrangement, a concept he referred to as *cutoff* or *emotional cutoff* (herein referred to as *cutoff*). His work primarily related to the relationship between parents and adult children, where children used varying degrees of cutoff to manage intense family relationships, but his theories are certainly relevant to other familial relationships. Bowen hypothesised that each person's emotional system – which consists of biologically driven instinctive, automatic responses – is 'governed by the interplay of two counterbalancing "life forces", individuality and togetherness' (Titelman, 2003a, pp. 19–20). The key concept, *differentiation of self*, then, refers to the way in which a person manages these tensions within the relationship system. According to this schema, individuals are placed along a continuum from *fusion* to *differentiation*. The most highly differentiated individual will be capable of separating their emotions from their family members and will respond to anxiety with logical reasoning, autonomous decision-making and adaptability. Conversely, the fused individual is more likely to be highly reactive to anxiety and have less capacity to recognise and self-regulate emotional or instinctive responses. Indicators of fusion include family members:

> (1) acting as if one can read the other's mind; (2) speaking or acting for the other; (3) automatically expressing emotional, social, or physical responses that are reactions to expressed or unexpressed behaviour or feelings of another family member; and (4) adopting or living out, automatically, a family belief, tradition, or lifestyle choice.
>
> (Titelman, 2003a, p. 22)

Bowen (1982) theorised that individuals in the fusion realm would be more susceptible to cutoff, which might take the form of emotional withdrawal and isolation, denying the importance of family, physical distancing or running away. Ultimately, cutoff serves to reduce the anxiety generated by intense familial contact, a concept Bowen referred to as *stuck-together fusion*.

Research also highlights that excessive contact, support and dependence have potentially negative effects on family relationships. For example, parents report more ambivalent feelings about their relationships when their adult children are more dependent, and there are a number of studies showing the development of tension and conflict when parents become more reliant on their adult children due to health deterioration or aging (Fingerman *et al.*, 2006; Ha & Ingersoll-Dayton, 2008; Kaufman & Uhlenberg, 1998; Pillemer *et al.*, 2007). Indeed, any condition that intensifies contact and dependence has the *potential* to undermine familial relationships – for example, working closely in family business. Conversely, research shows that when adult children are more autonomous they are less likely to rely on positive feedback from parents only and more likely to think positively about the parental relationship (Fingerman *et al.*, 2006).

Attachment and parenting

I always worried about Lawrence because I had a dreadful pregnancy with him ... the unhappiness level was extreme while I was pregnant with him. I couldn't bond with him for three or four days, and I couldn't call him by name and I couldn't – breastfeeding was difficult.... Did that impact on Lawrence's little personality? His [estrangement] decision?

(Lois)

Attachment Theory offers another way of examining estrangement between family members or attachment figures. It provides a lens to examine: (i) the conditions potentially leading to the development of estrangement; and (ii) the propensity of people with particular attachment models to estrange when conflict occurs (see also Chapter 5). Original ideas about attachment stemmed from theories of evolution and ethology. Bowlby's work suggests that when attachment figures are not reliably accessible, sensitive and responsive, secondary attachment strategies such as *hyper-activation and protest* or *deactivation and compulsive self-reliance* will be activated (Shaver *et al.*, 2009). Over time, these experiences will contribute to the child's relatively stable expectations or *working models* about self, others and relationships (Miller & Kaiser, 2001), and influence their propensity to estrange.

In the 1970s, Ainsworth and her associates identified three patterns of infant attachment to their primary caregivers – secure, anxious-resistant and avoidant – and these concepts have been further developed since that period (Bretherton, 1995). Basically, children with *avoidant attachment* appeared to lack connection with the caregiver, were unperturbed by strangers, did not appear distressed during separation and rejected or did not acknowledge the caregiver on reunion. Bowlby (1979) suggested conditions contributing to avoidant attachments in infancy through to adolescence included: persistent parental unresponsiveness; discontinuities of parent-ing; threats to withdraw love as a method of disciplining the child; threats to abandon the family as a method of discipline or coercing a spouse; parental threats of suicide, desertion or killing their spouse; telling a child his or her bad behaviour will contribute to the parent's illness or death; requiring the child to become the parent's caregiver; and asking a child to suppress memories of incidents he or she had witnessed.

It is now understood that attachment patterns or models remain open to the influence of new attachment experiences throughout adolescence and adulthood (and there may be a cumulative effect). For example, research confirms that having experienced adverse events, such as divorce, maternal depression, abuse, or death of a parent, is much more common in adolescents who exhibit avoidant and particu-larly anxious attachment patterns, regardless of early maternal sensitivity to the child (Beckwith *et al.*, 1999; Weinfield *et al.*, 2000). 'Parental attachment may be particularly important to children residing in conflictual homes because it communicates to the children that the family will continue to be a source of stability and support to them despite their sense of disrupted family relationships' (Formoso *et al.*, 2000, p. 177).

When people develop an avoidant attachment they may have a greater propensity to estrange in adulthood (Fiori *et al.*, 2009; Shaver *et al.*, 2009). Indeed, recent research showed that many adult children attributed their estrangement from parents to poor parenting practices, long-term disconnection and physical or emotional abandonment (Agllias, 2014, 2015b; Scharp *et al.*, 2014). Factors that they cited as undermining the childhood relationship included: an authoritarian parenting style, where parents were demanding and highly critical; shaming; scapegoating; favouritism; name calling; parentification, where the child was expected to exhibit adult-like behaviour and take on adult-like tasks and responsibilities; and when parental attention and affection was conditional on adherence to the opinions and demands of the parent. Additionally, when parents are physically absent in childhood, for whatever reason, this may have implications for the development, maintenance or reinstigation of estrangement in adulthood (see further discussion in Chapter 5).

A sense of long-term disconnection in childhood has been described as a precursor to estrangement in adulthood (Agllias, 2014). This disconnection may be characterised by a lack of early attachment experiences, a feeling of not 'belonging' to family, and a distinct lack of attention or actual presence by the parent or parents. This disconnection is often experienced as 'being the odd one out' during adolescence and adulthood as well as 'seeing things differently' to one's parents (including values, beliefs and ideas). In adulthood, it may also be described as a lack of parental support, as well as the parent's lack of interest in the adult child's nuclear family. While there are no current studies where parents attribute estrangement from an adult child to their own parenting style or disconnection, older parents in one study suggested that their parenting was possibly compromised, undermined or affected by a number of immediate and historic stressors that might have contributed to their child's feelings of rejection or betrayal (Agllias, 2011). Another study found that parents often referred to their adult children's *perception of being unloved* but provided little detail about the origins of this situation (Carr *et al.*, 2015). It is important to consider this in terms of Coleman's (2008) commentary on estranged parent and child relationships: 'as a therapist I've learned that something that may look trivial from the outside can be suffocating or hurtful to the child who lives inside that family' (p. 39).

Abuse

My step father abused me as a child, and I can't for the life of me work out how [my mother] didn't see that and I really think that that's where it all stemmed from to begin with, just the not getting along with her ... where my family fell apart a bit. Like where my aunty didn't talk to us for years ... because she was friends with him.

(Tracy)

There are situations where the permanent or temporary severing of family ties appears appropriate and necessary to promote healing from abuse. This is particularly so where destructive power imbalances and abuse continue into adulthood or the next generation may be at risk of similar abuse (LeBey, 2001; Sucov, 2006). Adolescents and adults often make conscious decisions to end familial relationships when the topic of current and previous abuse cannot be broached or will not be acknowledged. Adult children have cited abuse as a direct factor in their estrangement from parents – and in some cases other family members – in three recent studies (Agllias, 2014, 2015b; Carr *et al.*, 2015; Scharp *et al.*, 2014). However, abuse was not always perpetrated by the parent or sibling who was ultimately estranged. Rather, abuse was intricately linked to a sense of betrayal. For example, a family member might have estranged someone whom they believed to have minimised, overlooked or colluded in the abuse, failed to protect them from the abuse, or refused to take any responsibility for the abuse. In other instances the estrangement stemmed from a family member's inappropriate response to the disclosure of abuse, such as disbelief, blame or minimisation. This was usually perceived as a direct attack on the survivor's credibility, and viewed as a statement about their value in the family unit. Similarly, estrangement might develop when a family member discloses abuse and some family members side with that person, and others side with the accused.

19

Abuse might be core to the decision to estrange or it can be entwined with other factors that cumulate in estrangement. For example, neglect and abuse (physical, emotional and sexual), are regularly fuelled, maintained or complicated by addiction, poor mental health and family secrets. Research shows that childhood abuse and neglect potentially influence emotion processing in adulthood, which includes 'emotion perception, communication, interpretation, and regulation of emotion' (Cahall Young & Spatz Widom, 2014, p. 1369). The experience of childhood abuse might make some adult relationships more tenuous and vulnerable to emotional or physical estrangement. Additionally, estrangement might constitute an abusive act in itself if it is used deliberately to mistreat and harm another. For example, a parent might throw a young adolescent out of home, or an adult child might use estrangement to punish a grandparent who refuses to support them financially.

Life cycle events

> [My mother] made a choice to put Tammy as guardian, bad mistake in my view because you need someone to be rational ... Tammy wouldn't know how to. She has no idea about mortgages and rent or anything, just free board.
>
> (William)

Estrangement might be triggered during transition periods across the lifecycle, especially where individual needs and expectations are incompatible (Hargrave & Anderson, 1997). Family stress theory suggests that life-cycle changes cause stress in the family system as individuals adjust their roles and positions (Beaton et al., 2003). Critical periods, such as children leaving the nuclear family, marriage, birth, death, retirement and divorce, often alter family equilibrium. For example, striving for individuation and autonomy during adolescence might challenge parental authority. A marriage brings an in-law into the family, and possibly different values and beliefs that need to be accommodated. A marriage is likely to affect degrees of contact, as well as the emotional, practical and possibly financial support available to various members of the intergenerational family, which may or may not be viewed as acceptable. Excitement about a family member's pregnancy might be viewed as a direct betrayal or denial of the pain suffered by a childless or infertile sibling. Latent childhood sibling rivalry might reignite when an older family member needs care, resulting in conflicts about quality of care and end-of-life decision-making (Peisah et al., 2006), or when a family member appears to be taking advantage of an older person. Finally, the death of a family member can create family conflict and estrangement. Inheritance is the final transaction of power, love, loyalty and favour and any unexpected or uneven distribution can result in significant rivalry and feelings of injustice (Sucov, 2006).

Non-normative stressors and unanticipated losses

> I had [cancer]. . . . My poor son [Richard] is trying to have to grow up through teenage years. So I was injecting myself daily – well I started off I got Richard to inject me, which caused him great traumas. I never thought about that, I was just using him as a helper, a pair of hands.
>
> (Helen)

Significant non-normative stressors or unanticipated losses might also contribute to family tension, misunderstandings and perceptions of rejection and conflict. The effects of ill-health, disability and poor mental health, drug and alcohol issues, incarceration, untimely or violent deaths, divorce and domestic violence all have the potential to alter effective communication patterns, as well as perceptions of belonging, worthiness and betrayal in the intergenerational family. For example, the actions of a member involved in criminal activity might pose physical, emotional, financial and value threats to family solidarity to the point where estrangement is imposed to protect the family. Sometimes, a member who is perceived to be responsible for a non-normative event might choose to estrange to reduce familial tension or conflict. Some families might not have the resources or supports to work through significant traumatic events, such as the death of a child, and this can create an array of vulnerabilities and a series of threatening conditions within the remaining family system. Two commonly cited non-normative stressors that people attribute to family estrangement are divorce and domestic violence (Agllias, 2011, 2014, 2015a; Carr et al., 2015).

Divorce

She didn't want contact at all [after the divorce] and she told me that straight out, 'I don't want contact with you. I feel I'm cheating mum.'

(John)

Divorce can pose serious threats to intergenerational contact and communication, with research showing that divorced parents are more likely to become estranged from at least one of their children than their married counterparts (Shapiro, 2003). Children of divorce have a higher risk for depression and they are likely to experience lower levels of family solidarity during mid and later life (Uphold-Carrier & Utz, 2012). However, it is most likely marital discord that has a greater effect on intergenerational relationships than the actual divorce. Marital conflict has been repeatedly shown to disturb functioning of the automatic nervous system and contribute to a number of negative internalising and externalising behaviours in children and adolescents, and effects might even progress into adulthood (El-Shiekh & Erath, 2011; Luecken et al., 2009).

Studies have shown that a number of parents attribute their adult child's estrangement to their own conflictual marriages and difficult divorces (Agllias, 2011; Carr et al., 2015). While custody and visitation orders physically separate children from their parents, it is parental anger and resentment that is most likely to keep children emotionally distanced from one or both parents and lead to estrangement. Bitter divorces often require family members (including children) to make declarations of loyalty to one party or the other, which can lead to estrangement during childhood, adolescence and adulthood. When a choice is made, it is often maintained by the chosen parent's tainted or distorted views of the other party, and a lack of physical contact also prevents the other side of the story from being processed. Additionally, divorce and third party alienation can often lead to secondary and inherited estrangements between grandparents and grandchildren, when one of the divorced pair decides to keep grandchildren from their ex-partner's parents (Kruk, 1995; Sims & Rofail, 2013). (Also see 'Third party alienation, including parental alienation', p. 23). Children are at greater risk of becoming estranged from grandparents – particularly paternal ones – after divorce (see Chapter 6 for further discussion).

Research shows that parental divorce often contributes to children experiencing anger and disappointment, emotions associated with feeling rejected, abandoned or exploited (Bulduc *et al.*, 2007; Cartwright *et al.*, 2009). Non-residential parents are most likely to be viewed as the 'abandoning party' and children might keep them at a distance to avoid further hurt and rejection (Kurdek & Berg, 1987). Additionally, marriage breakdown often leads to a number of stressors for children and young adults that have the potential to undermine their relationship with the residential and non-residential parent (e.g. longer working hours and relocation). Remarriage can also disrupt family routines and introduce different family values and parental expectations, all with the potential to exacerbate young people's feelings of abandonment, rejection or low worth.

Domestic violence

> There was the violence threat ... that if I contacted the kids he would kill one of them. I knew he was capable of doing it because I had already experienced that [violence].
>
> (Joyce)

Domestic violence poses a serious threat to family solidarity, safety and communication. When there is high conflict or domestic violence in a marriage and subsequent divorce, children are more often subjected to divided loyalties, pressured to take sides or to decide which parent has the most to offer. Research about domestic violence reveals a number of negative effects on the victim of violence including affective conditions, such as depression and grief; cognitive changes, such as lowered self-esteem; physiological conditions, such as sleep disorders and increased drug and alcohol use; and behavioural effects, such as difficulties in normal daily functioning (Buchanan, 2008; Spitzberg, 2009). Parents who live in fear often unwittingly transfer these feelings to their children (Buchanan, 2008) and parental expressions of fear are linked to greater feelings of childhood insecurity (Cummings *et al.*, 2002). Many of these effects have the potential to significantly affect the relational aspects of parenting and children might perceive the abused parent as erratic, rejecting or of low worth. The child might determine that the offending parent is the most stable option and the one most able to protect them from danger. Some parents directly attribute their estrangement from an adult child to the deliberate long-term separation tactics used by a violent partner (Agllias, 2011).

Mental illness and addiction

Mental illness and addiction can contribute significantly to a family's stress load, potentially draining physical, emotional and financial resources. Mental illness and addiction have the *potential* to create and exacerbate existing tensions and conflicts between members, to affect attachment, parenting and care between family members. Drugs and alcohol may fuel abuse, betrayal and domestic violence. However, research with estranged family members showed that they rarely attributed estrangement to mental illness or addiction alone (Agllias, 2011, 2014). Rather, mental illness and addiction were often viewed as contributors to the estrangement, or as indicators of broader family issues that ultimately resulted in family estrangement (as indicated throughout the other sections in this chapter). For example, an adult child will often attribute estrangement from their father to parentification and parental absence rather than the gambling or alcohol use that most likely created and exacerbated these phenomena. Carr *et al.*'s (2015) research with people who were either estranged from a parent or adult child showed that 2.6 per cent of parents and 3.4 per cent of adult children attributed this to drug and or alcohol use, while 3.7 per cent of parents and 3.4 per cent of adult children attributed this to mental illness.

A final word about stress pile-up

We lived here and I had a series of pregnancies, miscarriages, premature, still birth – anything that could go wrong went wrong. . . . I had a little girl who survived. . . . My first husband had mental health problems.

(Elizabeth)

Research shows that many families experience multiple stressful events leading up to or around the time of estrangement, and some people directly attribute estrangement to family system *overload* (Agllias, 2011, 2014, 2015a, 2015b). Hill's (1947) original family stress model proposed that all families experience stressors that can be buffered by family resources, social supports, positive family perceptions of the situation and parental self-efficacy (Hill, 1947, 1957). However, when stressors are multiple and there is minimal recovery time, the family system becomes unbalanced and more susceptible to crisis or *stress pile-up* (Galvin *et al.*, 2008). When families are experiencing too many stressors, when stressors are significant and resources are depleted, a minor event can push the family beyond its management threshold. Family members can reach out for solutions to their pain in drugs, alcohol and a variety of unhealthy pursuits. In this state, roles, rules and boundaries are generally abandoned, and all members are at increased risk of negative health, mental health, and social outcomes (Segrin & Flora, 2005). During periods of stress pile-up and crisis 'families often have to deal with fundamental questions of whether people are good or bad, their spiritual beliefs, and how much emotional distance from family members is necessary and desirable' (Segrin & Flora, 2005, p. 210). Losses can reverberate throughout the intergenerational family, and acts of survival can easily be misconceived or historically reconfigured as gestures of betrayal or relational devaluation. Sometimes intergenerational issues are passed from generation to generation, weakening bonds and resulting in repetitions of abandonment and estrangement.

Third party alienation, including parental alienation

We were both living under the one roof. Every morning as I would go to work she would stand on the front veranda [and say]: 'You're a mongrel and a bastard and I hate your guts and so do the kids'.

(Gary)

Some people attribute estrangement to third party alienation, primarily where a family member is recruited or manipulated into an estrangement by another family member or *external party*, such as a romantic partner or family friend (Agllias, 2011, 2015a; Carr *et al.*, 2015). For example, an adult son might cut family ties soon after marrying, or a teenager might move in with his best friend's family and cease contact when his mother becomes engaged to a man he does not like. The third party might also be an ideological influence. For example, a woman might significantly decrease contact with her atheist siblings after joining a fundamentalist church, or a son might estrange after joining a motorcycle gang. In these cases, the remaining or cut off family members will often suggest that the estranger has been unduly influenced by the third party: given tainted information about family dynamics or inducements to estrange. These situations will often involve a clash of values, behaviours and lifestyles. The estranger appears unable to incorporate, integrate or manage the tension between the different parties or lifestyles resulting in a choice between them.

Parental alienation – or the concept that a parent might manipulate their child to choose sides against the other parent – is a controversial concept that has been recognised since the 1940s (Meier, 2009). Gardner (2001) claims that Parental Alienation Syndrome is a subtle but extreme form of child abuse arising:

> primarily in the context of child-custody disputes. Its primary manifestation is the child's campaign of denigration against a good, loving parent, a campaign that has no justification. It results from the combination of a programming (brainwashing) parent's indoctrinations and the child's own contributions to the vilification of the target parent.
>
> (p. 192)

Common tactics of alienating parents include: badmouthing the other parent; interfering with physical, mail, phone or online contact; emotional manipulation such as telling the child that the other parent does not love them or that they are dangerous; and developing an unhealthy alliance to estrange the other parent (Baker & Darnall, 2006). Estrangement studies show that some parents and adult children attribute parental alienation or a cluster of these tactics to the development and maintenance of their estrangement (Agllias, 2015a, 2015b; Carr *et al.*, 2015). Some estranged parents believe that their children are given inaccurate information about them – for example, that they had broken up the marriage, had an affair, had taken all the money, did not want the child anymore or did not pay maintenance. Others suggest that subtle acts of parental alienation occur throughout intact marriages, continue in the child's adulthood, and are often connected to elements of power and control associated with domestic violence and abuse. It is also possible that alienating tactics may contribute to and confirm the child or adolescent's existing perceptions, suspicions or beliefs about family rejection or relational devaluation.

Disparate values

> *He's moving along. . . . We're just not good enough, and when I'm with him I don't feel good enough. I don't feel – I've hit a nail on the head there haven't I? I feel socially inept . . . they're all in the cappuccino set.*
>
> (Trish)

People often attribute estrangement to *betrayal* by a family member or members. Perceptions of betrayal are bound to ideals and expectations about things like goals, obligations and family roles. Ideals and expectations are underpinned by values, and a belief in common values often contributes to a sense of safety within the family unit. However, a secure sense of common family values might also create blind spots and contribute to significant feelings of rejection and betrayal when these values are perceived to be disrespected. Sichel (2004) refers to the *family myth*, which is often based on the 'presumption that every family member is compatible, possesses the same goals, and loves the others without question' (p. 58). This myth is perpetuated by 'we' statements about shared values and behaviours and little tolerance for individual difference. Banishing members who challenge the family myth might be regarded as the only way to keep it intact (Sichel, 2004).

There is a commonly held expectation that when individuals radically challenge the family belief system – in areas such as politics, religion, sexuality, faithfulness and interracial marriage – there will be some degree of family dispute, distancing or corrective action (Sichel, 2004; Sucov, 2006). This is particularly so when families are more rigid, inflexible and heavily invested in their values and beliefs, and especially if the challenge is perceived as a threat to solidarity, identity and survival (Sucov, 2006). There is certainly evidence that some groups of people are more likely to be estranged by family members because some component of their being, behaviour or lifestyle challenges family values, including people who are homosexual, bisexual or transgender (Koken *et al.*, 2009; Pachankis *et al.*, 2008; Watson, 2014), people with HIV/AIDS (Swendeman *et al.*, 2006), and people with a mental health or substance use disorder (Pompili *et al.*, 2004; Winters *et al.*, 2008). Migration might pose threats to family values, as some family members, often younger members, acculturate faster than others (Netedu & Chimilevschi, 2012). So too, a dramatic shift in socio-economic status – often known as upward social mobility – has been shown to contribute to estrangement in some families (Agllias, 2011; Hoerning, 1985; Stewart, 2015). For example, an adult child might attain a professional qualification or marry a wealthy partner, essentially providing life experiences, values and opportunities that are unfamiliar to most other members in the family of origin.

Research shows that family conflict and estrangement is commonly attributed to disparate values, which often become apparent through acts of value betrayal (Agllias, 2011, 2014; Carr *et al.*, 2015; Robinson, 2011). For example, Helen said '*My brother has now been disowned because he is a compulsive gambler and stole from me when he came up. And I said, "that's it, I'm not helping you anymore" . . . because I can't trust him*'. However, acts of value betrayal are regularly less dramatic than the aforementioned one, and more often symbolic in nature. Examples include forgetting a birthday or dressing a grandchild in a $350 outfit when the grandparent is experiencing financial difficulties. It often relates to perceived hypocrisy (such as portraying oneself as a dedicated Christian and charity worker, but committing less than Christian-like acts within the family unit). Intergenerational disputes commonly coalesce around issues such as truth telling, keeping confidences, parenting practices, finances and cleanliness. In some cases, disparate values might be attributed to the mental health or addiction of the estranged person, and particularly resultant behaviours that transgress family or societal values (Agllias, 2011, 2014).

While significant value challenges might contribute to an immediate expulsion from the family, symbolic challenges are unlikely to contribute to a physical estrangement in the short term. Rather, they often contribute to feelings of discomfort, emotional estrangement and a widening gap between family members (with the potential to explode or dissolve into a physical estrangement at a later time). When people fear that any discussion of disparate values might contribute to conflict or a physical estrangement they often avoid these potentially controversial issues. However, individuals are usually alert to behaviours and non-verbal clues signalling that their values, beliefs and behaviours are not acceptable to the family, and they are 'often hurt by occurrences that are even more ephemeral and abstract than spoken words' (Leary *et al.*, 1998, p. 1233). Implied or actual judgement about such differences might be perceived as rejection and experienced as shame.

Unfulfilled expectations

We were expecting to move back and get the support. Michael was working and we had two children at the time with health issues as well and myself with my [illness] out of control and we were hoping for that support and there was no support really there and emotionally there were a lot of let downs.

(Lisa)

Unfulfilled expectations are commonly cited as contributors to estrangement, and they are often underpinned by disparate values (Agllias, 2011, 2014; Carr *et al.*, 2015). When an expectation – even an unrealistic one – is unmet, this is usually experienced as being rejected or defrauded of something one is entitled to, or as an indicator of a declining relationship. Unfulfilled expectations relate to rules and values about equity and fairness. For example, research showed that some parents attributed their estrangement from an adult child to mismatched expectations about the transfer of money or the repayment of loans, where the adult child expected the parent to provide a deposit for a house, or appeared affronted when asked to repay a loan (Agllias, 2011, 2015a). In different research, some adult children attributed their estrangement to unfulfilled expectations of parental support, and particularly emotional support, during periods of hardship (Agllias, 2014, 2015b). Perceptions of favouritism are also common in the intergenerational family. Children often have an expectation of continued and equitable parental availability and affection and are likely to estimate their importance to the parent by comparisons with their brothers and sisters (Kowal *et al.*, 2004). When a child or adult child perceives that a sibling is receiving preferential treatment, their expectation of equality is unfulfilled.

Secrets

[My brother] found this letter, an insurance company, where Dad had written down. . . . some weird name. . . . He had a newborn baby when I was graduating high school. Obviously I flipped my lid and got straight on the phone to him. . . . I said, 'Dad, do you have another family?' 'Yep, so?'

(Laura)

All families have secrets, hidden from the world and one another, that serve to either bond or distance particular members (Smart, 2011). Family secrets may serve to keep a family intact; as long as the secret is kept, the family system will remain stable (Imber-Black, 1998). Secrets can also bridge the gap between a family's private reality and public face (Smart, 2011). For example, concealment of an illegitimate child or a family member's homosexuality might be employed to avoid judgement and stigmatisation. Sometimes secrets are 'known' to all family members, but they are kept from the public sphere and remain unspoken within the family unit. For example, a father's alcoholism may be secreted through the adaption of family interactions that prevent or minimise public scrutiny. Some family secrets are historically derived and their effects may persist across generations. This is especially so if secrets emerge from trauma and oppression. For example, survivors of wartime atrocities or childhood abuse might suppress their experiences to survive trauma in the first instance and later keep the secret in an effort to protect future generations.

When family members are not privy to a secret they often sense that something is amiss and feel anxious, suspicious, doubtful and distant. On the other hand, keeping or living with a secret can increase a family member's power, as well as a sense of obligation to either reveal or keep the secret. Keeping a secret, such as a family member's alcoholism, within the confines of family, can create considerable stress for the individual and the group. When a person does not wish to keep a secret they might feel shame at so doing, exploited by the person requiring their complicity and weighed down by the associated burden. Betrayal is often intricately interwoven with family secrets and lies that, once exposed, contribute to shock, pain, embarrassment and perceptions of rejection and danger. Common secrets kept from children include the whereabouts or existence of a non-custodial parent, the existence of siblings and circumstances around family deaths (e.g. suicides). When children or adult children discover that important information has been withheld from them, it can significantly undermine trust and contribute to relationship breakdown. Withholding information in order to protect children might also contribute to a distorted view of a situation. For example, research showed that some women believed that their decision to protect their children from domestic violence might have inadvertently protected the perpetrator from scrutiny and opened a space for the development of parental alienation (Agllias, 2011). They suggested that their children were manipulated by their abusive partners into believing untruths about their parenting, faithfulness, loyalty and particularly their love for the child.

Ineffective communication patterns

I'm sure I've hurt my mother terribly in her mind. But at the same time ... I'm also emotional and I've been hurt by not having a mother that I could communicate with.

(Mark)

The conditions mentioned in this chapter – including fusion, abuse, stress pile-up and disparate values – are common in families where estrangement does *not* eventuate. Somehow ineffective communication patterns appear to exacerbate vulnerabilities, feelings of hurt and rejection in families who ultimately experience estrangement. As Davis (2002) claims:

Estrangements often start because we lack the communication skills to prevent them: we don't know how to apologise, listen or cool off and talk again tomorrow. Instead a harsh word gets set in stone. Small slights are whipped up into unforgivable injuries. Jealousy festers. Misunderstandings are never discussed or resolved. An ultimatum, made in anger, comes due (p. 14).

In some families, conflict is open, loud and aggressive, leading decisively to estrangement. In others, 'the wounds and the hurts tend to accumulate and grow in an unforgiving or distant family atmosphere; family relationships may suffer a slow, agonising death' (Hargrave & Anderson, 1992, p. 146). Indeed, silence appears to be a strong precursor to the development of estrangement, where hurts are often hidden or discussed with everyone except the person who initiated the hurt, where a lack of open discussion prevents new information being introduced, and where the initiator's silence is often perceived as a lack of contrition.

Survival and personal growth

It came to the point where I realised that [my] health and wellbeing would be better without them unfortunately. . . . I gave it one last effort. I did my utmost and my body started breaking down with the effort.

(Julie)

Research shows that people usually initiate a long-term or final estrangement after cycles of emotional and physical estrangement as well as reconciliation (Agllias, 2014, 2015b; Scharp *et al.*, 2014). Estrangement is usually enacted when the estranger believes that the relationship is immovable and when hurts are irreconcilable. This is generally accompanied by the strong belief that their personal or family health will benefit from the estrangement, or that the only way they can live a healthy and productive life is to cease contact with a destructive family member (see Chapter 4 for further detail).

Punishment

[My daughter-in-law said] I was punishing her by removing my babysitting services and that she would punish me; that I would never see those children again, and I haven't.

(Betty)

A number of people suggest that they have been estranged by a family member as a punishment for perceived wrongdoing (Agllias, 2011, 2014). *Wrongdoing* is often the refusal or inability to give money or support, as indicated by Betty's quote. Estrangement-like behaviours – such as rejection, ostracism and exclusion – are regularly used in social situations in order to highlight, correct and punish bad behaviour: children are sent to the *naughty corner*, lovers give each other the *silent treatment*, and church members are *excommunicated*. 'Ostracism represents one of the strongest, most effective, and efficient punishments available to group members' (Ouwerkerk *et al.*, 2005, p. 328). As a threat, it acts as a mechanism of control to encourage individuals to change their undesirable behaviours and to conform to social norms (Juvonen & Gross, 2005). Some suggest that the preventative or deterrent effect of potential exclusion or rejection is very strong. However, physical distance is often the core mechanism of estrangement, and this serves to punish more than correct behaviour. When 'individuals are cast out through silence they may lack vital information they could use to correct their behaviour, or to cope with their exclusion' (Williams *et al.*, 2005, p. 3). So estrangement can be a tactic used to punish and maintain control over the estranged person.

Inherited and secondary estrangement

Estrangement always has potential implications for inherited or secondary estrangements. Sometimes family members might be estranged from a person with an historically attributed 'problem status', without any knowledge of the person or witness to problem behaviours (Titelman, 2003a). In other words, the estrangement is inherited. In other cases people are drawn into secondary estrangements as they become involved with a primary estrangement or are recruited to take sides (see Chapter 5 for further explanation and discussion).

Socio-historic and political legacy

I certainly didn't marry out of love, I married to have children. In those days you couldn't sort of just do what you do today. So I'm sure I wouldn't have married the man I married.

(Jean)

Estrangement develops and occurs in a socio-historical and political context, a context that colours the way it is defined, understood and experienced. For example, Jerrome (1994) commented on the effect of Western society's promotion of independence, individualism, self-interest and autonomy on the estranged parent and adult child relationships uncovered in her research. She suggested that these values appeared to support a position of non-intervention and prevented parents from speaking about or negotiating notions of interference, challenging behaviours causing hurt, and making requests for help from their adult children (Jerrome, 1994). Parents might also be caught between societal values promoting and rewarding their adult child's achievement and self-interest and their own need for support and affection (ibid.). Different studies have concluded that parents tend to explain their adult child's distance or estrangement in terms of a socially acceptable 'busyness' rather than admitting their own feelings of abandonment or the possibility of family breakdown (Gabriel & Bowling, 2004; Jerrome, 1994; Peters *et al.*, 2006).

LeBey (2001) posited that the promotion of individualism emerging from social movements in the 1960s increased the disposability of relationships, and women in particular were more able to move away from unsatisfactory relationships. As Jerrome (1994) noted, 'the recognition of kin ties [became] a matter of personal discretion and individual choice' (p 250). The potential for estrangement between fathers and their children, and grandparents and their grandchildren, increased as a consequence (LeBey, 2001). However, these ideas should be viewed with caution because there is little evidence to suggest that estrangement is a new phenomenon, or that rates of estrangement have increased as a direct result of increased divorce rates. Additionally, family breakdown is not a recent occurrence. Early parental mortality, and particularly death during childbirth, have contributed to reconfigured family arrangements in the past.

Structural conditions, and particularly structural inequalities, that make some families more prone to stressors such as poverty, and reduce their access to society's commodities such as education, contribute to the likelihood of family estrangement. Power relations – connected to gender, race and class – significantly affect the ways that families are created, as well as the family rules and myths that keep them together and break them apart. For example, gendered ideologies highlighting the importance of the nuclear family, the breadwinner/homemaker model, the family as a private entity, the inevitability of marriage and the naturalness of motherhood persisted throughout the Western world in the 1950s and 1960s. Research with women who were parenting during this period – and were estranged from at least one adult child in 2009 – showed the significant influence of these ideologies on their conduct in romantic relationships, the timing of marriage and their capacity to leave abusive relationships (Agllias, 2011). While none of these women directly attributed estrangement to these factors, they were cognisant of such influences on the quality of their marital relationship, the impacts on their parenting capacity, their capacity to leave a problematic marriage, and the possible undermining of their long term relationships with children who later became estranged.

Conclusion

Estrangement is often portrayed as a communicative error, where a simple misunderstanding is maintained by parties who are too stubborn to *give in* or *play fair*. In other instances, and particularly in media portrayals, estrangement is viewed as the result of one selfish and dysfunctional member. As a consequence, individuals are often tainted by simplistic and stigmatising comments and assumptions about family estrangement. This chapter suggests that family estrangement is too complex to be a communicative error or psychological fault. Rather, it is likely to develop uniquely, from a complex interplay of long-term factors that erode relationships across time and even generations. A number of possible risk factors appear to precede estrangement, including challenges to attachment and differentiation, as well as the build-up of normative and non-normative stressors and losses intricately linked to sociohistorical and political conditions. Disparate values and unfulfilled expectations often create points of tension and conflict, where perceptions and sometimes misperceptions of danger, low worth, exploitation and rejection might be exacerbated by communication difficulties and family secrecy. The particular combination of any number of these issues ultimately culminates in estrangement. The following two chapters examine the experience of being estranged and the experience of initiating estrangement.

PRACTICE POINT 1: SITUATING THE ESTRANGEMENT

Family patterns and stressors

Estrangements often occur during stressful life periods. So it is important to look beyond the immediate relationship dynamic and to explore the broader family context in order to situate the estrangement. This practice point introduces the genogram, and uses exercises to map the dynamics, patterns and stressors evident in the intergenerational family. A sound starting point for assessing intergenerational estrangement is to create a basic genogram or family tree. At this stage, it is important to place individual blame on a temporary hold, and take some time to gain a broader understanding of intergenerational stressors that may have contributed to the primary person's estranged relationship(s), i.e. the reader's or client's estrangement(s). A closer examination of associated and intergenerational estrangements will be conducted progressively throughout the chapters, and more specifically in Chapter 6. (Note: While this chapter offers a basic guide to genograms, Chapter 8 provides further resources on this topic).

EXERCISE 1

Employ commonly used or personally meaningful symbols to document and visualise the intergenerational family and the primary person's estrangement(s). See Figure 2.1 for a list of commonly used symbols and refer to 'Case example (Jane)' for further guidance. The process of developing even the most basic genogram usually uncovers further insights into, and questions about, communication patterns, secrets and stressors within the family system. It can be useful to map these separately where possible or note them for future investigation and reflection (as guided in Chapter 6).

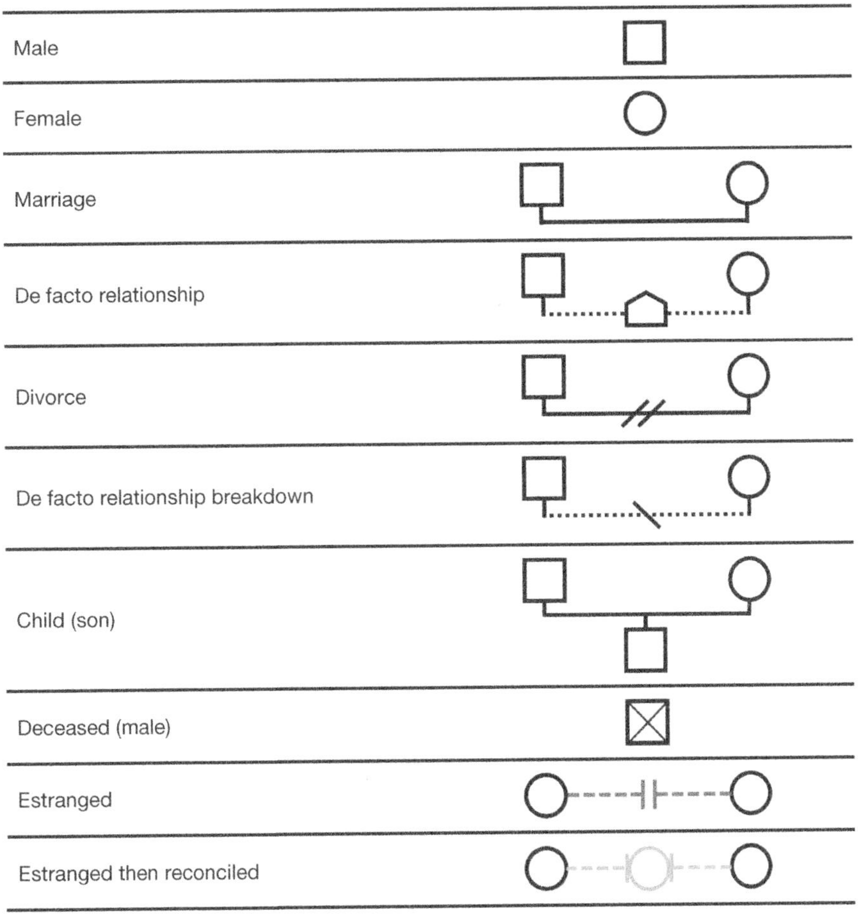

FIGURE 2.1 Commonly used symbols for genograms

Case example (Jane)

The genogram shows that Jane is a single woman. She is the second – or middle child – of three children born to Kat and Bill. Jane has one older brother, Sam, and one younger brother, Terry. Sam is in a de facto relationship with Scott, while Terry is married to Beth and they have one daughter, Ally. Kat and Bill are divorced and have both remarried. Kat's second marriage is to Ray. Bill's second marriage is to Carol and they have two daughters (Pia and Rose). Jane's maternal grandparents are Harold (deceased) and Katherine. Her paternal grandparents are Robert and Shirley (who no longer live together).

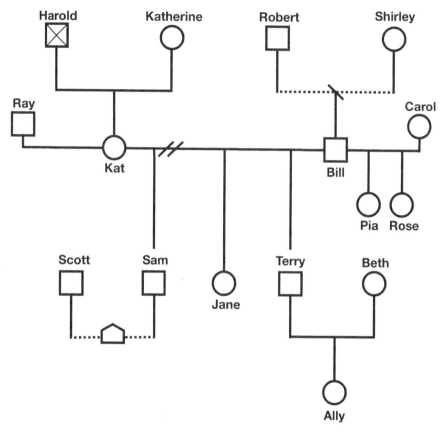

FIGURE 2.2 Example genogram

A genogram of Jane's primary estrangements (see Figure 2.3) shows that she is estranged from her mother and stepfather (Kat and Ray), her grandparents (Katherine and Harold, who is now deceased), and her younger brother and his nuclear family (Terry, wife Beth and daughter Ally). It is easy to view Jane as the common denominator in estrangement in this family; however, a more thorough mapping of relationship status across the generations provides a more accurate picture (see the Practice Point in Chapter 6 for a discussion about, and depiction of, intergenerational conflict and estrangement in Jane's family).

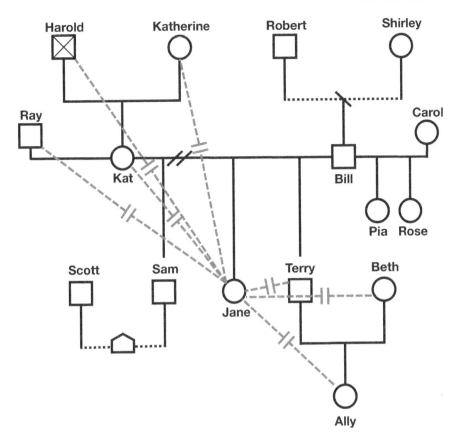

FIGURE 2.3 Jane's estranged relationships

The stress inventory

There are a number of stress, adversity, life-event and strengths inventories available to identify, map and assess individual/family stress loads and coping capacities (and many can be easily found on the Internet). These types of inventories are based on research findings that show that too much stress – and particularly too many stressful events in a short period of time – can place individuals and families at risk for a range of physical, emotional, relational and social difficulties. The following inventories are not diagnostic or predictive. They are a simple way of developing a deeper understanding of estrangement in context.

EXERCISE 2

Refer to the genogram that you drew in Exercise 1 and consider the occurrence of major non-normative events across the last three to four generations. How many times has this family system experienced any of the events in Table 2.1?

TABLE 2.1 Major non-normative events

Divorce		Remarriage	
Infertility		Infidelity	
Major illness		Significant injury	
Disability		Chronic illness	
Mental illness		Addiction (any type)	
Incarceration		Migration	
Domestic violence/assault		Poverty	
Child abuse (sexual, physical, emotional and neglect)		Significant loss of property (e.g. house or business)	
Traumatic death (e.g. car crash, accident, murder)		Untimely death (e.g. before old age and including miscarriage)	
Other		Other	

EXERCISE 3

Consider the estrangement that has been mapped on the genogram in Exercise 1 (or choose one of them) and think about the two years leading up to that relationship dissolution. Reflect on the stressors experienced by each party (using Table 2.2). This exercise can be repeated for additional estrangements.

TABLE 2.2 Stressors prior to estrangement

	Estrangee	Estranger
Death of a family member		
Death of a friend or acquaintance		
Divorce		
Separation from a marital/de facto partner or boyfriend/girlfriend		
Remarriage or re-partnering		
Traumatic death of family member, friend or associate (e.g. accident, murder)		
Untimely or unexpected death of family member, friend or associate (e.g. before old age or miscarriage)		
Major illness		
Significant injury		
Ongoing or new disability		

TABLE 2.2 *continued*

	Estrangee	Estranger
Chronic illness		
Mental illness		
Addiction (e.g. sex, drug, alcohol, gambling)		
Incarceration		
Migration		
Domestic violence/assault		
Disclosure of child abuse (self, family, friend or colleague)		
Poverty		
Significant loss of property (e.g. house or business)		
Loss of employment or significant role change		
Pregnancy		
Infertility (self or partner)		
Infidelity (self or partner)		
Significant or new caring role		
Significant or new concern about a family member or friend's situation (e.g. divorce, illness or mental health)		
Retirement		
Increased arguments/conflict with a family member or friend		
Taking out a moderate/large loan		
Child/ren leaving home		
Leaving home		
Another family member or friend moving into the home		
Change of residence		
Change of job/university		
Partner changing employment/retiring/starting or finishing university		
Changed behaviours or goals (e.g. dieting, stopping smoking)		
Other		

EXERCISE 4

Reflect on findings from the three exercises (and document if this is useful). Consider what stressors might have impacted on relationships in the intergenerational family. What stressors might have influenced specific estrangements? What questions remain and require further investigation and reflection?

Chapter 3   **Losing a loved one**

Nothing can describe the pain that you go through at that particular time. Nothing can describe that. . . . Just one of those things that people have to feel before they have an appreciation of it.

(Yvonne)

Being physically estranged by a loved one can be one of the most shocking and traumatic events a person experiences in their life. In contrast to the inevitability of death – even when untimely and unnatural – people usually do not expect to be estranged by a family member. Indeed, one woman who had experienced her son's traumatic death and her daughter's estrangement shortly afterwards, commented that: 'the pain of your child dying is incredible, but losing a child to estrangement is *unbearable* – it hurts so, so much more'. When a loved one chooses to walk away from a relationship the estrangee is generally faced with unimagined loss and grief. There are no socially sanctioned ways to mourn a loved one who has chosen to estrange, and this can result in isolation for many. Social responses to the loss are often inappropriate and unexpected, ranging from well-meaning advice to simple disregard, exclusion or ridicule. Despite the intense pain, estrangees generally remain drawn to the absent relative, while being pushed and pulled by a range of emotions across time. Emotional responses are often triggered by attachment cues and social reminders, including public holidays, special dates and personal memories. Many are consumed by understanding the estrangement, unsure of the motives and intentions for the dissolution and questioning their own possible contributions to the situation. This chapter discusses physical estrangement from the perspective of the estrangee, and primarily those who are negatively affected by the relationship dissolution. It examines estrangement-related grief through the lens of ambiguous and disenfranchised loss. It critiques society's ideal constructions of 'family' and how these ideas and discourses potentially contribute to guilt, shame and social withdrawal. Finally, a practice section encourages the reader or client to critically assess the current estrangement status and identify existing resilience, strengths and strategies that might be harnessed as they learn to live with estrangement.

The trauma of severance

[My mother] took off when I was probably 21 and nobody had contact with her for some time. . . . I can remember that she went to [another city] to live with this boyfriend . . . but [my sister and I] were almost hysterical in the rejection from her.

(Angela)

The rupture of the attachment bond has the potential to cause significant psychological damage. Most estrangees experience estrangement as a meaningless and traumatic loss. Many liken the realisation of physical estrangement to an assault: 'stabbed in the heart', 'torn apart', 'crushed', and 'buried alive'. Initial emotional responses might include shock, anger, anxiety and helplessness. Protest behaviours, such as crying and attempting to contact the other person, and cognitions, such as disbelief and pre-occupation with the estrangement, often occur. Sichel (2004) suggests that numbness, detachment and depersonalisation often provide emotional anaesthetic in the early stages of estrangement, and 'mastery and competence, ability to delay gratification, and tolerance for frustration' (p. 11) are likely to be negatively affected in the weeks following. Many experience weeks and months of disturbed sleep.

Physical estrangement is a particularly unimaginable and intense loss because of its *unexpectedness* and the fact that it is *intentionally* enacted by a *family member*. Estrangees often report that they were completely blindsided by their family member's decision to estrange and many claim that they are unable to comprehend the precise reason for that decision, even years later (Agllias, 2011, 2014; Carr *et al.*, 2015). Even when a person knows the estranger's reason for estrangement, when the relationship has been highly conflictual or the estrangee has experienced long-term disconnection from the family member, estrangement is rarely anticipated. Few want to entertain the idea that a family member might estrange, regardless of the magnitude of problems between them.

A loss that occurs without forewarning can increase traumatic responses, increase anxiety and feelings of vulnerability. While all losses have the potential to interfere with taken-for-granted assumptions about ourselves and the world (Charles-Edwards, 2007), estrangement has the potential to violate assumptions about the predictability, goodness and trustworthiness of one's own family. It is inconsistent with most people's deep-seated and often unconscious understandings and beliefs about family, including longevity and coherence, interdependence, mutual support, comfort and safety, shared activities and a shared historic narrative. Put simply, being estranged by a loved one *does not make sense*.

Note: It is important to recognise that some estrangees might experience physical estrangement primarily as a relief from the tension and anxiety surrounding the previous relationship. This chapter focuses on estrangees who are primarily dissatisfied with the new relational status, and those who experience emotional reactions to, and negative social consequences from, the estrangement.

A unique enduring loss

[Estrangement is a] stab in the heart which never goes away. It might close, but inside that wound goes deeper ... then there's the bruising that comes out. And I know I retreat like a wild animal back to its den. I have to do that occasionally. That's when it gets really bad.

(Joyce)

Physical estrangement is a unique type of ambiguous loss that is enacted and experienced within a complex family and social system. As the shock-induced anaesthetic begins to wear off and traumatic responses to estrangement lessen, estrangees will need to increase their reconnection with others, and this can create new anxieties, vulnerabilities, unexpected associated losses and triggers for pain. As a result, initial grief responses often become interspersed with, and generally succeeded by, emotions of anger, hurt, sadness, resentment, frustration, disappointment, bitterness and hate; new protest behaviours such as searching for, investigating and looking out for the estranger might become evident or problematic; and cognitions about personal worthiness, the meaning of life (and sometimes the point of living) may arise. The following section examines the conditions that make estrangement such a unique and enduring loss.

An ambiguous loss

I've thought, well probably the next time they'll turn up is when – if they get a message to say something's happened ... [because] either I'm in hospital or Leonard's in hospital.

(Elizabeth)

Successful or healthy grieving involves the reorganisation or reorientation of one's world without the absent person, but the nature of estrangement often interferes with this trajectory. Physical estrangement can be described as psychosocial death, where the estranged person is still alive, but their personality, essence and presence has gone (Doka & Aber, 2002). The estranger is physically absent but remains psychologically present due to the attachment bond and the family members' shared histories. The loss is ambiguous because the estrangee is caught between two opposing ideas simultaneously: the estranger might or might not return (Boss, 2006a). Research with older parents showed that many believed that their estranged adult child would return if they become seriously or terminally ill (Agllias, 2011). Additionally, estrangers might be sighted in the street or at family functions such as weddings and funerals, but remain incommunicative and *untouchable* to the estranged relative. Such ambiguity might prevent the estrangee from seeking support, taking on new roles or activities and adjusting to a new life without their loved one. Lack of clarity about the estranger's future intentions often stimulates hope for reconciliation, but it can also prevent people from fully acknowledging or grieving their loss: 'Without an overt death in the first case, it seems premature and even cruel to grieve in socially sanctioned ways; in the second, to begin to grieve would remove the hope of return of the lost one to the social milieu' (Walter & McCoyd, 2009, p. 20). Additionally, in Western society, the act of grieving tends to signal finality, and there are no social sanctioned rituals to acknowledge family estrangement. People often remain stranded between the hope they feel and the grief they need to experience in order to recreate a different life. It is important to understand that the experience of this type of grief is due to the external context or circumstances, not individual pathology.

Symbolic representations of family

> *I always wanted to be a good mother. I thought that not being a good mother was the worst thing that could happen, but not to be a mother is the worst thing ever.*

> (Dianne)

Our concept of *family,* and our *place* in relation to family, is closely aligned with our sense of self and safety in the world. Different types of relationships create different responses to rejection: people hold representations or mind associations of particular relationships and the roles they associate with them (Weiss, 2001). When people are estranged from a family member they might also lose identification with roles that hold considerable symbolic meaning, such as being a parent, sibling or child. For example, a parent might associate sound *parenting* with lifelong protection of, and support to, a child. Estrangees' responses might be closely associated with the obstruction of this role, as well as the actual loss of contact.

People also evaluate their own success in interpersonal relationships against these representations and socially accepted standards of familial behaviour, which might contribute to increased loss and grief responses in certain groups. For example, in one study, female estrangees who had married and had children in a period of considerable social conformity – where marriage was highly desirable and motherhood idealised – suggested that their adult child's decision to estrange them contributed to a generalised anxiety about their adequacy as mothers and guilt about their failure to preserve such an important relationship (Agllias, 2011). Women whose identities were aligned to motherhood primarily were more likely to report that estrangement impacted on their sense of self-identity and social connection than those whose identities were aligned with motherhood and career.

The power of silence

> *[The estranger has] complete control of you . . . that's annoying and maddening and saddening.*

> (Lois)

Physical estrangements are created and sustained by silence. While silence might initially provide relief from conflict, it rarely signals a truce. Over time, estrangees often interpret silence as an underhanded and dangerous weapon: 'silence speaks though it says nothing, grows though it has no substance, hurts though it can touch nothing, and conceals though it cannot hide from perception' (O'Grady & Meinecke, 2015, p. 1). Estrangement is an effective silencer, preventing one party from giving their perspective, and blocking their capacity to apologise or make things right. The estranger appears to have control over the flow of information and the power to prevent, reject or minimise input from the other party (including cards and presents, meetings or phone conversations). Over time, absence has the potential to create stronger barriers, where silence withholds information about the estranger's whereabouts, health and wellbeing. Thomas Carlyle (1997) suggests that it is impossible: 'to forget something you know, and to ignore silence without saying something' (in O'Grady & Meinecke, 2015, p. 4). This seems highly relevant to estrangement where *continuing bonds* render the estranger unforgettable. Their voice – and often their final words – remain present in the psyche, and the estrangee's imagination may fill in the gaps. However, the person who has been estranged is denied a reply, effectively rendering them susceptible to feelings of frustration, futility and powerlessness. Additionally, feelings of powerlessness were identified more strongly when there was a perceived third party influencing the estrangement in Robinson's (2011) study.

Some estrangees are also silenced by fear and hurt. The following quote shows how silence has contributed to an enduring estrangement through a lack of information and fear of further rejection:

I have been wanting to see who to get in touch with to start – make some enquiries as to where could I find out her address. But I have – don't know quite where to start, and I haven't quite got the courage to face it, if she didn't want to see me.

(Joyce)

Some are fearful of attempting contact in case they hear something too difficult to defend or too distressing to address. Others fear that their hurt or the issues that led up to the estrangement will not be fully acknowledged by the estranger and they will continue to be blamed for the relationship breakdown. Sometimes the hurt is so raw that the estrangee perceives silence as their only remaining protection.

An emotional tug of war

Mother's Day and once again I had hoped for that one phone call, but it didn't happen, so I have finally had to accept the 'fact' that Brett has no feelings towards me. Heartbroken of course, as I thought after my visit to his home with all the family he had decided to 'bury the hatchet' but obviously that's not the case. . . . All it did for me was to give me renewed hope that we could all be family once again. How cruel is that.

(Jean – diary entry)

People who have been physically estranged by a loved one often describe the experience as an emotional tug of war, where a range of factors contribute to fluctuating emotions which potentially slow or prevent closure (Agllias, 2011). The interplay of the attachment bond and social reminders appear to create painful reminders of the missing person, whilst keeping the estrangee emotionally drawn or *pulled towards* them. In the early stages of estrangement they might *reach out* to the estranger in an attempt to provoke some sort of response, to break the silence and start a dialogue towards reconciliation. Over time – and even when reconciliation seems remote – unexpected events might rekindle hope and the desire for contact. While these events often act as an emotional pull towards the estranger, they can also make estrangees highly susceptible to further rejection and loss experiences.

41

Reaching out

> *I've persevered, I've sent birthday and Christmas presents every year. I always make sure the cards have 'granddaughter, grandson' on them, to try to keep me in their mind; but they wouldn't know me.*
>
> (Betty)

Many people continue to reach out to the estranger, and their family, for years or decades, often sending cards, presents and invitations to mark special occasions, such as birthdays and Christmases. These gestures are generally offered as a symbol of goodwill and care. In other instances these offerings serve to reduce personal feelings of guilt, or to prevent accusations of neglect or feelings of bad will that are anticipated from the estranger (should they reunify at some point in the future). Estranged people often choose these items with much more care than they would for non-estranged family members. Some choose items unique to the relationship such as cards marked 'sister', or of particular significance to the estranger. Some choose gifts to say something memorable about the gift giver.

Sometimes estrangees continue to send texts, emails and even make phone calls in the hope of receiving a positive response. Messages often act as an olive branch in the initial stages of the estrangement, but as time progresses the tone of invitations often becomes more tentative as the following quote illustrates: '*I just think I will give her a little time and maybe I'll send off another timid little note or something or make an overture*' (Debra). Estrangees often mull over the timing and content of the messages and the anticipated reactions of the estranger for extended periods before taking such an action.

Pulled towards

> *Dear Lawrence, ... My worst time is your birthday.... This year I sent SMS messages to your [siblings] to share the importance of the day with them. I usually spend the day quiet and withdrawn, trying to connect with you in some way.*
>
> (Lois – diary entry)

There are a number of events and processes that pull the estrangee towards the estranger and reinvigorate feelings of hope and loss. The loss experience is determined, in part, by the extent of emotional dependency on the other party (Shaver & Tancredy, 2001). The duration and intensity of family relationships creates many more memories, social connections and memorabilia than a social relationship, and family photos and gatherings are constant reminders of the estranger. Birthdays, Christmases and Mothers and Fathers Days can be extremely difficult days due to the memories they invoke, the absence they highlight, and the anticipatory loss they often create.

Most people will experience some contact with the estranger after the physical estrangement: at a family occasion, such as a wedding or funeral; walking past each other in the local supermarket; or receiving a letter or text message. Unexpected contact has significant potential to unleash a plethora of emotions and previously experienced traumatic symptoms. Upcoming family events can be experienced as considerably stressful as the estrangee tries to anticipate and balance their hopes and fears about the possible encounter. This anticipation can become all-consuming leading up to the event, with the estranged person pondering or second guessing the likelihood of the estranger's actual attendance, the estranger's possible behaviour at the event, and rehearsing how they themselves might react to various scenarios.

A number of estranged people remain vigilant in their effort to 'look out' for the estranger. In the early stages, this might involve going to places where the other person might visit, in the hope of seeing them. In later stages, people often remain alert to accidental meetings with the estranger, particularly if they are going into suburbs or shopping centres close to their residence or workplace, or places they believe they might encounter or sight the estranger. Vigilance and unexpected cues might trigger unconscious attachment responses (including a range of bodily sensations and grief-related emotions). Technology, and particularly social media, has increasingly allowed estrangees to 'look out' for the estranger more easily than in the past. Internet *insights* play a significant part in some people's ongoing attachment to, and knowledge of, the missing family member.

In some instances, the estranger initiates contact. They might need information or some form of help. Recent research showed that some older estrangees suspected that their estranged adult child invited them to important events such as christenings and weddings to keep extended family happy or to keep up appearances with in-laws (Agllias, 2011). Estrangers might make contact when they are intoxicated or fuelled by anger and resentment, and in these instances contact is primarily aimed at accusations, revenge and retribution, or it may be an attempt to attain some sort of closure. Sometimes a meeting might be initiated and some indication made that the estranger wants to test the viability of some form of reconnection. In the case of estrangements occurring in childhood, an adolescent or adult child might reach out to fulfil a curiosity about their estranged parent. Regardless of the type of and reason for contact, and the outcome of such, the estrangee is drawn back into a range of often contradictory emotions and cognitions.

Estrangees often maintain a genuine emotional connection to and concern for the other party despite the pain the estrangement has inflicted. Many empathise with the estranger's situation and worry about the effects of the estrangement on his or her health/mental health, levels of emotional and practical support, and the quality of other family relationships. For example:

> I feel sorry for [my estranged daughter]. I feel like it must be lonely being this tough girl out there in a tough world. I thought, it is a bit sad to be so isolated, without family. . . . She's painted herself into a terrible corner really and you feel sorry. I would like to just give her a couple of hundred dollars for Christmas or something and I couldn't even do that.
>
> (Debra)

When third party influence is suspected as the primary contributor to physical estrangement people often oscillate between feeling disappointed at the estranger's perceived weakness, having empathy for their predicament and fears for their emotional safety.

Particular life stage events might draw the estrangee towards the other person. For example, the birth of a child might evoke memories of the estranger and become a salient reminder of the vacant family role the dissolution has created (e.g. the estranger might be the child's absent grandfather or aunt). Illness and reminders of mortality highlight one's limited time to resolve or make sense of estrangement. These events can create a particular pull, where the estrangee often thinks about one party dying without reconciliation or any form of resolution. They might engage in a type of anticipatory grieving, thinking about their own death without reconciliation, and how the estranger might continue without them. Considering legal decisions such as guardianship, and especially drawing up a legal will and testament, can be a particularly difficult time, where the estrangee needs to make decisions about their legacy and how this relates to and might possibly affect the estranger (and even the other potential beneficiaries). Research showed that many older people, estranged from their children spent considerable time worrying about their legacy, ruminating over the reduction or maintenance of the estranger's share and compiling letters and sometimes decades of legacy items – such as birthday and Christmas presents for the child and grandchildren – to be distributed after death (Agllias, 2011).

Pushed away

[Jennifer] hasn't spoken to us for many years. My mum died last year. She turned up at the funeral. But she never spoke to me.

(Frances)

Unfortunately, when estrangees reach out they are often rejected; cards and presents are returned or discarded; messages are ignored or rebuffed. Many of the hopes – stimulated by upcoming or actual events, processes and life stages – are short lived or dashed in some way. Meetings might highlight the distance between the parties, the brittleness of the relationship or the power of the estranger to reinstate the estrangement status. For example, one estrangee commented on a meeting with his adult daughter (whom he had not seen since a bitter divorce):

It had gone pretty right, a three-hour discussion. I think it's safe to call it a three-hour discussion, had gone okay. It had gone quite okay and she said, 'Look, I don't want you to contact me. If we're going to see each other again it will on my terms'.

(Gary)

In other instances, meetings might deteriorate into explicit conflict and further anger, insults, accusations and even violence. Sighting a loved one without their acknowledgement can be an intensely hollow experience that reinforces the powerlessness of the estrangee. Estranged people with serious illnesses or nearing death can be shocked to find out that the estranger has chosen not to return to make things right. Regardless of its nature or circumstance, further rejection has the potential to stimulate fresh and intense loss and grief responses, sometimes as powerful as the first. Any progress that has been made towards grieving and establishing a new life can be undone or reversed quite quickly in these circumstances.

A relational experience

It sounds so stupid but I wanted the facade to continue so [my estranged dad would be] at my wedding so I don't have to have a half arsed wedding. I know my mum should be enough because she did everything for me, but it's just so unfair . . . because no one knows [about the estrangement], what am I going to say? He didn't turn up? Like, my godparents and everyone, like no one knows.

(Laura)

Loss and grief is a process that occurs in a social and relational context. In the case of physical estrangement, it is a loss that is rarely recognised or understood by immediate family, let alone broader society. It is rarely spoken about in public, or formalised in family policy. Rather, society's vehement endorsement of the mythological and symbolic concepts of family, such as 'family unity', 'blood is thicker than water' and 'the home is where the heart is', often disguise, minimise and malign estrangement, effectively forming a rationale for social disenfranchisement. This disenfranchisement can have significant impacts on estranged people, who often perceive their situation – and themselves – as stigmatised as a result. It tends to reinforce a 'social silence', where estrangees are often reluctant to disclose their loss, potentially modifying and limiting their social experiences and even internalising stigmatised notions of self.

Stigmatised social interactions

For women who are estranged from their children there is something wrong with the woman and that's, I think, in everyone that I've talked to, is how people treat us. . . . You can nearly draw a circle around as to how far people get in touch with you and there's that line out there, they don't cross it because there's something wrong with us.

(Joyce)

Societies have ideologies and norms that shape, influence and govern how people feel, express and think about loss and grief (Doka, 2002). These ideas are widely recognised through social responses and mores and formalised in certain situations, such as one's entitlement to bereavement leave (ibid.). There are situations, however, where a person experiences loss but their grief 'is not openly acknowledged, socially validated or publicly observed' (ibid., p. 5), and in some cases it might be explicitly renounced or the person rejected. This is called *disenfranchised grief* and it occurs when the relationship between the person and the bereaved is not recognised; the loss is not recognised; the griever is not recognised; the circumstances surrounding the loss cause embarrassment, shame or stigma; or the person expresses their grief in ways not sanctioned by society (Walter & McCoyd, 2009). In Western society, the estrangement loss and the people who experience it are often unrecognised, and there is considerable stigma associated with the breakdown of biological relationships.

Clearly physical estrangement violates societal ideals about family togetherness and unity. The relationships and bonds between family members are portrayed as foundational and unbreakable, and family role divisions are often depicted as essential and universal (Connidis & Walker, 2009). Once aspects of family are regarded as *essential*, people are less likely to view them critically, and variances, such as estrange-ment, are more likely to be perceived as threats to traditional family life (ibid.). In its most fundamental form, estrangement might also be viewed as a threat to the human socialisation and survival process. It is a breakdown of the attachment bond protecting children in early life, older people in later life and the weak and ill throughout their lives. Once internalised, these ideological norms constitute a *stigmatised consciousness* which is suspicious and intolerant of family estrangement (Link & Phelan, 2001).

Goffman (1963) suggested that *stigma* was when a person possessed an attribute (such as a disfigurement or being estranged) that was deeply discredited by society, thus making the person 'not quite human'. Stigmatisation is a process of selectively labelling human differences, linking particular labels to negative stereotypes, placing labelled persons in a category with the purpose of separating them from those without the label, and exerting social, economic, and political power to create status loss, group discrimination and social exclusion (Link & Phelan, 2001; Major & Eccleston, 2005). People often disenfranchise or stigmatise others to feel better about themselves or to alleviate their own discomfort and anxiety (Major & Eccleston, 2005). Estrangement might remind the non-estranged of their mortality and vulnerability to a similar fate. A contagion mentality, where people subconsciously suspect that estrangement might be spread from one family to the other, might fuel avoidance and rejection of the estranged person.

Research showed that the stigma associated with estrangement positioned estrangees precariously for additional rejection in the familial and social sphere (Agllias, 2011, 2013b, 2014). Estrangees in these studies spoke of being embarrassed and marginalised in social situations and being judged or labelled as a dysfunctional family in professional interactions with doctors and hospital staff. Many believed that others would not be able to understand the notion of estrangement, might judge their capacity to maintain a relationship and possibly make unfavourable judgements about the actions of the estranger. When people experience perceived or actual stigmatisation and when they fear social disapproval or rejection, they are most likely to keep aspects of their identity secret (Major & Eccleston, 2005). Physical estrangement is concealable in many instances, so people are able to maintain their desirability as a relational partner by keeping the estrangement a secret. This requires that estrangees remain vigilant in social situations, where they redirect risky conversations, avoid questions, minimise the information they provide to new contacts or lie about their estrangement status. However, most people prefer to be honest about their lives and true identity and concealment can deprive them of feelings of integrity. According to Goffman (cited in Major & Eccleston, 2005), hidden or concealable stigma made one discreditable:

> Individuals who conceal or disguise a stigma may not only suffer from fear that their stigma will be discovered, but may also fear social disapproval for having tried to conceal it. This may lead to anxiety in social situations with the nonstigmatized.
>
> (ibid., p. 74)

Being able to disclose estrangement to someone who is trusting can be a very useful support and outlet for estrangees, but many feel wary of disclosing to someone who they fear might be subsequently dismissive, belittling or unsupportive. Concealment might actually prevent closeness from developing in potential relationships. The anticipation of a difficult question or awkward situation where estrangement might be revealed seems unfavourable to this end. Hiding estrangement, or making decisions about who to disclose to, potentially limits the number of social interactions estrangees choose to engage in, and this might be more so for some groups of people. For example, qualitative studies showed that older mothers reported more concerns about disclosing their estrangement from an adult child in social situations than older fathers (estranged from an adult child) and younger adults (estranged from a parent) (Agllias, 2011, 2013b, 2014). This might be due to the social expectations in such situations, where mothers are required to give more details about, and maybe even produce photos of, their adult children and grandchildren. Men may not be required to provide such details and conversations might be less family oriented. Adults who have been estranged by a parent or sibling might not be asked to disclose detailed information about such familial connections. Finally, when social situations are too distressing, some estrangees resort to alternative sources of inclusion, such as changing churches or moving locations to start afresh.

Relationships with family and friends

[My nephew] said to me one day when I was at a family function, 'What's wrong with [my estranged son], why doesn't he come to any of these things, what, is he ... [too good for us]?' ... And he said, 'Do you want me to go down and knock his fucking head off?'

(Carol)

Not surprisingly, members of one's intergenerational family and friendship group are also influenced by ideological expectations of family unity; however, disenfranchisement and stigmatisation by one's friends or non-estranged family members can be particularly distressing. Judgements about the cause of the estrangement and comments that infer some form of culpability can diminish the estrangee's trust and engagement with friends and family. Judgements and accusation about the estranger can be fraught with mixed feelings, but often the estrangee feels an overwhelming desire to protect the estranger's reputation. Additionally, competition and rivalry between friends and family are often activated when estrangement occurs, resulting in comparisons and putdowns about the person or family experiencing the estrangement. Unfortunately in some cases, this relational superiority seems to elicit unwanted advice and commentary about the estrangement, the estranger or the relationship. In some instances, well-meaning advice is uninformed or simplistic. A number of estranged people report that the depth of their loss is misunderstood by family and friends, who advise them to 'forget about' the estranger or 'move on' (Agllias, 2011).

Silence often settles on a family after estrangement in order to cover the tensions and in some way stabilise the relationships between existing members. The estrangee might feel responsible for the impact on other family members and any resultant secondary estrangements. They will often take on a protective role as a result. This might involve refraining from disclosing the degree of their own pain and minimising any reference to the estrangement for fear of upsetting or involving others (see Chapter 6). This can be highly problematic in terms of grieving within the family system. It can lead to even further discord when one of the estranged parties wishes to speak about the matter but others want to avoid any mention of the topic. The estrangee might also feel a need to hold on tightly to non-estranged relationships for fear of losing them too, which can exert significant pressure on family members to attend to their increased desire for closeness.

Additionally, the uncertainty about the state of the relationship might lead to role ambiguity, where friends and family are unsure about who is 'in' or 'out' of the family system, and what roles should be assumed or left unattended. They might not wish to offend the estrangee by assuming a role or duty previously carried out by the estranger or by acknowledging their absence. Friends and family are often 'perplexed about whether to express sympathy or maintain a solid sense of normalcy and/or hope' (Walter & McCoyd, 2009, p. 20). For example, Elizabeth stated:

> [My relative] sends a card to me . . . that says for Bill and family and she doesn't seem to get the message that we don't see Bill and the family. We said to her, 'We don't see them, you know, he doesn't want to know us anymore,' but she still sends the card.

In this instance, Elizabeth is annoyed by this action because she feels her loss has not been acknowledged or heard, and the card acts as an annual reminder of her son and grandchildren's absence. However, it is doubtful that the relative means to cause distress and it is more likely her lack of understanding and certainty, as well as the absence of rules for this type of situation, result in the maintenance of her usual festive practices.

Internalised guilt and shame

> I often think, who would want to be with you when your own child doesn't want you?

> (Dianne)

It is important to understand that generally the death of a family member does not impact on self-esteem or sense of self-worth the way that estrangement does. Estrangees subscribe to the standards of wider society that have been inculcated through socialisation across the lifetime. This can make them highly alert to the perceptions of others about their possible failings. Hence, shame and embarrassment are often central internalised aspects of estrangement. Interestingly, one study of parents who had been estranged by their adult children illuminated not only the internalised stigma they experienced, but their often stigmatising judgemental beliefs about other parents in the same situation (Agllias, 2011). Some related narratives about accidentally meeting another estrangee and their surprise at the *normality* of his or her behaviour. While these discoveries made the participants feel less alone, it did not necessarily mean that they were willing or able to engage in conversation about their own estrangement. Others made judgemental remarks about parents who had been estranged by more than one or two children, often suggesting that this indicated higher culpability or some form of parental deficiency.

According to Goffman's (1963) schema, estrangement might be seen as a 'stigma of character', a blemish closely associated with social expectations about family. Remennick (2000) said:

Stigma as a psychological state is only possible when its carriers adopt the mainstream social definitions of the norm; this is especially true about hidden conditions. In other words, stigma is a psychological corollary of conformity. The more a woman identifies with the universal expectation of motherhood, the deeper her perception of stigma in case she cannot meet this norm.

(p. 823)

So the more people conform to social ideologies about family and particular family roles, the more susceptible they will be to internalised shame, embarrassment and guilt about the estrangement. Additionally, social disenfranchisement and isolation creates a situation where people are more likely to have reduced self-esteem, internalise the shame and not view the stigma as an external imposition. They are prevented from sharing their stigmatised experience and from gaining an alternative narrative about family estrangement (Goffman, 1963). Finally the fear of further stigma might prevent some people from seeking further information about estrangement from books, groups, or websites.

Estrangement impacts on daily living

You can't really get over it, but I try not to let myself get really emotional about it anymore. Every now and then I do, but I try very hard not to.

(Beth)

When a loved one decides to estrange, it activates a set of biological responses and social consequences that potentially cumulate in some degree of generalised anxiety and vulnerability in the person who has been left behind. Physical estrangement has the potential to interact with existing stressors and vulnerabilities, to open old wounds, to reduce sources of emotional and physical support, and to stimulate behaviours that the estrangee would never have imagined. While some people adapt more quickly, and with fewer negative symptoms, the estrangement loss and its associated stressors can sneak up gradually or pounce unexpectedly across time. This section in no way suggests that all estrangees will experience the following impacts on daily living or that they will experience them in the same way. Rather it examines the vulnerabilities and risks that estrangement creates and exposes, as well as their potential to affect the estrangee's ongoing health and wellbeing. While there is minimal estrangement-specific research about the impacts of estrangement on health and wellbeing, there is sufficient transferrable evidence to indicate the potential for an array of possible negative outcomes.

Rejection, emotional reactivity, stress and anxiety

Well [my wife] says that she thinks that it's affecting my health. She thinks that I'm not a happy person anymore. She actually thinks that I'm suffering depression. That's her opinion. She thinks I'm suffering depression.

(John)

Research shows that physical estrangement can contribute to physiological changes in the individual, although the extent, progression and implications of these changes are not fully understood (Allen, 2003; Friesen, 2003; Harrison, 2003). Studies confirm that rejection produces negative physiological, cognitive and emotional responses, and even affects health-related behaviours in some vulnerable people (Ford & Collins, 2013). One commonly cited by-product of estrangement is emotional reactivity, which 'is built into biology and influences all internal states and behaviour' (Harrison, 2003, p. 247). The greater the emotional reactivity, the greater the likelihood that anxiety and stress will result (Klever, 2003). Bowen Family Systems Theory suggests that 'as stress and anxiety increase, there are greater pressures for humans to organize their lives and functioning around automatic responses to events, circumstances, and relationships' (Smith, 2003, p. 354), which might also suggest emotional reactivity and stress might be self-perpetuating in some estrangement contexts.

Chronic stress and anxiety resulting from estrangement will lead to different physiological, psychological and behavioural outcomes for different people. While there is some debate about how chronic stress and anxiety develop into problematic symptoms, there is sound evidence that chronic stress can lead to serious health conditions and illnesses, including a weakened immune system, insomnia, muscle pain, high blood pressure, cognitive impairment, anxiety, depression, diabetes, obesity and heart disease, to name a few (Baum & Polsusnzy, 1999; McEwen, 2007). There is also some evidence that chronic stress that results from interpersonal sources (from friends and family for example), is more likely to result in recurrent episodes of depression than non-interpersonal stress (Sheets & Craighead, 2014). Additionally, some ways that people try to manage stress – such as drug and alcohol use – can lead to further negative or cumulative consequences. It is also important to consider this in terms of the social consequences of estrangement, where a reduction in meaningful social interactions might minimise the buffering effects usually provided by social support.

Rumination

> And that's the thing, I don't know. And it drives me insane. The first thing you think of when you get up in the morning and the last thing you think of again at night, what have I done? What if I had done something different? What if? Why? Every day.
>
> (Marguerite)

Physical estrangement can result in considerable rumination in some estrangees:

> When an individual is in pain, he or she dwells on such emotion and its causes and various results instead of taking active measures to solve the problem. Several researchers regard rumination as a personal trait reflected by the condition where an individual overthinks pain and immerses himself in the circumstance to limit his motivation to communicate and curb his active behavior.
>
> (Sun et al., 2014, p. 53)

In the case of estrangement, rumination is the tendency to overly and repetitively focus one's attention on the relationship dissolution, including the events, thoughts and feelings that led up to it and resulted from it. Rumination has been linked to anxiety, anger, suicidal ideation, post-traumatic stress disorder and particularly as a risk factor in depression (Sun *et al.*, 2014). The unique conditions surrounding estrangement are likely to stimulate and maintain rumination in susceptible people. Primarily, estrangement is viewed as preventable because the estranger is still alive, albeit absent. It implies that one or both parties could have done something differently, which can lead to endless speculation about the estranger's health, mental health, exposure to third party influences, and examinations of personal responsibility. However, action or problem solving is prevented by the very nature of the estrangement situation, and people who determine that the only solution is reconciliation can become stuck in a rumination mindset.

Complicated grief

Semi trailers looked very attractive. It was very easy to do, all you had to do was line your car up.

(Lois)

Ambiguous and disenfranchised losses are likely to increase the likelihood of complicated grief. For example, research shows that a number of factors increase the likelihood of experiencing complicated grief: closeness to and dependency on the person who has been lost; personal avoidance of emotional issues; globalised negative feelings; and most importantly, inability to make meaning of the loss (Lobb *et al.*, 2010). All of these factors are inherent in the nature and context of estrangement (as described throughout this chapter). Complicated grief – which is most often examined and referred to in relation to death – is characterised by significant grief symptomatology which is distinct from depressive and anxiety clusters, and has endured past the expected range of norms, negatively impacting on daily living (Lobb *et al.*, 2010; Shear, 2015). Symptoms include 'intense yearning, longing, or emotional pain, frequent preoccupying thoughts and memories of the [absent] person, a feeling of disbelief or an inability to accept the loss, and difficulty imagining a meaningful future without the [absent] person' (Shear, 2015, p. 154).

Qualitative research with estrangees showed that many reported a number of these symptoms for weeks or months after the dissolution, which is to be expected, but several also reported a number of these symptoms years and decades afterwards (Agllias, 2011, 2014). In addition, people experiencing complicated grief might be more likely to estrange other family members or minimise social contact, in the belief that their happiness and recovery is solely dependent on reconnection with the estranger. Indeed, some older people estranged by adult children suggested that they felt guilty playing with or enjoying their non-estranged family members while the estranger remained absent (Agllias, 2011).

When Searching Becomes Problematic

I must admit, I used to prowl the shopping malls where I knew my daughter-in-law shopped to see if I could see the kids. I used to go and sit outside in the hope of seeing them.

(Betty)

Generally, losing an attachment figure activates the attachment system with the aim of re-establishing contact with the person (Field, 2006). Following a death, the permanence of the loss and the futility of proximity-seeking behaviours will be accepted over time and the bereaved will stop searching for his or her loved one (ibid.). However, the ambiguity of physical estrangement – and particularly signals of hope, such as a sighting or contact – might delay the deactivation of these systems and protest emotions like anxiety, anger and pining might be experienced for longer periods than they would after a death.

Estrangees need to be very careful that their natural responses to loss, such as searching and vigilance, do not start to dominate their thoughts and actions. In modern society, the capacity to easily make contact through email, texting and social media can be extremely tempting for estrangees, who may overuse these means to contact the estranger. These contacts will often reduce anxiety and feelings of loss in the short term because the estrangee feels that they are doing something towards reconciliation. Some will make contact multiple times per week, but they will most likely become more anxious and more desperate when there is no reply. Contacting the estranger can become a compulsive and self-perpetuating loss-related behaviour that can interfere with normal functioning. It potentially lessens the chance of reconciliation because the estranger is often experiencing this contact as invasive, insensitive and badgering (see Chapter 4).

Research with parents estranged by adult children showed that many used the Internet to search their child's whereabouts and ascertain their happiness (Agllias, 2011). Some placed boundaries around their searching, such as one man whose children's careers and achievements were highly visible in the public arena. He used the Internet every six months to 'check up' on their progress and success. However, some employed extreme actions – beyond the searching of publicly available information – to find out about their child's whereabouts beyond the immediate loss period. This included asking friends to go to the child's suspected residence to determine if they still lived there, using contacts in the police force or other government authorities to locate the child's address, and one woman who used the same medical practice as her estranged child and asked the doctor to report on the estranger and his family's wellbeing. Indeed, West and Hatters Friedman's (2008) research identified some estranged women whose rejection from their mothers resulted in stalking, which they defined as, 'the willful, malicious, and repeated following or harassing of another person that threatens his or her safety' (Meloy in West & Hatters Friedman, 2008, p. 37).

Reduced support and vulnerability

> When I was [a teenager] my mother kicked me out of home and I didn't have anywhere to go because I was alienated from my father at that time, so I lived at the top of town with anybody and everybody . . . I was bashed and assaulted very badly.
>
> (Angela)

Estrangement might result in fewer resources upon which to draw, both emotionally and practically. For younger members of the family, this could mean reduced support and advice about important decisions, such as purchasing a home, and fewer offers of practical assistance, such as helping with childcare. For older people, it might mean a reduction in assistance with labour intensive activities such as yard work, or technology such as computers. Social workers in palliative care positions reported that estranged clients often had fewer supports, or more conflicted support at the end of life, which potentially interfered with family decision-making, paying bills and maintaining the client's house while in hospital, as well as forward planning for funerals, and practical support on discharge (Agllias, 2013a). However, research showed that in most instances estranged people were able to fill the practical roles left void by the estranger (Agllias, 2011, 2014). They were generally more concerned with, and disturbed by, the lack of emotional resources, or the emotionally supportive elements tied to practical activities, than actual task completion.

Estrangement can also leave some estrangees exposed and vulnerable to an array of social risks, such as exploitation, financial and housing insecurity and loneliness. For example, research shows that family estrangement is one of four prime factors along a pathway to adolescent substance use disorder (Winters *et al.*, 2008). Young people who have been estranged from parents are increasingly disadvantaged by austerity measures in the Western world, which require parental support for longer periods of adulthood. Young estrangees often have to justify and prove their estranged status in order to receive welfare benefits, housing assistance and educational loans (National Union of Students, 2008). Estranged people can also become extremely vulnerable at times of emergency. While social support, which is generally based on reciprocity, can be sourced from a variety of relationships if necessary, 'people give more weight to kinship in awkward and emergency situations' (Neyer & Lang, 2003, p. 318). Short's (1996) interviews with clients of emergency relief centres revealed family relationships characterised by conflict and estrangement, resulting in an absence of family members with resources to share in times of crisis.

Conclusion

Most people describe physical estrangement as a unique and prolonged loss that poses considerable challenges when compared to other losses such as divorce or the death of a close relative. Estrangees might experience prolonged periods of grieving and an inability to fully adjust to, accept, or make sense of the loss, even when they have a fulfilling life outside of the estrangement. Grieving the estrangement and the loss of the estranger is an intrapersonal and interpersonal process that can continue until the end of life. Estrangement is a particularly difficult loss to accept because it has no predetermined outcomes or end points. Rather, estrangees often describe an ongoing process of: (i) acknowledging the reality of the estrangement; (ii) experiencing grief reactions; (iii) learning to live without the estranger; (iv) learning to live with new ways of relating socially; and (v) creating a fulfilling life while never knowing if the estranger will return. However, this is not a linear process because the nature of the relationship and particular triggers, as described above, often highlight the estrange-ment, refresh emotional reactions, and require remedial attention. Chapter 7 explores the methods that estranged people employ to grieve, increase their health and emotional wellbeing and *learn to live with estrangement* in the long term.

PRACTICE POINT 2: ASSESSING THE IMPACT OF THE ESTRANGEMENT

It is important to understand and assess the various effects of estrangement in order to: (i) acknowledge the personal loss experience (including the immediate and longer-term effects); (ii) establish a baseline of current functioning in order to measure progress/development across time; (iii) acknowledge the strengths, strategies and supports that have already been utilised to survive or live with estrangement (and those that have not been so useful); (iv) assess current priorities and areas that might need attention; and (v) assess this collective knowledge against information provided in Chapters 7 and 8, in order to incorporate some new strategies to maximise health and well-being, if warranted. The exercises in Practice Point 2 have been developed for people who found their relationship relatively satisfactory prior to the estrangement. Practice Point 3 – in Chapter 4 – is more suitable to those people who had a difficult relationship prior to the estrangement.

EXERCISE 1: REFLECTION ON THE EFFECTS OF ESTRANGEMENT

Think back to the days and weeks after you became estranged and reflect on the immediate effects of estrangement. Document these in Table 3.1 below – column (a). Then, think about your current situation and detail the current effects in column (b). Note: An example is provided to assist with this process (see Table 3.2).

EXERCISE 2: REFLECTION ON CHANGE

Look at the effects that you have documented in Table 3.1 and consider how these have changed over time (lessened, remained constant or increased). Reflect upon these changes and take a note of them at the bottom of the inventory. Have there been positive impacts? Make a note of these too.

TABLE 3.1 Impacts of estrangement inventory 1

	(a) Immediate effects	(b) Current effects
Emotional e.g. anger, anxiety, relief, emotional shock, fear, sadness, hurt, frustration, irritability, guilt, denial, uncertainty, apprehension, agitation.		
Physical e.g. difficulty breathing, nausea, fatigue, headaches, weakness, twitches, grinding teeth, sweating, chest pain.		
Cognitive e.g. hypervigilance, changes in memory, lack of concentration, confusion, nightmares, flashbacks, blaming the other person, poor attention.		
Behavioural e.g. withdrawal, emotional outbursts, change in appetite, pacing, increased drug or alcohol use, change in activity, acting out, change in communication patterns.		
Spiritual e.g. loss of meaning, loss of trust, questioning meaning of life, questioning spiritual beliefs, questioning God (or Deity).		
Social e.g. socialising less, avoiding people and social functions, taking time off work, being less engaged at family, work and social events, not answering the phone.		
2. Reflection on changes over time (including any positive effects)		

TABLE 3.2 Impacts of estrangement inventory 1 (example)

	(a) Immediate effects	(b) Current effects
Emotional e.g. anger, anxiety, relief, emotional shock, fear, sadness, hurt, frustration, irritability, guilt, denial, uncertainty, apprehension, agitation.	*Anger* *Sadness* *Hurt* *Shock*	*Anger* *Sadness* *Hurt*
Physical e.g. difficulty breathing, nausea, fatigue, headaches, weakness, twitches, grinding teeth, sweating, chest pain.	*Weakness* *Fatigue*	*N/A*
Cognitive e.g. hypervigilance, changes in memory, lack of concentration, confusion, nightmares, flashbacks, blaming the other person, poor attention.	*Hypervigilance* *Blaming the other* *Poor attention* *Confusion* *Nightmares*	*Hypervigilance* *Blaming the other*
Behavioural e.g. withdrawal, emotional outbursts, change in appetite, pacing, increased drug or alcohol use, change in activity, acting out, change in communication patterns.	*Withdrawal* *Change in appetite* *Pacing*	*Withdrawal* *Increased drug and alcohol use*
Spiritual e.g. loss of meaning, loss of trust, questioning meaning of life, questioning spiritual beliefs, questioning God (or Deity).	*Loss of meaning* *Questioning meaning of life*	*Questioning meaning of life*
Social e.g. socialising less, avoiding people and social functions, taking time off work, being less engaged at family, work and social events, not answering the phone.	*Socialising less* *Taking time off work* *Not answering the phone*	*Socialising less*

2. Reflection on changes over time (including any positive effects)

Became less angry and had less physical responses, but grew increasingly sad and hurt by everything. . . . I still blame my brother for the estrangement but not everything bad that happened around that time. Have started to socialise more because I know I should. My wife makes me go out now, but I tend to drink a lot at these events (I know this is a problem). I don't miss the confrontations and bullying from my brother.

EXERCISE 3: REFLECTION ON RESILIENCE

All people draw on strengths, strategies and supports to work through estrangement.

- *Strengths* are the positive personal traits and virtues that people employ in a balanced life, and they can be drawn upon as a guide to, or motivation for, action during times of confusion and distress.
- *Strategies* are the simple and complex plans for action that we develop to bring about positive change, achieve a goal or solve a problem.
- *Supports* are people or things that provide assistance, that buffer or hold some of the weight of negative experiences.

First, reflect on the changes identified in Exercise 2. Then consider the strengths, strategies and supports that positively influenced those changes. Document these in the Table 3.3 'Resilience inventory' below. Finally, reflect upon and document any traits/strengths, strategies or potential supports that were not so useful – or became less

TABLE 3.3 **Resilience inventory**

Strengths that I have drawn upon Strengths might include things like open-mindedness, curiosity, integrity, persistence, social intelligence, forgiveness, self-regulation, gratitude, humour, spirituality.	
Strategies that I have used These might include: setting up a more structured routine; planning meals and sitting down to eat regardless of appetite; challenging black-and-white thoughts whenever they arise; taking a friend/partner to difficult social situations; taking up a new activity such as meditation or yoga; and using a diary to let go of, or contain, worry.	
Supports that I have employed These might include: adequate finances; people such as family, friends, neighbours and work colleagues; therapeutic interventions such as counselling; church or social groups; educative supports like documentaries, movies, books and websites; and natural or manmade resources such as beaches, parks, sunsets (and time itself).	
Traits/strengths, strategies and supports that were not useful or became less useful over time 	

useful – across the estrangement journey. These might include things like: the strength of independence (which can become problematic if it prevents help-seeking), the trait of stubbornness, or strategies such as social withdrawal and unsupportive influences such as one-way friendships. Note: An example is also provided to assist with this process (see Table 3.4).

TABLE 3.4 Resilience inventory (example 1)

Strengths that I have drawn upon Strengths might include things like open-mindedness, curiosity, integrity, persistence, social intelligence, forgiveness, self-regulation, gratitude, humour, spirituality.	*Integrity and humour*
Strategies that I have used These might include: setting up a more structured routine; planning meals and sitting down to eat regardless of appetite; challenging black-and-white thoughts whenever they arise; taking a friend/partner to difficult social situations; taking up a new activity such as meditation or yoga; and using a diary to let go of, or contain, worry.	*Staying away from negative and judgemental people*
Supports that I have employed These might include: adequate finances; people such as family, friends, neighbours and work colleagues; therapeutic interventions such as counselling; church or social groups; educative supports like documentaries, movies, books and websites; and natural or manmade resources such as beaches, parks, sunsets (and time itself).	*Sister, wife and my boat (going fishing has been important).*
Traits/strengths, strategies and supports that were not useful or became less useful over time *Hiding estrangement from my more supportive friends (pride)* *Drinking*	

EXERCISE 4: AREAS FOR ATTENTION

Look back at column (b) in Table 3.1. Identify two to five areas that might require further consideration or attention. Consider the strengths, strategies and supports that you mapped in Table 3.3 and how these might be helpful.

Chapter 4   **Deciding to leave family**

It's not as if it was this hugely earth shattering thing, I think it was just the straw that broke the camel's back. I had had so many years of it, of crap from her and always being made to feel that I wasn't important, and that really got to me.

(Linda)

'People stay in relationships for two major reasons: because they want to; and because they have to' (Johnson, 1982, p. 52). Physical estrangement rarely occurs after one disagreement, conflict or betrayal. Generally, it is a protracted process foregrounded by a long-term sense of disconnection between the parties; this is most often and deeply felt by the person who ultimately chooses to estrange, but it might also be core to the estrangee's experience. Physical estrangement is often preceded by cycles of emotional and physical distancing which serve protective and preparatory functions for the relationship dissolution and especially the estranger. The person who chooses to estrange another usually experiences considerable anticipatory loss prior to the estrangement. The catalyst for severing ties completely is often a relatively minor incident, although sometimes it might be one significant act of betrayal. Regardless of the stimulus, it is at this point that the estranger decides that negative or destructive elements of the relationship – which they consider to outweigh the positive, supportive and obligatory elements – are immovable or beyond repair. Despite having more preparation for, information about and agency in the decision to estrange, the estranger usually experiences similar personal and interpersonal losses to the person they estrange. This chapter discusses physical estrangement from the perspective of the estranger. It commences with Paul's story, which is illustrative of the long-term processes involved in estranging others. It then explores the ambiguous and disenfranchised nature of estrangement loss. The chapter examines the estranger's rollercoaster of emotions, where feelings of relief, opportunities for growth and newfound independence may be intermingled with feelings of guilt, regret and questioning about the decision. Additionally, the post-estrangement relationship often involves considerable management, where the estranger is required to preserve the estrangement and uphold or instate further boundaries between the parties. Finally, a practice section encourages the reader or client to critically assess the current estrangement status and identify existing resilience, strengths and strategies that might be harnessed as they learn to live with estrangement.

Paul's story

Well I was pretty much emotionally estranged from my parents for a lot of my life. At the age of 18 when I moved out of home, that's when the physical estrangement started for a period of about five or six years. Then I met my wife, who talked me into having another go at it. . . . [My parents and I reconciled briefly], but no they haven't changed, they will never change and I certainly don't want these people anywhere near me and my family and my kids under any circumstances and that was when I said no, that's it, they're out of my life, I'm gone. Yeah, I couldn't bring myself to say it to their face so I sent them a fairly lengthy email. It said, this is what I feel about the past from when I was young, this is what I feel about what's happened since we started catching up to each other. I think some of the stuff that you've done is just absolutely unacceptable and I don't want you in my life.

Estrangement is a long and complex process

Much of the literature about the dissolution of relationships takes a *dissatisfaction* or *economic* focus, where costs are weighed against benefits and the relationship is simplistically evaluated: as beneficial, possibly salvageable, or not worth continuing. However, Johnson's (1982) work on personal relationships draws attention to factors beyond a dyadic evaluation of satisfaction that are potentially pertinent to family estrangement. In particular, one's personal and structural *commitment* to a relationship, in this case a familial relationship, must be considered:

> [P]ersonal commitment is an internalized sense of moral commitment to the maintenance of the relationship. This may be derived from . . . moral strictures focused on the maintenance of specific types of relationships, or perhaps from the perception of the relationship as involving an implicit contract, obliging one to its maintenance even in the face of declining dissatisfaction.
>
> (Johnson, 1982, p. 54)

One's structural commitment to family is embedded in: a network of interdependent and primarily beneficial family relationships (others often have a stake in network stability); cultural ideologies and social expectations of continuing bonds; and the poor likelihood of finding an available relationship alternative (such as a *new* mother or brother). In other words, family relationships are particularly difficult to terminate, even when dissatisfaction is high, due to a number of personal, interpersonal and ideological factors. In addition, there are a number of factors that will physically or emotionally pull even the most determined estranger back into the family relationship across time. There is often a long and complex process that occurs between the stirrings of relationship dissatisfaction where the desire to make things different, experimenting with relationship distancing, and the accumulation of enough personally and structurally acceptable *evidence* for public disclosure of dissolution, all take place prior to the actual estrangement.

Long-term disconnection

That closeness [within the family] was really never there. It wasn't really there. Maybe because I was working very hard or I didn't want to be interested and because basically, this is an awful thing to say, I don't like children.

(Robert, reflecting on the precursors to his children's
decision to physically estrange him)

People who choose physical estrangement often cite a poor familial bond or disconnection as the backdrop to family conflict and eventual estrangement (Agllias, 2008, 2014; Robinson, 2011; Scharp *et al.*, 2014). They often suggest that they were never fully connected to the other party, that the bond has disintegrated or that one or both parties have changed over time. Many say that they feel different to, or somehow apart from, the estrangee. They might also feel disconnected from the larger family or removed from the closeness and intimacy that they share. This might be relayed conversationally in comments such as; 'I never felt like I belonged to this family', 'I'm the odd one out', and 'I always felt like a visitor in my own home'. They might describe themselves as the 'lone wolf', 'the agitator', or the 'scapegoat'. Feeling disconnected is often related to having different ideas, opinions, preferences or talents, or raising uncomfortable issues. Sometimes people describe this difference in terms of their role or actions in the family, such as: 'I spent a lot of my time in my room as a child', or 'I was nothing but the breadwinner to those children', or 'I was mum's carer while my sister was having a great life'. However, disconnection can develop from physical differences too; e.g. 'my sisters all had boobs but I looked like a boy'. Adult children might suggest that they were never close to a parent or sibling. A parent might suggest that they never truly bonded with their infant child or describe an adolescent who became increasingly different, unresponsive or unreachable across time. Siblings might refer to differences in temperament, parental favour and affection that set them apart.

Long-term disconnection between parents and children, as well as siblings, might be related to early attachment experiences. They might arise from external events, such as working long hours, or issues, such as mental illness, that potentially interfere with the parent's capacity to parent, and other family members' capacity to bond and share intimate moments. Stressors that affect family connectedness not only affect feelings of closeness between parents and children, but also have the potential to affect sibling and extended family relationships. For example, the competition for adult attention and affection increases when it is scarce, creating sibling rivalry and suspicions of favouritism that can affect relationships across generations. Regardless of origin, when feelings of belongingness, acceptance and fairness are replaced with feelings of discomfort and disconnection the potential estranger starts to view their familial connection from an outsider perspective. They may start to evaluate it differently. They often seek information from alternate sources, and become alert to further signs of disconnection or exclusion.

New ways of being

[My parents thought] it just wasn't a real job. But the people I met, I was mixing with these highly intelligent people and it was fantastic. They're my intellect. . . . I was conversing daily with professors and CEOs. . . . These people would come to me and ask my advice. For me, who had been called an idiot. . . . It was about [my parents'] own selfishness, outside their realm of understanding.

(David)

There is some evidence that people who choose to estrange evaluate their familial dissatisfaction more intensely at different periods (Agllias, 2008, 2014; Robinson, 2011). When viewed through a new lens, their suspicions of disconnection might be recognised, re-evaluated and renamed as less favourable conditions such as rejection, neglect and disrespect. There are key periods when new people, perspectives and ideas are introduced into the family system and when relationship discomfort or dissatisfaction might be evaluated more critically. This is particularly so at developmental periods such as adolescence and early adulthood: greater freedoms, a more diverse friendship set, starting employment and going to university all offer new perspectives about familial closeness. For example, an adolescent who previously enjoyed significant freedom outside of the family home due to a sole parent working long hours might re-evaluate this as a lack of parental care and concern for his safety when he starts socialising with, and observing, others who are satisfied with more conservative parenting practices and restrictions. Or a value, belief or talent not previously recognised by the family might be appreciated or acknowledged in a new context, potentially highlighting the young person's negative experience of being misunderstood by parents or teased by a sibling (see David's experience above).

In later life, a parent's remarriage – and the new parenting perspectives introduced by the spouse – might influence the renaming of an adult child's contacts and requests for support as *selfishness* and *greed*. A number of estrangers in one study suggested that their new partner and in-laws provided different insights into family connectedness and ways of relating (Agllias, 2014). These insights provoked comparisons with their own family of origin and particularly relationships that were considered unsatisfactory. Comparative data served as a benchmark for evaluating *good enough* relationships and collecting evidence of wrongdoing in their own family. Indeed, some research suggests that some transferring of emotional and ideological attachment often occurs during these periods (Robinson, 2011).

Testing the water

I've gone back [and forth] to mum for 20 years, you know. I've been there done that . . . when you're loyal and you have real emotions it is hard to fight them because it's your family and you're supposed to love your mum.

(Donna)

Estrangers often describe cycles of estrangement and reconciliation before (what they consider to be) a final physical estrangement. (It is important to remember that the term *reconciliation* in this book refers to a continuum of relational states from the resumption of contact without acknowledgement of previous conflict or dissatisfaction, to the acknowledgement and resolution of previous issues). Estrangers often assess the strained relationship on an ongoing basis, weighing up conflicting feelings of love and hate. They will crave the *belonging* associated with family while simultaneously seeking *relief* from the strained relationship. There may be times when they feel so worn down by the demands or experiences of the relationship that they need to distance themselves in some way in order to evaluate the relationship and to regroup before trying again. Sometimes, after long periods of estrangement, they need to go back to the relationship to test their reality or perception of previous events and to assess the potential for reconciliation. In some instances, the estranger communicates the expectations for the relationship at that point, giving a warning or ultimatum that reconciliation is conditional and physical estrangement possibly imminent if conditions are not met.

Research showed that many families experience cycles of emotional estrangement, physical estrangement and reconciliation before a more serious or long-term rupture occurred (Agllias, 2011, 2014; Scharp *et al.*, 2014). However, estrangers were more likely to perceive these cycles as contributors to a difficult relationship, whereas the estrangee was more likely to view these as discrete periods of conflict and reconciliation, where problems have been resolved or put aside (Agllias, 2011, 2014).

Estrangers might *experiment* with differentiation – and estrangement – through very simple distancing practices or mechanisms such as reducing times between visits or changing the type of visit. For example, a man who is having relationship difficulties with his cousin might start requesting that they meet in a busy cafeteria on a work day, so that the event is time bounded and intimacy is unlikely, compared to a meeting in the family home. One commonly cited distancing opportunity occurs in adolescence or young adulthood where leaving home for college or entering a romantic relationship might serve as *legitimate* relief from a difficult relationship. These practices may or may not be recognised as a precursor to estrangement by the estranger or the other party. They are usually not deliberate or planned actions to test life without the other party, rather they operate at the subconscious level, where the dissatisfied party – who has been socialised to understand and abide by family codes of unity and good will – takes measures to preserve their familial contract while relieving their discomfort, avoiding confrontation, and preventing overt conflict or estrangement.

However, when periods of contact emphasise previous areas of dispute, when problematic issues or behaviours are not addressed and conciliatory promises are not kept, dissatisfaction and the desire to distance permanently is likely to increase considerably. Robinson's (2011) research showed that people were often able to conceal the depth of their relationship dissatisfaction as well as their gradual emotional and ideological transfer to a lifestyle without the strained relationship. So, relationships might be able to operate at a level of emotional distance or cyclical distancing for decades, but most will come to a point where it is likely that one party will want more contact or less contact, where issues need to be discussed and resolved, or where the estranger evaluates their life as more satisfactory without the other party (also see 'Emotional Estrangement' in Chapter 5).

The catalyst

I started to see, it didn't matter that I got a degree, it didn't matter that I bought [expensive presents]. It didn't matter what I did. I could do backflips and I was still not going to be loved, and it started to sink in.

(Angela)

The catalyst for physical estrangement is often perceived and portrayed as an insignificant event, a childish reaction or a significant betrayal. In reality the catalyst is more likely to be *a new way of thinking* about and prioritising the relationship or *a new found confidence* in one's capacity to survive without the other person. The aforementioned processes of *disconnection, new ways of being* and *testing the waters* have usually coalesced into a feeling of deep dissatisfaction with the relationship – and in some cases open conflict – well before the estrangement is enacted. Indeed, many estrangers describe a period of growth and healing where they have acquired enough strength, independence and resolve to raise their relationship complaints, or live without what they perceive to be a dysfunctional family relationship.

The estrangement decision or announcement is rarely planned. It is more likely to happen when the estranger feels exhausted by relationship demands or is caught off guard by an often symbolic action that results in a final hurt. For example, Helen felt that she had to estrange her brother 'because he is a compulsive gambler and stole from me'. In this case, Helen said that she had given her brother considerable financial assistance, and would have given him more had he asked, but his theft was an intolerable breach of trust that recast her previous contributions as *taken for granted*. Research with adult children who chose to physically estrange from their parent or sibling showed that this *last straw* moment often occurred during a period of contact or reconciliation, when they felt that they – or their child or partner – had been rebuffed, insulted or unappreciated, or when they were silenced from speaking about previous hurts and estrangements (Agllias, 2014; Scharp *et al.*, 2014). In other instances estrangement is enacted when the parties are engaging in conflict about something that might or might not be related to the estranger's primary complaints and concerns. Regardless, *deep hurt* is core to the estrangement decision: 'Studies on the features of hurt feelings suggest that hurt is a distinct negative emotion that is associated with feeling devalued, unwanted, and rejected' (Smart *et al.*, 2009, p. 368).

A note on ultimate betrayal

Originally [estrangement] was [my father's] decision when I first confronted him with the sexual abuse. That was his decision not to speak to me for five years. I decided to forgive him and went back and then about four years later realised it was better I didn't speak to him.

(Julie)

Many people suggest or presume that physical estrangement is – or should *only* be enacted as – a result of ultimate betrayal. Indeed, some people suggest that they had a strong historical bond with the estrangee prior to an *ultimate betrayal*: an act that they perceived to be unforgiveable. However, most estrangements should be considered in terms of relationship quality prior to the betrayal (whether this is a disconnected or fused relationship). For example, society views infidelity as the ultimate betrayal of romantic and marital type relationships, and some relationships will disintegrate on the discovery of such a transgression. However, many more couples are able to withstand and work through infidelity (as long as it discontinues and reparation is made). So too, with familial relationships, it is rare that estrangement occurs after one act of betrayal in an otherwise well-functioning and balanced relationship. As Julie's comments (at the begining of this section) show, even abuse perpetrated by another family member can be forgiven in certain circumstances. It is the reaction to this confrontation and or forgiveness, and the actions after it, that are most likely to influence the continuation of the relationship. This is discussed further in Chapter 8.

Anticipatory grieving and loss reality

Many estrangers experience a form of anticipatory loss prior to the final dissolution (and elements of ambiguous loss might also be experienced during cycles of emotional and physical estrangement). The processes involved in assessing, testing and ultimately physically estranging from the family relationship potentially incur a number of losses that might be experienced across decades. Anticipatory loss is the cognitive realisation of impending death or loss – or in this case physical estrangement – and the associated grief that is experienced (Rando, 1986; Rolland, 1990). It involves grieving for: (i) the past, which might include grief pertaining to painful relational episodes and regret about the inability to change the past, or periods of joy that are unlikely to reoccur; (ii) the present, which includes the experiences of an eroding relationship; and (iii) the future, where the anticipated loss of relationship, or the continuation of an unsatisfactory one, act as a reminder of positive family experiences that will never be shared or repeated (Agllias, 2014; Rando, 1986).

While the concept of anticipatory grief is generally applied to terminal illness and bereavement, where loss is imminent and certain, it has been applied to disability and other permanent living losses. The development of anticipatory loss and the associated processes are highly applicable to estrangement. For example, the threat of the estrangement loss is often protracted, where the potential estranger moves from, and between, the notion that physical estrangement is a *possibility* and *inevitable*. The existential elements of possible or impending relationship death, and the conflicting desires for closeness and relief, might make denial a comfortable default position at times. Unexpected moments of joy or peace during periods of reconciliation – similar to a *remission period* during an illness – might result in ambivalence, where hope for the relationship is often tempered by apprehension about its longevity. This hope can be quickly sullied when a family member's *behavioural relapse* highlights the reality of the impending loss. Associated 'feelings may include: separation anxiety, existential aloneness, denial, sadness, disappointment, anger, resentment, guilt, exhaustion and desperation' (Rolland, 1990, p. 229). Numbness and premature detachment can occur, which might be interpreted as callousness in the estranger, and result in less empathic responses from family and friends when the estrangement is enacted.

The estrangement event

After that disconnection in July I really grieved. I was just – have I done the right thing? I was shaking. I was anxious all the time.

(Donna)

There is often an assumption that the estranger will experience fewer loss and grief responses than the person they estrange because of their *choice* in the final decision, and their capacity to *prepare* for the ending, but research about anticipatory grief shows mixed responses (Reynolds & Botha, 2006). Some people who chose estrangement suggest that their foremost response to the dissolution is *relief* from a primarily hurtful and dysfunctional relationship. In these cases, estrangers appear to have gradually detached from the family member across long periods of time, and the final estrangement announcement is often a more planned or less reactive event. For example, the estranger might take time to write a final letter of complaint and severance to the family member, they might move away without leaving a forwarding address, or they might signify the estrangement symbolically, such as a bride who does not ask her father to walk her down the aisle. In these instances, the estranger does not deny feelings of loss and sadness, but tends to suggest the estrangement is inevitable, and their grieving for the relationship has been an ongoing process. They might be observed by their social network, and particularly the estranged relative and other family members, to be calmly going about their activities of daily living unaffected by the relationship dissolution, but this is rarely the case.

However, research also shows that anticipatory grief does not always take the place of post-loss grief, nor does it lessen the associated effects (Rando, 1986; Reynolds & Botha, 2006). Knowing or suspecting that a loss is about to occur does not necessarily ensure emotional preparation or processing in all individuals. Many estrangers experience remarkable shock at their decision if it occurs unexpectedly. They often confront significant loss and grief reactions immediately after the physical estrangement has been announced, even when that declaration is symbolic or in text rather than face to face.

While many estrangers cite 'relief' as the primary response to the estrangement, many more report that the initial sense of relief is quickly overridden by – or experienced alongside – overwhelming and often unexpected grief responses. Shock responses are common in the initial stages, including bodily symptoms such as shaking, disorientation and faintness. Emotional responses often include feelings of helplessness, anger and particularly disbelief at the magnitude of the decision that they have enacted. Protest behaviours such as crying are common. People who choose estrangement are rarely prepared for the depth of their own responses. Many ruminate about their decision, with repeated cognitions such as 'what have I done?' in the days after estrangement. Similar to the estrangee experience, estrangers report numbness, detachment and depersonalisation in the weeks following estrangement, as well as somatic disturbance (Agllias, 2014).

Over time, acute emotions and bodily responses seem to decrease in intensity or frequency for most estrangers. However, anger and rumination that has been experienced early in the estrangement process might continue to be disruptive for longer periods. They might feel anger towards the estrangee, not only for the behaviour that contributed the estrangement, but because this behaviour has situated the estranger in what they perceive to be an unwinnable – and somewhat stigmatised – position. Many perceive an injustice because they have had no option but to make the final decision and take the final actions to cease the relationship. Rumination may continue with estrangers going over and over the catalyst or estrangement event, questioning why this has happened and revisiting the behaviours and events leading up to the final declaration. Some continue to question whether they have done the right thing in dissolving the relationship.

Many estrangers experience self-conscious emotions after the estrangement, including guilt, shame and embarrassment. Even when people firmly believe that they have made the correct decision, the belief or knowledge that others *blame* them for the estrangement will result in the internalisation of the aforementioned emotions. Self-conscious emotions are often evoked by implicit or explicit self-evaluation and self-reflection (Price Tangney *et al.*, 2007). They are influenced by 'an individual's knowledge and internalization of moral norms and conventions', and particularly when 'behaviors [are] likely to have negative consequences for the well-being of others' and where 'there is broad social consensus that such behaviors are "wrong"' (ibid., p. 345). It appears that estrangers will often revisit negative aspects of the estranged relationship, and particularly negative elements of the estrangee's personality, to remind themselves of the transgressions and hurts that led to the estrangement decision (and maybe this minimises self-conscious emotions in some way).

Many people who choose estrangement suggest that they experience a considerable *loss of self* after the dissolution (although some suggest this loss is well embedded in their psyche before the final declaration). The meaning that estrangers attribute to their estranged relationship, and particularly the meaning attributed to their familial role, needs considerable re-evaluation and readjustment during the weeks, months and maybe years after estrangement. Social mores suggest that our sense of self is initially borne and developed in the family. However, core components of the estranger's identity are often altered through the estrangement process, possibly contributing to confusion and anxiety about the future. Ideologies pertaining to *family* may be questioned and evaluated against the reality of the estrangement, and the person who chooses estrangement might internalise a sense of failure as a result.

'Close relationships do not end – they merely change. Insofar as the relationship exists in the mind(s) of the participant(s), it continues to exist cognitively. . . . Relationships are as much symbolic events and images' (Harvey, *et al.*, 1982, p. 119). One study found that some adult children reported 'hearing' the estrangee's voice, words or sentiments after the estrangement (Agllias, 2014). While they recognised these 'voices' as internalised messages about their worthiness, attractiveness or intelligence, they had to work actively to dispel the negative impact this had on their continued sense of self in the post-estrangement period. Additionally, many estrangers *imagine* the other person's responses to the estrangement and even their day-to-day choices following the separation. For example, 'I know what my father would say if he knew I had left university'. As a result, this estranger continues to feel his father's disappointment and his own shame even though his father is absent due to the estrangement.

People who choose estrangement might also experience generalised feelings of interpersonal and social vulnerability for long periods after the estrangement. They might feel *nervous* or *exposed* in social situations, and wary of any form of rejection or confrontation. This might develop from the negative precursors to estrangement, the actual loss, the ongoing relational and ideological challenges of estrangement, as well as specific triggers (all described in more detail further in this chapter).

A note on choice

If I have to choose between my family – myself, family and the world – family goes, absolutely.

(Brenda)

This chapter often refers to the estranger 'choosing' estrangement. This is based on research with estrangers who often describe estrangement as the most appropriate way forward when faced with two – usually negative – alternatives (Agllias, 2014). However, the phrase 'choosing estrangement' is not meant to negate the belief of some, who would suggest that they had *no choice* but to estrange a family member. Regardless, *choice* infers the taking of responsibility. When we choose something we are electing to take responsibility for that choice (e.g. choosing to get married or have a baby). Other choices are more limited; they are made out of necessity, and they are likely to incur more feelings of burden and distress (e.g. choosing whether to euthanize a beloved, but seriously injured, pet). Estrangement is often experienced as a *choice* that must be made, and one that incurs considerable unwanted emotional, physical and relational responsibilities.

Triggers for pain

I sometimes feel angry if I think about [my mother], which I hardly do. She got breast cancer . . . she rang my daughter and said I'm letting you know because you need to go and get checked, but I'm not telling your mother because she doesn't deserve to know. . . . Of course my daughter gets on the phone and rings me.

(Linda)

Estrangers are potentially exposed to a number of triggers that can reinvigorate disorientation, pain and hurt after the estrangement, including events such as birthdays, weddings and Christmases. Expected family celebrations – to which the estranger is uninvited – often trigger thoughts about, and images of, the estrangee(s). This might elicit negative ponderings about the way their absence is noticed, regarded or spoken about at these events. Visiting the area, state or country that an estrangee resides in has the potential to trigger stress prior to, and vigilance or hypervigilance upon, entering the relevant zone.

Symbols of love and affection from other relatives can highlight the estrangement. For example, a niece who is particularly kind to her aunt might trigger sadness and regret in the aunt who has chosen to estrange her own daughter. Recalling particular memories – whether they are joyous or painful – can retrigger loss and grief responses. Questions from strangers about the status of the relationship or questions from children about their estranged relatives can trigger sadness and anger. Periods of crisis can be particularly difficult for estrangers, especially if they require extra assistance. Not only does their need for support highlight the estrangement but it might also highlight the fact that their relative is absent due to *a choice they made* (which may contribute to renewed feelings of guilt, regret and shame).

Contact is a notable trigger for pain. An invitation to a family event, when an estrangee is likely to attend, can create a significant life disruption in the years after the estrangement. The estranger is often burdened with an array of complex dilemmas in response to such an invitation: weighing up the possible effects on their personal health, wellbeing and grief process; considering the feelings of non-estranged family members and the possibility that non-attendance will lead to judgement and additional familial rejection; and fears about the messages that attendance or non-attendance will send to the estrangee. Gifts or letters might bring mixed emotions; a combination of relief that the estrangee has thought about them (or their family) and a feeling that the contact is inadequate or 'too little too late'. Gifts and contacts will be viewed particularly negatively if they do not attempt to address the issue that the estranger regards as the catalyst for estrangement. Indeed, many estrangers perceive any form of contact as an affront.

Symbolic and actual reminders of mortality will often trigger loss and grief responses in estrangers, similar to the experience of estrangees (Agllias, 2008, 2014; Robinson, 2011). Many are triggered by personal health events or second-hand or third party messages about the health status of the estrangee. While committed to the finality of the estrangement, many estrangers think about the potential death of the estrangee – or their own death – and how they might react if it occurs. They might play out illness, dying or death scenarios, anticipating and maybe even practising their desired responses. However, Karen's story shows that the actual loss of an estranged family member can evoke unimagined responses, years after contact has ceased.

Karen's story

Well I didn't think I cared . . . the more time you're apart from people, the less you feel. Well that's what you think. . . . I didn't know I was going to react. So I went to [my estranged mother's] funeral and organised everything and you're allowed to view the body and that. I didn't know how I was going to react and stuff and I had a panic attack. I passed out and everything and I've never had that before. . . . Here she is, she's died and nothing's been resolved. Nothing's been resolved. . . . I want to know why she hated me, why she treated us the way she did. [In the weeks afterwards I felt] weird, disconnected. Just like, that was so surreal, did that really happen? I kind of joked about how I reacted. You know, oh like I fainted, as you do to try and lessen, I don't know, the trauma or something.

Missing 'a' family

> But when Jim and I were first together, for quite a number of years there, I'd just cry and cry and he'd go, what's wrong, and I'd go, none of my family talk to each other and you know . . . I want a family
>
> (Tracy)

'The notion of "family" is deeply tied to the sense of who we are in the world. . . . No matter how old we are, no matter how distant emotionally or physically, we seem unable to get away from the importance of family' (McGoldrick, 1995, p. 22). People who choose estrangement often report missing 'a' family, despite their decision. Even those who suggest that they 'never had a family' have symbolic notions of this ideal, including the things a family can provide and how it feels to be supported by one. Most estrangers are adamant that they do not miss their *own* family member or members – and particularly the issues that led to the estrangement – but they do miss some or all of the *family experience*. This includes the emotional, educational and physical support that family members, and particularly the family unit, can afford. It is particularly important to highlight that many estrangers lose more than one family member after the estrangement, and they often exclude themselves or are excluded from family activities to varying degrees. The chasm often develops beyond the person they have estranged, so the loss of *family* is a very real experience. (This is discussed in detail in Chapter 6).

Estrangers often miss the family activities and particularly the comfort attached to those events, and this might also affect their feelings and associations with friends who have a unified family or are perceived as taking family for granted. Research with adult children who chose physical estrangement found that several missed simple things, such as having someone else make dinner for them, or being able to spend the weekend with family (Agllias, 2014). It was interesting how being parented, supported or feeling comfortable was so closely connected to meals and gatherings for some. Historic familiarity is also lost when estrangement occurs. Historic familiarity includes the importance of having someone who *knows* you, and knows your history. Beyond this, family history can be lost when families don't communicate anymore, and this can be a considerable source of loss and sadness when, for example, children ask about their family tree or estrangers are asked about their genetic history during periods of illness.

Practical issues, problem solving and decision-making are also associated with estrangement from family, and a reduction in intergenerational support often requires the estranger to become very independent, resourceful and capable in many areas. This independence can be a source of real pride and celebration for estrangers but it also places considerable stress on them, and particularly in the early stages of adjustment. People who choose to estrange have rarely been prepared – nor could they have been prepared – for a life without backup. Estrangers might become intensely aware of their vulnerability and the notion that they have no one to fall back on if they fail. A lack of family can exacerbate social isolation in some instances. For example, couples may be unable to socialise because they do not have babysitters for their children.

A relational experience

Occasionally I'll think, maybe I should make an effort to have him as part of my life, but I don't know. I think it's more of people's expectations.

(Kim)

Physical estrangement is a decision that is not made in a vacuum. Like all other relationship dissolutions it 'has to be managed and dealt with in a teeming social context. Real friends, real relatives, real social institutions may have to be informed about the dissolution and, if the relationship was a significant one, these social entities will probably have a strong view about the whole thing' (Duck, 1982, p. 8). A final estrangement decision marks a new or renewed period of self-evaluation, reassessment and even behaviour modification that is influenced by, and occurs within, *a social and relational context*.

Estrangers often describe and experience estrangement as a disenfranchised loss because it violates societal ideals about the family as *essential, inevitable* and *everlasting*. It is rarely recognised by others and the perception of choice can establish the estranger as the perpetrator of a significant and unnecessary relational transgression. Estrangers often report that the estrangement process erodes their general level of trust, often narrows the breadth of their social circle and precludes conversational depth when familial topics are introduced in social situations (Agllias, 2014). While most are cautious about disclosing their relational status freely, they tend not to actively hide their decision from others either. They are most likely to disclose this information when it is bounded by private and trusting arrangements. Fully aware that estrangement carries a stigmatised burden and might elicit possibly negative reactions to their decision, estrangers *manage* the release of information. This usually means providing the minimum information that is required and acceptable within each particular social situation, and rarely offering information about their role in the estrangement decision. Many estrangers do not fully disclose the details or extent of the estrangement to extended family and friends, for a variety of reasons (Agllias, 2014; Scharp, 2014). However, estrangement has the potential to become *highly visible* or come *under public scrutiny* in certain circumstances. For example, a wedding is a prime example of an event where family and friends observe and question who is – and who is not – in attendance (or sitting in the first row at the church ceremony). These types of events may have the potential to expose and embarrass the estranger publicly, as well as altering their self-perception or actual social standing in their relational context.

One of the most significant effects of physical estrangement is the potential reduction of support from family and friends. Relationships are likely to be affected when estrangers: avoid others who they presume to be angry or disappointed; avoid people who they believe are more closely aligned with the estrangee(s); and are given clear messages that they are no longer welcome by certain members of family or friends. Additionally, estrangement in one familial relationship is destined to impact on the whole family system, where positions of allegiance and favour can contribute to impermeable boundaries and triangular interactions that often create and contribute to additional estrangements within the intergenerational family (this is discussed at length in Chapter 6).

Close and trusting relationships

I have huge trust issues. Huge trust issues. That's why I've got two girlfriends. I've tried to branch out and have other friends and then I feel betrayed.

(Karen)

Interestingly, people who choose estrangement often describe their relational network as consisting of a few very intense relationships and a number of somewhat superficial relationships (Agllias, 2014). While it is difficult to determine how and why this develops, a number of estrangement-related issues and processes are likely to contribute. First, estrangers often believe that other people do not and would not understand estrangement, and particularly the decision to estrange a family member or members (Agllias, 2014; Scharp, 2014). For some this is an intrinsic belief that they are being judged by dominant social discourses, while others have actually experienced judgemental comments or exclusionary behaviours from others.

Second, many estrangers suggest that the precursors to estrangement – primarily experiences of rejection – contribute to a generalised reduction in trust, which may affect their capacity to engage fully or openly in new relationships. Research suggests 'that when a sense of disconnection and rejection develops during childhood and adolescence, individuals show a relatively stable tendency to either avoid or overvalue interpersonal relationships' (Yoo *et al.*, 2014, p. 1377). This might be exacerbated by the impact of estrangement on the estranger's sense of self (and internalised feelings of low worth). In these instances defensive posturing or emotional withdrawal might serve to protect them from public exposure and embarrassment, but it might also be interpreted as coldness or disinterest to potential friends. Others suggest that previous rejection experiences contribute to *people-pleasing behaviours* and developing very close but potentially unsustainable relationships too quickly. For example a number of adult children who chose to estrange said that their feelings of rejection by a parent, as well as the isolating conditions inherent in estrangement, made them vulnerable to the exploitation of others (Agllias, 2014). For some, this involved developing intense 'friendships' with people who took advantage of them financially or sexually. For others, this involved marrying the first person who said 'I love you'. In these cases the desire for a *new chance* at love and family were often quashed on the discovery that the spouse was unsuitable, rejecting or abusive.

The primary effect of these factors might be a reduced, tentative or superficial engagement with new people, which can lead to a greater reliance on established friendships. However, the drawn-out and traumatic nature of estrangement also has the potential to *burn out* or reduce tolerance in these relationships. When a person only has a small network of friends to support them during stressful periods – and they also have a reduced family network – this can place additional emotional and physical burdens on existing alliances. In one study, some estrangers believed that the weight of their demands and expectations – and especially those derived from their estrangement-related emotional needs – contributed to the demise of certain close friendships (Agllias, 2014). Some estrangers make concerted efforts not to bring up or discuss the estrangement for fear of burdening others or contaminating the relationship.

Intense nuclear family or marital relationships

With my husband, I constantly have to have him telling me he loves me.

(Rita)

When people become estranged, the concept of intergenerational family changes and the desire for a new or different family often emerges. However, this can exert considerable pressure on the estranger to 'get it right' in the new configuration. While there are a number of social pressures on parents and couples to succeed in their relationships and roles in everyday life, estrangement can exacerbate these expectations. First, the estranger often sees estrangement as an opportunity – or obligation – to stop destructive patterns in the *new family* or *new relationships*. Second, the estranger might consider the new configuration as a way of alleviating internalised shame and guilt, or highlighting the necessity of the estrangement: when future relationships are primarily successful and harmonious this can act as proof that the estrangee was the problem after all. Third, they might feel a need to fill the void of the estrangee in the new configuration. Last, estrangers might feel obligated to keep their estrangement-related emotions to themselves to protect members in the new configuration.

As a result, estrangers may feel under considerable pressure not to make the same mistakes that were made in the estranged relationship(s), not to repeat undesirable behaviours attributed to the estrangee, to provide additional resources in new relationships, and to absorb or suppress emotional distress. For example, one study showed that some adult children who chose physical estrangement from a parent or parents felt enormous pressure to parent their children differently to their own experiences (see Chapter 6 for detailed discussion). Additionally, estrangement has the potential to place enormous stress on the new family due to the reality of depleted emotional and physical resources. The marital-type partners of estrangers can be subjected to a number of additional stressors. They may need to buffer the anger and outbursts of the estranger, or respond to internalised expressions of loss, such as withdrawal. Indeed, a number of adult children in one study suggested that their partners were required to do a lot more *emotional lifting* after they chose estrangement (Agllias, 2014). Estranger's partners might experience attacks and boundary violations from the estrangee, be required to draw more heavily on their extended family and friendship networks to compensate for diminished support, and take over particular roles to cover for the estrangee(s).

Maintaining boundaries

I haven't seen her [since I was 20] but of course I heard from her and she came to my door yelling and crying and whatever. Also I received a letter . . . that said that it was my fault that [my brother] had run away and I had set him up to doing that.

(Tina)

Estrangers often suggest that they need to protect themselves from further injury and pain, which makes them vigilant for any form of boundary violation that might pose a threat to their health and well-being. A core component of the post-estrangement period, then, is *maintaining the estrangement*. This can involve the exertion of considerable emotional, strategic and practical energy. Indeed Scharp's (2014) research confirms that the maintenance of estrangement requires ongoing negotiation and significant communicative work on the part of the estranger. While this work might lessen across decades, it rarely ceases. It usually involves preventing the estrangee from making contact or breaching boundaries through practical strategies and symbolic gestures. It involves managing internalised ideologies about family, as well as the expectations of others, when there are psychological and physical pressures to reunite. It involves the anticipatory and actual management of events that are unavoidable, and a commitment to manage self-healing and growth.

Managing the estrangee

> *Some clients feel relieved to not have the 'difficult' person in their lives, [but they] worry about them coming back towards the end or claiming money off the estate.*
>
> (Peta, Social Worker)

Estrangers often experience contacts from the estrangee after the estrangement announcement that can range from letters, phone calls, texts and gifts, to stalking, threats, being approached and physical violence. Such contacts require them to make decisions about taking action or sitting with inaction. The most common way that estrangers manage this is through practical strategies that prevent communication, such as not answering the door or the phone. This often involves changing phone numbers or moving locations without informing the estrangee, and sometimes changing surnames to avoid detection. This might also require the collusion and management of others in keeping this type of information private. The estranger will also need to remain vigilant in public if the other person lives nearby, and they may need to change their daily routine. The use of social media often becomes more restrictive for estrangers, where they are likely to employ strict privacy settings to prevent the estrangee from viewing their new life. They might also screen and manage other people who have access to this information in order to protect it from being shared. Interestingly, research with adult estrangers found that some used social media to check on the status and whereabouts of estrangees, which acted as an assurance that their boundaries were unlikely to be breached in the near future (Agllias, 2014; Scharp, 2014).

Creating symbolic boundaries

> *[My estranged daughter said], 'By the way dad, my middle name is not Elizabeth now', because I gave her her middle name, Elizabeth. 'Mum made me change it to her name, Clare.'*
>
> (Robert)

Estrangers might also create symbolic boundaries to maintain the estrangement. As noted in Robert's quote above, symbolic boundaries might serve to keep the estrangee 'out'. In Robert's case, his daughter's name change acts to delete his historic connection to her rather than keeping her identity obscured. However, symbolic boundaries can also be created to keep family members 'in'. In Robert's case, his daughter's name change also indicates a strong alliance with, and allegiance to, her mother. Other legal actions, such as changing wills and guardianship arrangements, might serve similar purposes. Estrangers might create symbolic boundaries through new traditions and rituals that would potentially offend or annoy the estrangee (e.g. having their wedding on the beach or getting a tattoo). Some use social media to deliberately display their successful and happy life without the estrangee and despite the estrangement. This acts as a symbolic gesture of rejection, where the estranged person sees that they are no longer included or needed, and that the estranger is no longer mourning their loss.

Managing the expectations of others

I have seen [my father] and spoken to him within that period but only when it's been kind of forced on me. . . . His wife contacts me and there's been one occasion where she's made me speak to him on the phone and one time my Pop brought him around [unannounced].

(Kim)

Estrangers often need to manage the expectations and actions of family and friends who might encourage, expect or enforce conciliatory attempts. Some get 'tricked' into meeting with the estranged relative, which makes them sensitive and cautious about similar situations. Periods of crisis and illness often contribute to third party pressure to reunite with an estrangee. Additionally, new intimates (such as partners and friends) can be considerable sources of pressure to reunite with an estranged relative even though they might have no historic understanding of the relationship dynamic. Research shows that spouses – and particularly ones who have a positive experience of family – can place considerable pressure on estrangers to *try again* (Agllias, 2014; Robinson, 2011; Scharp, 2014). This might be driven by a selfless and naive effort to reduce some of their partner's hurt, or involve more selfish motives such as improving the family's social status. Estrangers might have to create and maintain 'no go zones' in some relationships, where the estrangee is not mentioned at all. However, the management of friends and relatives can often become so difficult that those relationships also become strained and lead to distancing or dissolution.

Additionally, estrangers often struggle with their own internalised responses to dominant social messages about the inevitability of the genetic bond. Their moral beliefs about personal and structural commitment – as described previously – can be triggered by a number of events and processes, and these conflicting ideas need to be managed if the estrangement is to remain intact. Estrangers often need to challenge their own ideas about family, and remind themselves of the precursors to estrangement, in order to maintain it. They can do this by creating new narratives about family, and they might also share these narratives with others. For example, estrangers might recite the importance of personal health over family obligation, denounce the acceptability of familial abuse, and promote the notion of *families of choice*.

Managing events

> So I went to this birthday party with a strategic plan, and one of them was to stay very grounded. . . . So I just kept moving. . . . So I ended up having quite an okay time with the camera in hand. So that was the way I managed it.
>
> (Angela)

As mentioned previously, family events are often a considerable source of rumination and pondering for estrangers, and many choose not to attend due to the stressors involved and the fear of confrontation. However, some do attend certain functions, and they do this through active management strategies (as detailed in Angela's comments above). Quite often *event management* involves arriving at events early or late to ensure a seat or position away from the estrangee or arriving with a support person to prevent feelings of isolation and to ward off the estranged person. In many instances, family events are managed by the collusion with, or assistance from, other relatives. Generally there is a peacemaker or an ally who will smooth the way, act as a lookout, or keep the estrangee at bay. Some people who choose estrangement manage particular occasions by holding their own separate event.

Maintaining a differentiated self

> I didn't run away and break off all contact to hurt her. I did it to protect myself and to become a person.
>
> (Tina)

Most estrangers view estrangement as the only avenue to health, happiness and personal growth. The decision to estrange, then, often involves an obligation to a *differentiated self*. Similar to the commitment to a new and different family, this involves a commitment to developing and maintaining a new and different non-conformist self. Associated discoveries can be intoxicating for some, and new-found freedoms and strengths can become self-perpetuating. The further the estranger moves from family norms, the more dysfunctional the previous relationship – and the estrangee's behaviours – might appear. Personal growth might also act as some sort of assurance that a difficult decision was not made in vain. However, the differentiation and maintenance of an autonomous self can act as a burden for some estrangers. For example, the estranger's success may become a guilty burden if the estrangee's life circumstances are less prosperous or more problematic. The differentiation process can also become problematic for those who reconceptualise independence as *isolation* from others. Indeed, research with adult estrangers showed that some viewed any form of contact or reconciliation with the estrangee(s) as a potential step backwards from healing and personal growth (Agllias, 2014). On the other hand, some suggested that the differentiation and maintenance of self assisted them to view the estrangee's actions more empathically (see Chapter 7 for connections to personal growth and healing). Regardless, the maintenance of self can be an arduous task because it requires some degree of interdependence at a time when relational trust may be low. It might require the ongoing renegotiation – or breaking – of family norms and actions that may have been prevented or punished in the past.

Impacts on daily living

So today hurts like hell but I will just get on with it – there is no other choice, my own family needs me and I need to work to escape and not think about the hurt.

(Rita, diary entry)

This section examines the vulnerabilities and risks that are created and exposed when estrangement is enacted. While there is minimal estrangement-specific research about the effects of estrangement on health and well-being, transferrable evidence is used to explore the potential impacts on daily living. Estrangers will experience similar physiological responses to estrangement as the person they estrange, including emotional reactivity, anxiety and stress (Agllias, 2014; Bowen, 1982; Harrison, 2003). Stress and anxiety are often by-products of the estrangement loss, a reduced support system and the vigilance required to maintain the estrangement. As a result, some estrangers might be susceptible to the illnesses and serious health conditions that develop from chronic stress and rumination, such as a weakened immune system, insomnia, muscle pain, high blood pressure, cognitive impairment, anxiety, depression, suicidal ideation, diabetes, obesity and heart disease (McEwen, 2007; Sheets & Craighead, 2014; Sun *et al.*, 2014).

Estranging a family member might increase susceptibility to a complicated grief trajectory, brought about by long-term, cumulative and cyclical loss occurrences, as well as the ambiguous nature and disenfranchised status of estrangement. Estrangers in one qualitative study reported a number of post-traumatic symptoms in the years after the estrangement, including: flashbacks; hypervigilance; being oversensitive to the remarks and actions of others; feelings of nervousness; high levels of shame and embarrassment; a form of survivor guilt, where they thought maybe they should have done more for the relationship; feeling like they had been given a second chance and needing to make the most of it; avoidance of anything related to the experience; and low self-esteem (Agllias, 2014).

Despite their assumed position as the primary source of rejection in the relationship dynamic, estrangers employ estrangement as a way of *ending* their experience of long-term rejection. However, the nature of the attachment relationship and the social ideologies associated with family are unlikely to dissipate quickly after relationship dissolution, where the intrinsic memory and imaginings of the estrangee might keep rejection responses alive indefinitely. Additionally, the very act of estrangement can create additional rejection, or gestures of disapproval, from family members, friends and associates. As a result, estrangers are likely to have experienced, and continue to experience, the emotions associated with rejection and betrayal – such as hurt, anger, sadness, distress and numbness – across long periods of time.

Smart Richman and Leary (2009) suggest that chronic experiences of rejection 'will predict withdrawal and avoidant patterns of responses', and subsequent 'behaviors that undermine physical health' (Smart Richman & Leary, 2009, p. 373). Rejection has been reliably shown to undermine self-esteem in social situations, so it is reasonable to assume familial rejection would produce a greater effect (Vandevelde & Miyahara, 2005; Zadro *et al.*, 2005). Similarly, internalised moral ideologies that have been contradicted by the act of estrangement can negatively affect the estranger's sense of self and social acceptability, and result in internalised feelings of guilt, regret and failure. These elements combined might contribute to a form of rejection sensitivity in some, as well as isolation and reliance on a small number of trusted relationships (Agllias, 2014; Robinson, 2011). Rejection sensitivity is when a person anxiously expects rejection, perceives intentional rejection in ambiguous behaviours, and reacts intensely to perceived rejection (Downey & Feldman, 1996; Downey et al., 2004). This can create a cyclical situation for estrangers where a prophecy of rejection is fulfilled when anxious or defensive behaviours prevent others from getting too close.

Rejection and betrayal threatens our primitive, as well as social, *sense of belonging* and *sense of safety*, both elements core to psychological and physical well-being (Baumeister & Leary, 1995). A number of post-estrangement conditions have the potential to reactivate earlier rejection experiences and threaten feelings of safety and belonging. First, a stigmatised consciousness warns estrangers that their choice is aberrant and dangerous. Second, the isolating conditions of estrangement often reduce access to the resources necessary for survival. Even if this is a temporary state, limited resources can remind the estranger of their vulnerability and outsider status. Third, the relief that many find in relationship dissolution fuels a belief that the estrangement must be maintained in order to preserve safety. However, maintenance, too, comes at a cost, with many estrangers reporting hypervigilance for years after the estrangement decision. Research about the connection between hypervigilance and anxiety is mixed (Beck et al., 2005; Cisler & Koster, 2010), but estrangers certainly report the experience as personally exhausting and possibly detrimental to their new family dynamic (Agllias, 2014). It should also be noted that hypervigilance is a very real response to feeling under attack or anticipating attack, but this, too, can be viewed as unnecessary or paranoia by significant others, and may become another source of the estranger's isolation and secrecy. Finally, the reliance on a small network of supports has the potential to place a great deal of stress on these relationships, making them vulnerable to dissolution. Indeed, Bowen Family Systems theorists suspect that estrangement can have considerably negative effects on marital and parent/child relationships where increased emotional reactivity and interdependence (or togetherness stress), without support from the intergenerational family, can increase vulnerability to relationship breakdown (see Chapter 6 for further detail).

Conclusion

Deciding to physically estrange a family member is a significant and difficult action, usually taken as a last resort after cycles of distancing and reconciliation. In other instances it is a reaction to a significant betrayal. It is a unique and protracted loss that poses considerable challenges because it contradicts the conditioned consciousness, stigmatised awareness and social experiences of family. The estranger has often experienced considerable anticipatory loss prior to the estrangement decision, but this does not necessarily negate the traumatic reality of being responsible for cutting ties with a family member. Grieving the estrangement, the inevitability of the decision, and the loss of a unified family is an intrapersonal and interpersonal process that can continue until the end of life. Estrangers often describe an ongoing process of: (i) acknowledging the lived reality of the relationship; (ii) experiencing grief reactions; (iii) learning to differentiate with limited support; (iv) developing a new sense of self and family; (v) maintaining distance from the estrangee; and (vi) creating a fulfilling life without the estrangee. However, this is not a linear process, because the nature of the relationship and particular triggers regularly highlight the estrangement decision, refresh emotional reactions and require remedial attention. Chapter 7 explores the methods that estranged people employ to grieve, increase their health and emotional well-being and *learn to live with estrangement* in the long term.

PRACTICE POINT 3: ASSESSING THE IMPACT OF THE ESTRANGEMENT

It is important to understand and assess the various effects of estrangement in order to: (i) acknowledge the personal loss experience (including the prior, immediate and longer-term effects); (ii) establish a baseline of current functioning in order to measure progress/development across time; (iii) acknowledge strengths, strategies and supports that have already been utilised to survive or live with estrangement (and those that have not been so useful); (iv) assess current priorities and areas that might need attention; and (v) assess this collective knowledge against information provided in Chapters 7 and 8, in order to incorporate some new strategies to maximise health and well-being, if warranted. The exercises in Practice Point 3 have been developed for people who had a difficult relationship prior to the estrangement. Practice Point 2 – in Chapter 3 – is more suitable for those people who found their relationship relatively satisfactory prior to the estrangement.

EXERCISE 1: REFLECTION ON THE EFFECTS OF ESTRANGEMENT

Think back to your first memory of distancing from the person who you eventually became estranged from and reflect on the effects that you can recall up to the point of estrangement. Document these in the Table 4.1 'Impacts of estrangement inventory 2' – column (a). Now, think back to the days and weeks after the estrangement and detail the impacts you can recall in column (b). Finally, think about your current situation and detail the current effects in column (c). Note: An example is provided to assist with this process (see Table 4.2).

EXERCISE 2: REFLECTION ON CHANGE

Look at the effects that you have documented in Table 4.1 and consider how these have changed over time (lessened, remained constant or increased). Reflect upon these changes and take a note of them at the bottom of the inventory. Have there been positive impacts? Make a note of these too.

TABLE 4.1 Impacts of estrangement inventory 2

	(a) Prior effects	(b) Immediate effects	(c) Current effects
Emotional e.g. anger, anxiety, relief, emotional shock, fear, sadness, hurt, frustration, irritability, guilt, denial, uncertainty, apprehension, agitation.			
Physical e.g. difficulty breathing, nausea, fatigue, headaches, weakness, twitches, grinding teeth, sweating, chest pain.			
Cognitive e.g. hypervigilance, changes in memory, lack of concentration, confusion, nightmares, flashbacks, blaming the other person, poor attention.			
Behavioural e.g. withdrawal, emotional outbursts, change in appetite, pacing, increased drug or alcohol use, change in activity, acting out, change in communication patterns.			
Spiritual e.g. loss of meaning, loss of trust, questioning meaning of life, questioning spiritual beliefs, questioning God (or Deity).			
Social e.g. socialising less, avoiding people and social functions, taking time off work, being less engaged at family, work and social events, not answering the phone.			

2. Reflection on changes over time (including any positive effects)

TABLE 4.2 Impacts of estrangement inventory 2 (example)

	(a) Prior effects	(b) Immediate effects	(c) Current effects
Emotional e.g. anger, anxiety, relief, emotional shock, fear, sadness, hurt, frustration, irritability, guilt, denial, uncertainty, apprehension, agitation.	*Frustration* *Sadness*	*Anger* *Sadness* *Hurt* *Shock*	*Sadness* *Hurt*
Physical e.g. difficulty breathing, nausea, fatigue, headaches, weakness, twitches, grinding teeth, sweating, chest pain.	*Headaches*	*Weakness* *Fatigue*	*N/A*
Cognitive e.g. hypervigilance, changes in memory, lack of concentration, confusion, nightmares, flashbacks, blaming the other person, poor attention.	*Blaming the other* *Poor attention*	*Hypervigilance* *Blaming the other* *Poor attention* *Confusion* *Nightmares*	*Hypervigilance* *Lack of concentration at times*
Behavioural e.g. withdrawal, emotional outbursts, change in appetite, pacing, increased drug or alcohol use, change in activity, acting out, change in communication patterns.	*Withdrawal* *Emotional outbursts*	*Withdrawal* *Change in appetite* *Pacing*	*Increased prescription drug use*
Spiritual e.g. loss of meaning, loss of trust, questioning meaning of life, questioning spiritual beliefs, questioning God (or Deity).	*Loss of trust*	*Loss of meaning* *Questioning meaning of life*	*Questioning meaning of life*
Social e.g. socialising less, avoiding people and social functions, taking time off work, being less engaged at family, work and social events, not answering the phone.	*Avoiding people and social functions* *Being less engaged at family events* *Not answering the phone*	*Socialising less* *Taking time off work* *Not answering the phone*	*Taking time off work*

2. Reflection on changes over time (including any positive effects)

I was really frustrated before the estrangement, and then very angry at the time of the estrangement. Became less frustrated/angry and had less physical responses over time, but grew increasingly sad and hurt by everything. I still blame my parents for the estrangement but not my decision to estrange. I have started to socialise more because I know I should. I also had a car accident around this time and have increasingly used prescription drugs to numb some physical and emotional pain. I know I take more time off work than I should (just can't face it some days). Positive things – well the split and the counselling has made me really interested in psychology and I have been reading and learning a lot.

EXERCISE 3: REFLECTION ON RESILIENCE

All people draw on strengths, strategies and supports to work through estrangement.

- *Strengths* are the positive personal traits and virtues that people employ in a balanced life, and they can be drawn upon as a guide to, or motivation for, action during times of confusion and distress.
- *Strategies* are the simple and complex plans for action that we develop to bring about positive change, achieve a goal or solve a problem.
- *Supports* are people or things that provide assistance, that buffer or hold some of the weight of negative experiences.

First, reflect on the changes identified in Exercise 2. Then consider the strengths, strategies and supports that positively influenced those changes. Document these in the Table 4.3 'Resilience inventory' below. Finally, reflect upon and document any

TABLE 4.3 Resilience inventory

Strengths that I have drawn upon Strengths might include things like open-mindedness, curiosity, integrity, persistence, social intelligence, forgiveness, self-regulation, gratitude, humour, spirituality.	
Strategies that I have used These might include: setting up a more structured routine; planning meals and sitting down to eat regardless of appetite; challenging black-and-white thoughts whenever they arise; taking a friend/partner to difficult social situations; taking up a new activity such as meditation or yoga; and using a diary to let go of, or contain, worry.	
Supports that I have employed These might include: adequate finances; people such as family, friends, neighbours and work colleagues; therapeutic interventions such as counselling; church or social groups; educative supports like documentaries, movies, books and websites; and natural or manmade resources such as beaches, parks, sunsets (and time itself).	
Traits/strengths, strategies and supports that were not useful or became less useful over time	

traits/strengths, strategies or potential supports that were not so useful – or became less useful – across the estrangement journey. These might include things like: the strength of independence (which can become problematic if it prevents help-seeking), the trait of stubbornness, or strategies such as social withdrawal and unsupportive influences such as one-way friendships. Note: an example is provided to assist with this process (see Table 4.4).

EXERCISE 4: AREAS FOR ATTENTION

Look back at column (c) in Table 4.1. Identify two to five areas that might require further consideration or attention. Consider the strengths, strategies and supports that you mapped in Table 4.3 and how these might be helpful.

TABLE 4.4 Resilience inventory (example 2)

Strengths that I have drawn upon Strengths might include things like open-mindedness, curiosity, integrity, persistence, social intelligence, forgiveness, self-regulation, gratitude, humour, spirituality.	*Self-regulation, open-mindedness and humour*
Strategies that I have used These might include: setting up a more structured routine; planning meals and sitting down to eat regardless of appetite; challenging black-and-white thoughts whenever they arise; taking a friend/partner to difficult social situations; taking up a new activity such as meditation or yoga; and using a diary to let go of, or contain, worry.	*I use a diary a lot to work through my feelings and challenge my negative thoughts. I make myself walk when I feel too sad or depressed.*
Supports that I have employed These might include: adequate finances; people such as family, friends, neighbours and work colleagues; therapeutic interventions such as counselling; church or social groups; educative supports like documentaries, movies, books and websites; and natural or manmade resources such as beaches, parks, sunsets (and time itself).	*I had some counselling after a car accident and talked about the estrangement a little. I also have a good group of friends who have listened to me, and I read a lot of psychology books.*
Traits/strengths, strategies and supports that were not useful or became less useful over time *The car accident gave me a lot of time to think about the estrangement and the drug use afterwards has become a bit of a problem. I also have one friend who tends to take more than they give, and this has become very draining recently. Taking time off work can be a vicious cycle where I get behind and dread going there, and it gives me more time to feel sad too.*	

Chapter 5   When there are few shared experiences

There's always trepidation. There's always fear. You don't go with a freedom, you don't go with a joy in your heart. . . . Even that time I went to Brett's . . . I didn't bring up any politics, I didn't bring up religion.

(Jean)

Social research suggests that our experiences are amplified, and may even be perceived to be more enjoyable, when they are shared (Boothby *et al.*, 2014). Additionally, sharing painful experiences with others can increase trust, cooperation and cohesion (Bastian *et al.*, 2014). When we think about sharing in the family context it usually involves the joint enjoyment of a belief, experience or activity. In times of crisis or stress, sharing involves the distribution of emotional and physical support to the family member(s) in need. In the intergenerational family, shared experiences are fundamental to the development and maintenance of bonding, belonging and cohesion as well as the transmission of important historic and genetic knowledge. Shared experiences assist in the acculturation of family values, expectations, support and care. While the cessation of sharing is fundamental to physical estrangement, this chapter examines three types of estrangement that are characterised by 'few' shared experiences, and where the absence of sharing appears more prominent than open conflict and overt accusations of rejection, abuse and betrayal. In the first instance, emotional estrangement is discussed. Emotionally estranged family members remain in contact, and they might even reside in the same residence, but they cite strained, meaningless and arduous relationships. In the second instance, family members appear to have so few shared experiences that relationships almost dissolve over time, and neither party feels inclined or able to contact the other (resulting in estrangement). Finally, when estrangements commence in childhood, due to factors such as parental abandonment or adoption, the establishment or continuation of this familial connection may be affected in adulthood. While these three estrangements might appear unique, they are highlighted and discussed in this chapter due to their similarities. The three types of estrangement, referred henceforth as (i) emotional estrangement; (ii) mutually disengaged estrangement; and (iii) absent estrangement, will be described in the first section of the chapter. This will be followed by a general discussion about the loss experience of estrangements characterised by few shared experiences. Finally, a practice section encourages the reader or client to critically assess the current estrangement status – including the practices and processes being employed to maintain emotional distancing – and identify existing resilience, strengths and strategies that might be harnessed as they learn to live with estrangement.

Emotional estrangement: Walking on eggshells

Like my husband comments ... it's so bizarre to be around family and be uncomfortable. To be nervous, scared, on edge is just bizarre to him. . . . He's like [it is as if] you're on audition or something or you're going to be thrown out the door any minute.

(Debbie)

The term *emotional estrangement* refers to a range of distancing behaviours as well as blocking and avoidance strategies that are usually employed in an effort to avoid hurt and relieve unresolved tensions between family members. Emotional estrangement is often cited as a core element in physical and cyclical estrangements. It might be described as a *precursor to* physical estrangement as well as the *reason for* physical estrangement. However, it can also be experienced in a relationship that never proceeds to open conflict, physical or cyclical estrangement. While emotional estrangement often involves a lessening of physical contact between the parties over time, the parties might actually live in the same home and participate in regular perfunctory contact.

Bowen Family Systems Theory, while primarily relating to the parent and child relationship, offers some possible insights into the development of emotional estrangement (Bowen, 1982). As detailed more thoroughly in Chapter 2, the theory suggests that emotional and physical distancing is an aspect of human adaptation that serves to regulate levels of attachment and dependency between parents and their adolescents or young adult children (Smith, 1998; Titelman, 2003b). Along the estrangement continuum, *covert cutoff* (or emotional estrangement) is considered to be a problematic relational state (Titelman, 2003b). Emotional withdrawal – through often covert practices – effectively reduces the immediate anxiety and stress associated with fused relationships, without overt conflict and complete physical withdrawal. However, unresolved issues remain in the long term.

Adult attachment theories might also provide some insight into emotional estrangement. For example, people with avoidant models of attachment are likely to experience a deactivation or flight response to distress, and a propensity to estrange. 'Deactivation involves inhibition of proximity-seeking inclinations, actions and emotional expressions and the determination to handle stress and distress alone' (Shaver *et al.*, p. 96). The *fearful-avoidant* person often has a negative self-view and view of others, resulting in high levels of anxiety and avoidance (Fiori *et al.*, 2009). They will exhibit a lack of assertiveness and feel insecure in social situations. While they crave intimacy, the possibility or realisation of closeness will often result in their fearful withdrawal. When observed, the person's fearful-avoidant response might be perceived as independence and confidence, but they are often 'deeply distrustful of close relationships and terrified of allowing themselves to rely on anyone else, in some cases in order to avoid the pain of being rejected and in others to avoid being subjected to pressure to become someone else's caretaker' (Bowlby, 1979, p. 138). The *dismissive-avoidant* person will have a positive self-view, but a negative view of others, generally downplaying the importance of rejection to maintain high self-esteem, and the appearance of independence and confidence (Fiori *et al.*, 2009). It is theorised that people with dismissive-avoidant attachments might have developed pre-emptive defences to suppress memory recall and keep the attachment system relatively suppressed during stressful events (Fraley & Brumbaugh, 2007).

While Attachment and Bowen Family Systems theories offer some useful insights, it is important to evaluate these in a broader and intergenerational family context, and beyond psychopathology. According to these theories, emotional estrangement might be regarded as a physiological response derived from an insecure attachment during childhood, or one that develops across time and presents in adolescence in families where intense emotional interdependence is present. It is also important to note that in some circumstances people may have the inability to connect emotionally with others or a condition that may be associated with depersonalisation and dissociation. However, when people have the capacity to engage in secure attachments and emotionally fulfilling relationships with others (outside of the family estrangement dynamic), it might be possible that emotional estrangement is a learned response within a particular relationship or a situational protective mechanism. Emotional estrangement might protect secrets or the personal safety of others (although this is unlikely to be a conscious action or viable long-term solution to the presenting issue). For example, a woman experiencing domestic violence who emotionally estranges her daughter and grandchildren effectively avoids disclosing the actuality or severity of her situation. As a result, the daughter and grandchildren are less likely to ask questions, attend the home or take action against the perpetrator, which probably reduces their potential exposure to violence (and may also protect the victim from violence in the short term). Additionally, given the significant social and internalised pressures to maintain biological relationships – as described in Chapters 3 and 4 – emotional estrangement might be viewed as the most effective way to *end* an unwanted relationship when physical estrangement is not considered a viable option.

It is also important to recognise that all types of social and familial relationships – beyond the parent and child – are susceptible to emotional estrangement, and relationships have varying degrees of emotional interaction across a lifetime. Families often utilise distancing behaviours and processes to 'keep the peace' and reduce tension in certain situations. Distancing is an important component of differentiation in adolescence, and also in creating social and professional boundaries outside of the family. 'Flight' is a legitimate physiological response to the threat of danger, and many people use withdrawal to take a break from a dispute or uncomfortable situation before regrouping and attending to the issue. People often use withdrawal to signify their hurt, to punish the other for wrongdoing, and in the hope that the other person will correct their errant behaviour, in order for the relationship to be resumed.

However, emotional estrangement is the *problematic prolonged overuse* of distancing practices to avoid closeness, tension or hurt. It effectively blocks any discussion or resolution of important underlying issues, and it tends to have negative emotional consequences for both parties. The emotionally estranged person may appear unaffected by an interaction but they are often experiencing or reacting to intense emotion. Emotional estrangement can be used to protect the self and it can also be used as an effective tool to punish another. It is unlikely that emotional estrangement can be achieved by one person alone. Rather, there are a number of actions and behaviours – as described in the following sections – that appear to engage the other in a cycle of outwardly tense and emotionally devoid interactions (although inwardly, negative emotion is core to each individual's experience of the exchange).

Indicators of emotional estrangement

> *I could see which way [my son] was going and I just cut him out of my heart. . . .*
> *It's as simple as that. You can't linger longer with these things.*
>
> (Stephen)

There are a number of practices that create, maintain and indicate emotional estrangement, ranging from avoiding and delaying contact, changing the nature of the relationship through language and symbolic acts, to intimidating behaviours and imminent threats. This section examines emotional estrangement from two distinct perspectives: (i) the perspective of the estrangee, who usually suggests that the other person is psychologically absent, changed, unreachable, incommunicative and rejecting; and (ii) the perspective of the estranger, who usually suggests that the other person is unreasonable, difficult, in denial and rejecting, and from whom they need to protect themselves. However, it should be highlighted that this is an artificial distinction for the purpose of examining the indicators of emotional estrangement. It is most likely that both parties use at least some of the behaviours and tactics cited in the following sections to maintain distance, to protect themselves from rejection and hurt and to punish the other for perceived wrongs. The next section examines the characteristics of emotional estrangement, which is followed by the unique perspectives and experiences of the estranger and estrangee.

Avoiding, delaying and altering contact

> *So I would call [my mother] and say, look, we haven't seen each other for maybe a month. Time for me to come over and spend some time with you, with the children and, 'Oh, I've got a cold. I don't want to see them.' Over a window of 18 months it happened time and time again. . . . It was her birthday, 'I'm sick, I don't want to see anyone.'*
>
> (Mark)

People often notice a decrease in contact when emotional estrangement is evident. Estrangers might choose to distance themselves geographically, by living a long way from the estrangee. Or they might choose to estrange through *activity* (e.g. too busy at work or university to visit), *adverse circumstance* (e.g. too unwell to have visitors), or disguised as an act of *goodwill* (e.g. I didn't want to bother you). When people live together, they might still employ methods of physical distancing such as bounded spaces (e.g. a bedroom or a shed becomes a no go zone for the estrangee). Regardless of proximity, the estranger usually avoids and delays contact, often increasing the time between visits or interactions. The estrangee might find it more and more difficult to find a mutually suitable time to meet, or share some sort of conversation or activity in a co-habiting situation. Over time, the estrangee is likely to discover that they are the primary instigator, and arranger, of contact. In other instances, contact might be formalised (e.g. dinner on the first Monday of each month). Some emotionally estranged parents in one study suggested that they often engaged more with voicemail than their adult child, and messages went unanswered, or were only answered after a number of messages were left (Agllias, 2011). The estranger will often make 'other plans' if they expect to be invited to a particular family event (such as Christmas), or 'say' that they have already made plans if invited unexpectedly.

The duration of contact usually decreases also, and the estranger often dashes in and out of planned contact, sometimes announcing that they have to be somewhere else at a certain time. Or contact arrangements might become more formal, where the estranger makes a pre-event announcement about how long they will be staying (e.g. 'we'll be there but we can only stay until 2pm'). The estranger will most likely avoid spontaneous interactions or contact that extends beyond the originally agreed upon arrangements. When the parties are cohabiting, the estranger might become intensely absorbed in a particular activity, such as reading or woodwork, to appear busy and counteract invitations for shared interactions.

Physical proximity often alters in emotional estrangement, where the estranger stands or sits further away than previously. Eye contact may be reduced. Miller and Parks (1982) suggest that relationship dissolution may be signified by tense bodily markers such as fidgeting (particularly of the legs and feet), increased walking around or pacing, as well as increased self-touch movements. The estranger might ignore the estrangee's words or pretend that they did not hear them. The estranger will engage in less physical contact, and touch might be briefer or more rigid than previously. Some estrangees suggest that they can feel the estranger pull away, fidget or flinch during an embrace or they might resist any touch that is offered (Agllias, 2011).

Distancing language and topic avoidance

Anyway, so I've tried to keep in touch with him. I ring him up and I say how are you going? All right. Where are you living? Not telling you. He's outright with it, you know, he's not – not a fluffy thing. What are you doing? I don't know.

(Helen)

Estrangees often notice topic avoidance when an emotional estrangement becomes more evident. Estrangers will avoid, change the subject or directly refuse to engage in topics that have the potential to breach their privacy, or cause disagreement, conflict, hurt or rejection. They tend to keep the topic of conversation quite general, rarely discussing emotions or opinions. Conversation might be marked by generalisations or vagueness when asked an opinion. For example, Miller and Parks (1982) suggest that dissolving relationships will involve the increasing use of over-inclusive or under-inclusive statements: 'responding to a question regarding how one liked dinner at a particular restaurant by saying, "the whole evening was nice" would count as an instance of over-inclusiveness. Conversely, under-inclusiveness occurs when the subject refers to just a part or attribute of an implied whole (e.g., "I liked the salad")' (p. 137).

The estranger's language is likely to become more ambiguous, non-committal and evasive, where the terms, 'maybe', 'not sure', and 'we'll see' are increasingly employed (usually to delay and avoid contact as described above). The amount of speaking often reduces and long or awkward silences become more frequent. The emotional and verbal tone may become less lively, and the estranger appears less interested, impressed or empathically engaged in the conversation. Estrangers might shift from 'we' and 'us' references to more 'you' and 'I' statements, clearly showing a separation from the other. They might refrain from calling the other person by their name or relational name (such as father).

Conversations might become one sided, where the estranger keeps control of the conversation so that topic boundaries are kept intact. Alternatively, the estrangee might enter a monologue as they try to fill the silence and encourage some sort of reaction from the estranger. The parties might increasingly speak through a third person, such as a partner or child in some instances (e.g. getting a spouse to make transport arrangements with the estrangee, or asking a child to tell an estranger that dinner is ready). The estranger is likely to focus attention on other parties in the room, rather than speaking directly to the estrangee.

Secrets and 'no go zones'

I never run their father down to them, but I don't talk to them about him either – and the other three are happy that way. If they bring – if they brought it up I'd talk to them, but they never bring it up so I don't.

(Lois)

Some emotional estrangements are marked by secrets and 'no go zones', where both parties are aware of the unspoken rules around particular topics that might cause embarrassment, hurt feelings and misunderstanding. It appears that one or both parties consider the topic to be a significant threat to the stability or continuance of the relationship if it were discussed. In other instances, discussion might require action that the parties feel unable to take. In many cases the estrangee is the person keeping a secret, fearing the consequences if it were to be discussed, but the estranger actually considers the secret as the primary relational threat. For example, a father who considers himself to be emotionally estranged from his son has never spoken about his wartime experiences in order to protect his son from the trauma, but the son interprets his non-disclosure as a negative and unnecessary boundary representative of his father's rejection and mistrust.

Lies and exaggeration

She just exaggerates. . . . Whenever I talked to her about what she does, it's always – oh she could be [the prime minister's] secretary one minute, you know, it's just unbelievable . . . she [actually] works in a shop.

(Beth)

Estrangers often tell simple lies to maintain their own privacy and create and maintain distance (e.g. I cannot attend because I have to work). They might also feel the need to develop more complex lies in order to distance themselves from the estrangee's assistance, interference or judgement, or to avoid a difficult conversation. So some estrangers might tell the estrangee things that they think they wish to hear (e.g. 'I have a good job and I am financially stable', when in fact the person is living on a friend's couch). However, it should be noted that some estranger's lying or exaggeration might not be a conscious action, and may be attributed to mental illness.

Regardless, the behaviour inadvertently achieves the same end – it creates distrust and keeps the other party from getting too close.

From intimacy to functionality

Estrangees might start to notice that they are being regarded more like an acquaintance than a family member, and that their knowledge of the estranger is decreasing. The estranger might maintain strict privacy around the simplest of information, effectively keeping the estrangee from understanding their personal circumstances. They might also reduce the exposure that the estrangee has to information about them or to people with such information. They might avoid events or gatherings where mutual relationships might require them to interact more cordially with the estrangee.

Estrangers often start to treat the connection more as an *exchange* relationship, where they expect to benefit equally from the other person, rather than in a *communal* relationship, where exchange is generally founded on a consideration of the other's welfare and without the expectation of immediate and equivalent reward. Arrangements about and access to shared property is likely to become more formalised, where people are less likely to assume access, but revert to asking in the way they would with a friend or acquaintance. Less shared property is likely to be accumulated. As a result, estrangers are less likely to ask for, or take, advice, assistance or help, and are more likely to use substitutes in times of need. Estrangers might decline the smallest of previously assumed familial goodwill so that they do not feel indebted to the estrangee.

Not attending or acknowledging important events

But just prior to my surgery I made mum and dad aware ... I'd had some counselling and I thought I'd give mum and dad – try to reconnect with them. ... They just couldn't be bothered coming around and it was too much for them to come and see me, even though I said I may not [live].

(Lisa)

Estrangees often notice that their emotionally estranged relative stops attending important events over time, often using some of the aforementioned excuses. Estrangers might 'forget' important occasions such as birthdays or anniversaries or their acknowledgement might be less personal than previously (e.g. sending a text instead of phoning). They might suggest that they are no longer interested in, or downplay the importance of, family activities such as Christmas. Or they might openly disparage such activities. Similarly, estrangers might reduce their response to illness or crisis events (e.g. sending flowers to the hospital instead of attending).

Enforcing the status quo

[He gave my husband] a very aggressive handshake ... a form of saying, up you, because [my husband] had to let go first, because it was a form of, don't think you're going to boss me around. And [his wife] was very confident. He was so terrible. He was so awful. He was sarcastic.

(Carol)

In some instances, estrangers might use intimidating actions to maintain control of the emotionally estranged relationship status. This can be achieved by words and actions that are clearly designed to infer and highlight the estranger's superiority and the estrangee's inferiority. Estranged parents in one study (Agllias, 2011) gave examples of their adult children flaunting their financial successes and deliberately raising topics outside of the parent's experience (e.g. investment, overseas travel or culinary knowledge). If the parent showed interest or curiosity in these topics, the child might dismiss these queries as ignorant or not worth addressing. In some instances estrangers might put the estrangee in a situation that is clearly uncomfortable for them without warning or assistance (e.g. inviting them to an event without explaining the purpose, expectations or dress code and then judging or embarrassing them for an aberrant presentation). Intimidation might also occur through physical dominance and bullying (see quote at the begining of this section). Regardless of the form, these types of actions often accompany an implied threat pertaining to the relational status quo. They suggest that the estrangee must remain silent and subservient in order to have contact with the estranger. In these instances the unspoken threat of physical estrangement is often palpable, and may work very effectively to keep the estrangee from challenging the relational status.

The cyclical experience of emotional estrangement

So I then sent him an email saying, I have tried to ring you on several occasions, on many occasions. Maybe it's because there is no reception . . . now please either email me or contact me in some way to let me know how you are. So I then received a forwarded email, which was like a Christmas card, you know, and that was it. Not even . . . nothing.

(Beth)

Emotional estrangement appears to develop from perceived rejection and counter rejection, and is perpetuated by both parties through acts of distancing and avoidance (which constitute ongoing acts of rejection and counter-rejection in themselves). Neither party appears able to address these rejections overtly – or the issues underlying them – for fear that their words or actions might result in even greater hurt or physical estrangement. Over time, almost every action is interpreted as a deliberate affront and an irritation. Parties are often left at an impasse where resentment, animosity and feelings of powerlessness sustain an unsatisfactory relationship. While the parties remain emotionally detached, there is some form of obligation to the other that prevents total relationship dissolution. However, encounters might also become a reminder of what is absent or what has been lost.

The estrangee's pursuit

There's a certain element of pain that I don't need to continue to re-experience every time I visit her. So I must admit, I had a lot of trepidation driving down there. . . . I got within 100 metres of home, my family home and I'm thinking, I just don't want to do this. . . . So I've always found it unpleasant.

(Mark)

Emotional estrangement generally sneaks up on the estrangee. They often explain away the disintegrating relationship for a long period (e.g. the estranger is too busy, stressed or unwell to engage) before openly acknowledging that something is seriously wrong. Over time, they increasingly notice a reduction in warmth and intimacy, a coldness or dismissiveness, the estranger's need to control interactions, and possibly their own feelings of impending anxiousness. When emotional distancing is eventually acknowledged, estrangees usually consider themselves to be a victim of the estranger's unwanted, disconcerting and indiscernible behaviour.

Fear is often core to the estrangee's experience, many of whom describe feelings of trepidation before an encounter. Some fear rejection, outright conflict or aggression and some fear physical estrangement. Encounters are often characterised as unnerving, tense and stressful as the estrangee assumes a vigilant position, monitoring the estranger for signs of withdrawal or displeasure and altering their own behaviours in an effort to mitigate any escalating tension. For example, estranged parents in one study said that they rarely or never confronted their estranged adult children about rejecting behaviour such as not returning phone calls (Agllias, 2011). It is also likely that both parties sense and smell each other's fear, a contagion that grows with each encounter. Some estrangees enter these encounters with a sense of purpose and hope for a positive outcome, but intense disillusionment if these aspirations are stonewalled. Anger is often the result of feeling deeply compromised by the encounter.

Similar to the experience of those who have been physically estranged, the emotional estrangee often spends considerable time trying to understand the estranger's behaviour and its origin. They will try to pinpoint the exact reason for the other's antagonism, and may feel frustrated and angry at the tactics the estranger uses to maintain this *secret*. Estrangees might experiment with different approaches and tactics to emotionally engage the other person, ranging from additional acts of care and concern, giving special gifts, offering extra material or financial assistance, to acts of confrontation and punishment. Many believe that they must have a legitimate reason to contact the estranger, so they are often on the lookout for, or creative in the pursuit of, sound 'non-threatening' contacts. These acts, as well as ruminating over the cause of the emotional estrangement, can become all-encompassing and exhausting activities. However, as time progresses and rejection persists or increases, many estrangees experience feelings of defeat, and become more timid in their words and actions. They might reduce expectations of the other party, and invitations to participate in shared activity. Estrangees are less likely to ask for help but may also continue to be affronted or hurt when their expectations of help, support or care are not forthcoming voluntarily. This might also leave some estrangees vulnerable to emotional and material deprivation.

The estranger's distance

The feelings of rejection, hurt and betrayal described by people who physically estrange are also core to the emotional estranger's distancing behaviours. However, the emotional estranger often describes a generalised experience of estrangee absence, and a multitude of ongoing slights and offenses which increasingly irritate and disturb, but may not be considered enough to legitimate confrontation or physical estrangement. The estranger might find it easier to describe the feelings they experience when in contact with the estrangee (e.g. irritation, disgust, impatience, anger and physical symptoms such as skin crawling and nausea), than to name the specific reasons underlying these responses. Ironically, the very things that estrangees do to gain respect and emotional reconnection often achieve the opposite result (e.g. gifts may be interpreted as guilty payoffs for past wrongdoings and confrontations may be perceived as bullying). Affection is almost always interpreted as a sign that the estrangee 'just doesn't get it'. When the estrangee also starts to withdraw from the relationship due to disillusionment, exhaustion, or to avoid further hurt, estrangers will often interpret or classify these behaviours as *evidence* of further indifference or lack of care.

Regardless of the origins of the emotional estrangement, the estranger remains in some way committed to the strained relationship due to a number of factors, including: perceived pressure to remain in the relationship, including personal and cultural beliefs about familial obligation and commitment; financial necessity; obligations to other family members (e.g. ensuring that their children have a relationship with the estrangee grandparent); to maintain other important and valued familial relationships; and fear about the potential consequences of physical estrangement. In other words, there is some positive element or gain from remaining in the relationship (e.g. financial stability, maintaining cultural norms and a positive public image, remaining a valued family member).

It appears that the estranger's distancing actions may be enacted as a defense mechanism to avoid further rejection, betrayal or hurt, as a form of punishment for wrongdoing, or to enhance their independence or personal authority. The need to control interactions – an evolutionary response to perceived threat – may provide a sense of certainty or calm prior to and during the interaction. However, it takes considerable effort to maintain an emotional estrangement. Distancing and control strategies take thought, time and effort to develop, implement and maintain, and this might explain the general decline in estranger-initiated interactions over time. Additionally, deception might go against the values of the estranger, who either struggles with their duplicity or works considerably hard to find relatively truthful avenues of escape. Contacts can be highly distressing for estrangers, who need to remain vigilant to any changes in the environment that may induce some form of emotional response (e.g. limiting physical contact to avoid the uncomfortable positive or negative emotional reactions this might produce). The estranger's need for control and independence might also leave them highly vulnerable during periods of crisis, where they are reluctant to ask for help and support from the estrangee.

Mutual Disengagement

> Lisa: *We never got upset, we never got angry. I never had an argument, got abusive with her. Is that right?*
> Michael: *You disengaged. It was too much energy to harbour anything and our priorities were [the children].*

There are instances where familial relationships seem to dissolve or disappear over time. Often there have been a series of losses, differences, slights and grievances, but these have not resulted in open conflict or deep-seated resentments worthy of *announcing* a physical estrangement. Neither party seems overly dissatisfied with, or let down by, the other person, but trust has been eroded and shared experiences are minimal or non-existent. In some instances one party may feel let down, but this appears to be in an ongoing sense, and one that they do not anticipate changing. It is almost as if they have grown used to, and accepting of, the distant relationship status. Generally, contacts become less and less, to the point where neither party has the desire to continue or re-establish a relationship. Previous or anticipated shared experiences tend not to hold enough joy or benefit to warrant an effort to (re)create them.

In many instances, different values and priorities may have initially created or exaggerated barriers to contact. When people have vastly different ideas, interests and practices, contact can be uncomfortable or unsatisfactory, so they reduce time with each other. In some instances, one or both parties have more important priorities than the relationship. For example, when a family is in crisis, and their primary goal is to manage the situation on a day-to-day basis, they will have little time to reach out to – let alone maintain relationships with – extended family. This is particularly so if they believe that they will not be supported or might be viewed as a burden by asking for assistance. If the family does reach out, and extended family members are unable or unwilling to provide support, then the relational chasm is likely to increase.

Mutual disengagement might be stimulated by divorce and separation, particularly when second families develop. When one or more family members develop a new life, their capacity and desire to actively maintain previous relationships might decline. Some family members might feel unwelcome – or simply uncomfortable – with the new arrangements. The introduction of new family members might also bring new traditions and values that produce discomfort or a desire to avoid contact. When separate lives develop over time, mutual disengagement can become a permanent state.

Regardless of the origin, people often describe the mutually disengaged estrangement as a 'non-event'. Over time, the desire for shared experiences depletes and the relationship status becomes more accepted. However, this differs from a distant relationship because the relationship is experienced as unsatisfactory at some level. Mutually disengaged people tend to feel sadness that they no longer have the relationship and the benefits that the particular relationship might provide (e.g. having a brother to go to the football with). However, they tend not to feel strong emotions for the loss of the other person.

Absent estrangement: When connection was never established

[I left my family because I fell in love with Selina]. I didn't care; it's an awful thing to say, I did not care because, as I say, Selina and I were like teenagers. . . . I used to phone up and the phone was put down straight away, my ex-wife wouldn't talk to me. The children wouldn't talk to me. I stopped sending them birthday cards. . . . I got transferred to [another city].

(Robert)

Some family estrangements develop and continue on from parental absence during childhood. Parents may be absent from their children's lives for a variety of reasons, including: adoption; voluntary abandonment; child removal; no knowledge of the child's existence; migration; incarceration; complications resulting from separation and divorce (such as a non-residential parent's relocation and safety issues related to domestic violence); and third party interference, including parental alienation. Parents might estrange their child, the child might define the parent's absence as rejection and estrangement, or the parties might receive information or experience difficult or conflictual interactions that ultimately result in estrangement. As Mary explains:

> My father apparently left just before I turned one, and went off to make his fortune. . . . Showed up again when I was 13, furious with my mother that I was in the local public school and terrible grades and, 'She's capable of so much better and why aren't you providing an education for her?' So, the [argument] started: 'Why haven't you paid child support?' Na-na-na . . .

In some cases, children decide to estrange from their absent parent. For example, Rebecca refused to visit or interact with her father when she found out that he had sexually abused a child in her intergenerational family:

> Actually I didn't want to [see him again], because even though I was only nine or ten, I knew that – Mum sat me down and told me everything that had happened. She was honest, and I knew that it was very wrong, very bad. She never said to me, you can't see this guy anymore, but I never wanted to anyway.

Regardless of origin and form, parental absence can affect the intergenerational bond resulting in estrangement. It should be noted that parental absence alone does not necessarily create or indicate an estrangement (as per original definition of estrangement).

While there is significant debate about causality, practitioners and researchers claim that parental absence is a variable that potentially contributes to a number of detrimental effects during childhood and adolescence. Associations have been made to lowered scholastic achievement, sleep disturbance, poorer socialisation, lowered self-esteem, higher teenage pregnancy, involvement in criminal activity and mental health issues (particularly anxiety, depression and addiction), as well as generalised feelings of insecurity, guilt, anger and inadequacy (Culpin *et al.*, 2013; Khaleque & Rohner, 2002; McLanahan *et al.*, 2013). Parental absence during childhood has also been associated with longer-term effects in adulthood, including mental health conditions and a range of relational difficulties that appear to be the result of insecurity, fear of abandonment, emotional detachment, intense premature attachments, stress response management and self-defeating behaviours (Arshad & Naz, 2014; Khaleque & Rohner, 2002; McLanahan *et al.*, 2013; Quirk *et al.*, 2015). While it is beyond this book to cover and analyse these topics in depth, the author suggests that some of these effects may have the potential to continue to influence pathways of estrangement in adulthood.

Adolescence and adulthood often provide new opportunities for parents and children to rethink their relationship, reconnect in some way, and potentially end an absent estrangement. The decision to re-contact and attempt some form of reconciliation with parent or adult child is often fuelled by questions about the period of absence, the reasons for ongoing distance, and curiosity about the other person. In some cases the decision is stimulated by the removal of existing barriers, a longing for family or a desire to belong. Both the parent and the adult child are often wracked with indecision about re-contacting the other, pondering the awkwardness of difficult conversations, the revisiting of trauma related to the separation or the re-storying of an event that may have been minimised or 'forgotten'. Contact opens up the opportunity for rejection or further rejection, and the initiation or acceptance of an encounter may depend largely on the parent or child's perceived capacity to tolerate further rejection. While there might be a successful reunion for some, this section deals with estrangements that continue into adulthood, and those where temporary reconciliation leads to what often appears to be a more resigned estrangement.

Maintaining the status quo

The estranged member of the family is my biological father ... whom I have had no contact with since I was about three I think it was. So I have no memory really of him.... For a while there I was adamant I wanted to face him. Then I thought realistically, what good is that going to do? It wouldn't gain anything.
(Kelly)

People generally do not attempt reconciliation when they feel there is nothing to gain, or that there is the possibility of losing something. In some cases, adult children might believe that their estranged parent is a 'bad seed', whether they have come to this conclusion by themselves or whether this message has been introduced and reinforced by others. Parents, too, might believe that their child's behaviours (particularly those that they have interpreted as rejection) are likely to be indicative of a problematic or difficult adult child. They might consider previous rejections by the child as indicative of the adult child's likely response to contact. They might have information or have heard rumours that their child exhibits current behaviours that they find unacceptable or too challenging to engage with (e.g. drug use). Or they might believe that the child has been so indoctrinated by others that any attempts at providing an alternative story would be futile.

Adult children might voluntarily decide to maintain the absent estrangement status quo because of their loyalty to a non-estranged parent (who they believe has been wronged), or to a step-parent who has accepted and parented them as 'their own child'. Additionally, some non-estranged parents can exert considerable pressure on their adult children not to reconnect with the estranged parent, making their choice highly problematic and potentially dangerous to their current familial status. Potential reconciliations can fail if either party feels that an approach is inappropriate or their privacy has been breached:

Unbeknownst to me [my father] found where I lived and spied on me from across the road and actually waved at me. I didn't know that it was him until mum and I had spoken later on and I felt violated that he'd been spying on me'
(Kelly)

Some say that 'too much time has passed' to start a relationship with a person who they do not know, or want to know.

Attempts to reconcile

I just thought everyone else knows what their dad looks like, and I know nothing about him. I didn't know his birthday or anything.... I just didn't want to die and not know what my own dad looks like, [so I went to see him].... So he was homeless and he lives in a caravan and he hasn't got any money. But it was good to see him. . . . He kept on writing and we wrote things but he sort of said, 'I don't want to go back to the past as well because it's too painful.' . . . But I'm really glad that I did that.

(Lori)

Reconciliation will not occur if the other party cannot be located or if they reject the offer of contact, but in many instances some degree of contact is achieved. Many adult children wish to meet due to curiosity about their parent's personality traits, talents and history (and particularly those that the two might share). Experience, independence and the birth of children often stimulate the adult child's questioning of preconceptions about the parent (e.g. whether their parent is the virtuous victim that they always imagined or really the villain portrayed by others). Some choose to make contact in an attempt to show the parent 'what they have missed out on', or how successful they have become despite abandonment. Parents are often stimulated to make contact when their life circumstances change (e.g. second-hand information triggers curiosity about the child or mortality-related events highlight time constraints).

However, reconciliation is often short lived when parents cannot meet the needs of their adult child (due to emotional, financial or time capacity). Parents might not have the answers to the questions that adult children ask (or the answers they wish to hear). They might find it too difficult to engage in difficult conversations about the past or take responsibility for the harms that the adult child has incurred. Some parents might find it too difficult to refute accusations made by ex-partners or find it too unpalatable to defend themselves against what they might consider a dogmatic narrative. Second families can interfere with reconciliation in a variety of ways. Adult children might consider their parent's second family an affront compared to their own abandonment. Being the outsider or a competitor for their parent's attention and affection might become too difficult. Second families may not be welcoming of the previously estranged adult child and might actively discourage reconciliation, especially if they appear to be absorbing scarce emotional and physical family resources. Reconciliation can be temporary when it creates tensions between the adult child's two parents, and the child feels the need to reinstate the estrangement in order to demonstrate loyalty to the originally non-estranged party.

Contact might cease when parties are unable to negotiate vastly different ideas about the type, pace and intensity of the potential new relationship. Adult children can be highly sensitive to any form of rejection during the reconciliation period and any act that might constitute betrayal, rejection, or neglect has the potential to result in the swift re-establishment of the estrangement with the parent. In some cases, it is enough for parties to visit, gain the information they require, and cease further contact. Sometimes people describe their periods of contact or reconnection with the other person as a 'nothing experience', where there is not enough common ground, affection or possibility in the relationship to pursue further contact:

The fact that [my father] is not part of my life is a nothing experience. There is no feelings around anything . . . I think he's losing out. I know we're losing out, but as an individual there's no emotional attachment at all.

(Mary)

In these cases, it appears that a lack of shared experience prevents the relationship from being established or re-established to a level that warrants continuation.

Grieving the loss of shared experiences

Well there is a lot of emotion there. As I said I'm angry and then the next minute I feel relieved knowing that they're not there, and then the next minute I'm upset, I'm crying, thinking they should be there for me.

(Lisa)

The loss experience associated with *emotional, mutually disengaged* and *absent* estrangements has many commonalities with physical estrangements (as described in Chapters 3 and 4). However, these estrangements differ in that they generally lack a 'crisis moment', tending to be characterised more by a series of loss *events* or *realisations*. This has implications for the nature of loss, the way it is experienced by the individual, and the way that it is recognised and acknowledged by other family members and society more broadly. This section describes the potentially complicated losses associated with estrangements that are characterised by few shared experiences, including: prolonged injustice, ambiguity, ambivalence and disenfranchisement. Finally, this section concludes with a commentary on the possible effects of ongoing negative interactions commonly associated with an emotional estrangement.

Prolonged – and often observable – injustice

There seem to have always been these replacements and it's almost easier for them to relate to the stepchildren because there's not that, I don't know, there's not that blood. There's not that fire. There's not that passion. . . . They somehow seem to fall into those relationships quite easily.

(Debbie)

Emotional, mutually disengaged and *absent* estrangements may be very difficult to recognise, and define, by the people experiencing them, let alone outsiders. Emotionally and mutually disengaged estrangements lack a crisis moment: estrangement is rarely 'declared'. Absent estrangements, too, are rarely announced between the two primary parties because they occur in childhood. Children are rarely *told* that their parent has 'left for good' due to the uncertainty surrounding its finality, and they will generally learn of, or increasingly recognise, the abandonment as time passes. Even when children are told that a parent has left, when they are highly distressed, or when they perceive some degree of finality, they may not have the capacity to understand the full implications – or reality – of such a loss. In most of these cases, estrangement is increasingly 'discovered' and 'acknowledged' over time. People often find it difficult to determine when it commenced, but they usually have a strong sense of when they *realised* something was unsatisfactory, abnormal or wrong.

Accusations, conflicts and betrayals are likely to occur across decades, making them less visible – and certainly less audible – in these types of estrangements. Grieving is likely to be prolonged and minimised by others (see 'Disenfranchised loss' later in this chapter). People are more likely to mourn what they do not have as a result of the relationship, than the actual estrangement or estrangement event (which may be regarded as inevitable or a non-event for many). Experiences of 'retrospective loss' are common for people in mutually disengaged or absent estrangements, where they mourn the shared experiences they *might* have had or *should* have had. Conversely, emotionally estranged parties might resent, regret and mourn the difficult interactions that they 'have' endured across time. Some encounters might act as reminders of what has been lost.

Many will mourn the loss of a normal relationship – or the symbolic meaning associated with a particular relational role – more than the loss of the actual person. This might be due to the non- or brief establishment of a parent–child relationship in an absent estrangement, the perception that the relationship is unworthy or meaningless in a mutually disengaged estrangement or the difficulties experienced during contact in an emotional estrangement. Consequently these losses are often tied to a sense of prolonged injustice, where the estranged are regularly reminded of the things they have 'missed out on' or 'have had to endure' because of the relationship status. This sense of injustice can also be triggered or exaggerated by external events, and particularly where the other party appears to have successful relationships with others, or appears to 'replace' estranged family members. Debbie's comments at the beginning of this section highlight her estranged parent's comparatively positive relationships with stepchildren. Such observations, which might be more visible than in a physically estranged relationship, can be intricately linked to an ongoing sense of injustice, injury and offense.

These losses might also be associated with anticipatory loss for some. Emotionally estranged parties often anticipate the continued dissolution of the relationship or a physical estrangement. So, too, people experiencing mutually disengaged and absent estrangements often acknowledge that they anticipate – and sometimes dread – future events that might ignite or exacerbate hurt, disappointment and loss experiences. These include key events such as upcoming weddings (where a young woman anticipates the pain associated with walking down the aisle without her biological father), the birth of a child (where people anticipate the emptiness associated with the absence of a proud and doting grandparent), and ageing events such as relocation to a residential facility (where an older person anticipates potential loneliness and isolation without a child to visit), or death of the other party (where a significant resurgence of cumulative grief may be anticipated).

Finally, it should be re-acknowledged that there are a number of potential losses and injustices associated with growing up with an absent parent (although it is beyond this chapter to examine these in depth). While a number of studies offer an insight into the variety of possible vulnerabilities posed by absence, findings should be viewed with caution because the causal pathways through which these issues coalesce and manifest are often difficult to determine. Additionally, many of these studies define 'absence' to varying degrees, and there are few studies that exclusively examine the effects of abandonment (i.e. full or significant absence). With this established, the research on parental absence, which predominantly focuses on fathers, indicates risk for an number of emotional, psychological, and social issues that might contribute to poorer outcomes from childhood and into adulthood, as well as the maintenance of absent estrangement in adulthood (Culpin *et al.*, 2015; Luo *et al.*, 2012; McLanahan *et al.*, 2013). There may also be a number of prolonged injustices for parents whose absence and subsequent estrangement has resulted from parental alienation (see resources in Chapter 8).

An Ambiguous Loss

[My estranged son] keeps that door open. He always just keeps it open that fraction.

(Sandra)

Emotional, mutually disengaged and *absent* estrangements are potentially ambiguous losses, often characterised by the physical presence, proximity or availability of the estranged party which contrasts with or contradicts their emotional unavailability or psychological absence. These estrangements tend to differ slightly from physical estrangements where the parties are generally prevented from reaching out to the other due to the strict rules of non engagement established at the time the estrangement is enacted. Rather, the *possibility* of contact, and the actuality of contact in the case of emotional estrangements, can make the relationship's status highly unsettling, unpredictable and difficult to explain to self and others.

Another element of ambiguity in these types of estrangements relates to delays or barriers to information processing. The loss of shared experience is often very difficult to make sense of, to rationalise, and to come to terms with. For example, when a person chooses to physically estrange another person there is usually a clear reason for doing so (such as betrayal, hurt, conflict), but this does not always apply to the estrangements referred to in this chapter. People in emotional, mutually disengaged and absent estrangements are often confronted by a lack of information, or facts that are clouded or difficult to sort through. The information that does exist is often contrary to socially conditioned expectations of familial relationships (e.g. mothers love their children unconditionally, sisters share lifelong loyalty), and may be contradictory according to the source. This type of ambiguity about the relationship status can slow closure and diminish grieving for the loss, and this may be particularly so for people with 'strong values of mastery and control' (Boss, 2004, p. 239).

Ambivalence

I know I should visit them, and sometimes I even want to go back, but it isn't long before I need to get out. I actually feel sick sometimes and I can't wait to get away. Afterwards, I ask why I put myself through that again.

(Leslie)

Emotional, mutually disengaged and *absent* estrangements are often characterised by ambivalence, and there may be particular losses associated with this conflicting position. Ambivalence is 'the state of having mixed feelings or contradictory ideas about something or someone' (Oxford Dictionaries, 2015), often manifesting in psychological conflict and indecision. Societal values and norms may have an enormous influence on feeling ambivalent. For example, a person's values and intentions about family unity and contact might contradict their actions and behaviours towards the estranged person. Additionally, the source of the ambivalence might differ, where people might feel ambivalent about the estranged 'person' or about the estranged 'relationship'. For example, one emotionally estranged person might experience ambivalent feelings about their sister (a conflict derived from both positive and negative interpersonal interactions with her), while another might have ambivalent

101

feelings about remaining in the relationship with their sister (a conflict derived from solely negative interactions with their sister, but feeling positive about being a good sibling and aunt). Regardless, this type of cognitive dissonance can contribute to questioning, indecision and further avoidance of the ambivalent situation.

The definition and associated measurement of ambivalence is complex and controversial, and research is often directed to a specific topic of conflict (e.g. ambivalent feelings about food or exercise) or type of ambivalence (e.g. Ingersoll-Dayton et al.'s [2011] research on sociological ambivalence and intergenerational role conflict). So it is difficult to obtain enough relevant research to make definitive statements about the impact of ambivalent components of estranged relationships on health and well-being. However, some early research might offer clues into the possible effects of emotional estrangement, relationships that fade away and relationships that are non-existent or underdeveloped due to absence. For example:

> When adults feel both positive and negative feelings toward a parent or offspring, they may experience lower psychological well-being because they care about the other party's feelings and desire a positive connection. Not knowing what to expect during each encounter (e.g. conflict or a positive interaction) also may engender stress. In addition, ambivalence may involve love for a person who does not reciprocate that affection or who is disappointing in some other respect.
>
> (Fingerman et al., 2008, p. 369)

Research shows that ambivalent friendships affect the individual's capacity to relax and feel supported during interactions when they are recounting a negative event (Holt-Lunstad et al., 2007). Ambivalent friendship and family ties have been linked to increased disease progression (Uchino et al., 2012). Hence, it appears that the stress involved with ambivalent family interactions has the potential to affect health and loss experiences.

Disenfranchised loss

Those in the public sphere might be less likely to acknowledge or understand the types of estrangements described in this chapter than they are a physical estrangement (where it is often presumed that a significant conflict or betrayal is core). It is difficult for outsiders to understand the enormity of pain and loss associated with emotional estrangement, especially if the emotionally estranged complainant actually sees their relative on a regular basis. It is difficult for outsiders to understand the emptiness and loss associated with absent relationships or mutual disengagement, when it appears that the complainant *could* choose to engage at any time, but refrains from doing so. In our goal-oriented society, people are taught that they can have almost anything they desire as long as they work hard enough. While it is understood that a deceased relative cannot be revived, it is rarely accepted that a family relationship is immovable or irreconcilable. Rather, the physical existence of the other is enough to minimise or dismiss the pain of the person who is grieving over, or aggrieved by, the estrangement. In some cases it appears easier to attribute blame for lack of effort than to empathise with the estrangement loss.

In addition, there is often a popular belief that if you grow up without 'knowing' or 'having' something then you cannot miss it retrospectively. Research showed that the losses associated with absent estrangements were often underestimated, overlooked or dismissed by other family members, and particularly non-estranged parents (Agllias, 2008, 2014). The loss associated with an absent parent might also be minimised if a step-parent is involved, and particularly if that person is perceived to be a better parental candidate than the biological one. Similarly, the loss of an ideal or expectation is regularly experienced by people who are emotionally estranged or mutually disengaged. The fact that a person has never experienced a close relationship with their family member does not negate their desire for one or their experience of loss for that type of relationship.

As a consequence of the ambiguous nature of *emotional, mutually disengaged* and *absent* estrangements, and the difficulty in recognising them, the associated losses can be overlooked by outsiders. Additionally, people are often assessed against cultural norms and judged for their actions – or inactions – towards a relative, without consideration of the relevant relational challenges, which can negatively affect the estranged person's sense of self and capacity to engage fully with others.

The physical and emotional effects of negative interactions

Every time I'd ring her or anything, I'd get off the phone and cry.

(Beth)

The losses associated with emotional estrangement, and specifically the ongoing experience of negative interpersonal interactions, have a potentially long-term effect on health and well-being. Negative exchanges include interactions that are uncomfortable, unpleasant, intrusive or demanding, critical, exclusionary, or where the person feels disappointed or let down. Negative exchanges can create a significant amount of stress on the individual (Rook *et al.*, 2012). For example, an abundance of research shows that family discord and adversity in childhood is associated with a number of internalising and externalising behaviours exhibited that are likely to originate from the dysregulation of the hypothalamic–pituitary–adrenal (HPA) stress system (Anda *et al.*, 2008; Luecken *et al.*, 2009; McEwen & Wingfield, 2003). Findings suggest that 'exposure to chronic and/or acute stress can interfere with HPA axis activity, resulting in cortisol levels that are either too high or too low to adequately prepare the individual to meet situational demands' (Luecken *et al.*, 2009, p. 412) Luecken *et al.*,'s (2009) work found attenuated cortisol in young adults who had experienced high levels of conflict, low cohesion, and low expressiveness in their family of origin (even after controlling for sexual and physical abuse, anxiety and depression).

Negative interactions with family during adulthood have been associated with increased health problems (Newsom *et al.*, 2008; Walen & Lachman, 2000), lower self-health ratings (Newsom *et al.*, 2008), psychological distress (Zhang, 2012) and negative affect (Russell *et al.*, 2012). While results have been inconsistent, there is some evidence to suggest a 'negativity affect' in some groups and situations, where the impact of negative social interactions is more predictive of well-being than positive social interactions over time (Newsom *et al.*, 2003; Walen & Lachman, 2000). Additionally, there is some evidence that negative interactions with family members may affect women's health status and mood more than men's (Walen & Lachman, 2000), and may be experienced more negatively by adults who are lonely (Russell *et al.*, 2012).

Rook *et al.*,'s (2012) research with older people experiencing ambivalent and solely problematic interactions found that: problematic ties with friends, and particularly family members, were more likely to cause and prolong psychological distress and interfere with the person's sense of coping and increased avoidance responses than ambivalent relationships. It has been suggested that older people are less likely to confront or attempt to alter the relational dynamic in these situations, rather adopting avoidant coping and managing their own emotional distress (Compas *et al.*, 1991; Rook *et al.*, 2012). Additionally, some research has found that the communication styles and personality traits of elders might be associated with risks for particular types of elder abuse (Comijs *et al.*, 1999). It appears that long-standing communication patterns might predict mistreatment and abuse, where elders who utilise passive and avoidant approaches to interactions and problem solving, are more vulnerable to physical abuse from their carers (ibid.).

Conclusion

Emotional, mutually disengaged and *absent* estrangements, often characterised by a lack of shared experience, can be the source of considerable loss and grief. They rarely have a defining moment. Rather, they emerge across the lifespan, often through a series of loss experiences, making it almost impossible to pinpoint the origin of disengagement. They are ambiguous loss experiences, where the estranged parties are often in contact – or could make contact – but emotional connection is minimal or non-existent. Additionally, their incompatibility with common ideologies of familial relationships means that they are rarely understood or recognised by others, potentially affecting long-term health and well-being. Chapter 7 explores the methods that estranged people – including those in emotional, mutually disengaged and absent estrangements – employ as they learn to live with relationship dissolution in a meaningful way.

PRACTICE POINT 4: ASSESSING THE IMPACT OF FEW SHARED EXPERIENCES

It is important to understand and assess the various effects of estrangement in order to: (i) acknowledge the personal loss experience (including the immediate and longer-term effects); (ii) establish a baseline of current functioning in order to measure progress/development across time; (iii) acknowledge strengths, strategies and supports that have already been utilised to survive or live with estrangement (and those that have not been so useful); (iv) assess current priorities and areas that might need attention; and (v) assess this collective knowledge against information provided in Chapters 7 and 8, in order to incorporate some new strategies to maximise health and well-being, if warranted. This section offers one reflective exercise for people who believe that they are experiencing emotional estrangement, and a series of exercises – similar to those in Chapters 3 and 4 – that examine the loss effects of emotional, mutually disengaged and absent estrangements.

EXERCISE 1: ASSESSING EMOTIONAL ESTRANGEMENT

This exercise requires a thoughtful and honest reflection on the practices and strategies that maintain emotional distancing and estrangement.

(a) Choose one family relationship that you consider to be emotionally distanced, strained, passive-aggressive or emotionally estranged. Tick the strategies and practices that apply in Table 5.1 'Distancing practices and strategies'.

(b) Now note the strategies and practices that both parties employ. Reflect on the cyclical nature of this estrangement. Does one party rely more heavily on particular practices and strategies? How might each party interpret the practices and strategies of the other? Which practices and strategies have increased or decreased over time?

(c) Are some of these practices and strategies possibly learned? For example, do other family members use these types of practices and strategies? Are there practices and strategies that are commonly used in this family? Are there particular situations where these strategies are employed more frequently?

(d) Reflect on learning from this exercise: Has this exercise made you curious about the distancing practices and strategies used between the estranged parties and the intergenerational family? If so, how might you employ this curiosity? (E.g. you might like to commit to observing these practices and strategies in self and others.) Did you identify additional distancing practices and strategies that are employed between the estranged parties or intergenerational family (and if so, what are they)?

TABLE 5.1 Distancing practices and strategies

	I observe myself using this practice or strategy	I observe my family member using this practice or strategy
Avoiding meetings		
Delaying meetings		
Putting limits on contact (duration, place etc).		
Reducing the time between contact		
Limiting spontaneous contact		
Increasing physical distance during interactions		
Avoiding physical contact		
Reducing eye contact		
Tense bodily markers (e.g. fidgeting, pacing)		
Pulling away during embrace		
Avoiding particular topics		

TABLE 5.1 continued

	I observe myself using this practice or strategy	I observe my family member using this practice or strategy
Avoiding emotional topics		
Avoiding contentious topics		
Keeping conversation quite generalised		
Speaking/answering in vague terms		
Frequently using non-committal and evasive language 'maybe', 'not sure'		
Frequently using over-inclusive statements		
Frequently using under-inclusive statements		
Using monologue to fill the silence		
Speaking through a third person		
Focusing on others in the room		
Keeping secrets		
Suspecting the other person is keeping secrets		
Lying or exaggerating about important things		
Lying or exaggerating about minor things		
Telling the other person 'what they want to hear'		
Treating the other as an acquaintance		
Maintaining excessive privacy		
Avoiding events where privacy might be breached		
Considering the relationship to be based on equal exchange (rather than communal exchange)		
Reducing shared property		
Sharing property through formalised arrangements only		
Refusing or avoiding advice, assistance or help		

TABLE 5.1 continued

	I observe myself using this practice or strategy	I observe my family member using this practice or strategy
Avoiding or refusing to attend important events		
Forgetting or minimising important occasions		
Minimal or reduced responses to crisis events (e.g. family member's hospitalisation)		
Using intimidating words		
Using intimidating actions		
Raising topics to show superiority and potentially belittle or embarrass the other		
Making threats or implied threats about physical estrangement		

EXERCISE 2: REFLECTION ON THE EFFECTS OF ESTRANGEMENT

Emotional, *mutually disengaged* and *absent* estrangements are rarely 'announced' and it is often difficult for people to determine a clear 'starting point'. So this exercise requires you to think about a time that you 'realised' that the relationship was distanced, different, problematic or estranged. The 'realisation period' might be different for each person. This might be an event, a moment of clarity or a vague recollection. For those who are unable to recall a precise memory, just choose a relevant time period to reflect upon. Think back to the days and weeks after you 'realised' that you were emotionally estranged, mutually disengaged or in an absent estrangement, and reflect on the effects at that time. Document these in Table 5.2 'Impacts of estrangement inventory 3' – column (a). Now, think about your current situation and detail the current effects in column (b). Note: An example is provided to assist with this process (see Table 5.3).

EXERCISE 3: REFLECTION ON CHANGE

Look at the effects you have documented in Table 5.2 and consider how these have changed over time (lessened, remained constant or increased). Reflect upon these changes and take a note of them at the bottom of the inventory. Have there been positive impacts? Make a note of these too.

TABLE 5.2 Impacts of estrangement inventory 3

	(a) Effects immediately after the realisation	(b) Current effects
Emotional e.g. anger, anxiety, relief, emotional shock, fear, sadness, hurt, frustration, irritability, guilt, denial, uncertainty, apprehension, agitation.		
Physical e.g. difficulty breathing, nausea, fatigue, headaches, weakness, twitches, grinding teeth, sweating, chest pain.		
Cognitive e.g. hypervigilance, changes in memory, lack of concentration, confusion, nightmares, flashbacks, blaming the other person, poor attention.		
Behavioural e.g. withdrawal, emotional outbursts, change in appetite, pacing, increased drug or alcohol use, change in activity, acting out, change in communication patterns.		
Spiritual e.g. loss of meaning, loss of trust, questioning meaning of life, questioning spiritual beliefs, questioning God (or Deity).		
Social e.g. socialising less, avoiding people and social functions, taking time off work, being less engaged at family, work and social events, not answering the phone.		
2. Reflection on changes over time (including any positive effects)		

TABLE **5.3** Impacts of estrangement inventory 3 (example)

	(a) Effects immediately after the realisation	(b) Current effects
Emotional e.g. anger, anxiety, relief, emotional shock, fear, sadness, hurt, frustration, irritability, guilt, denial, uncertainty, apprehension, agitation.	*Anger* *Sadness* *Hurt* *Shock* *Jealous*	*Anger* *Sadness* *Hurt*
Physical e.g. difficulty breathing, nausea, fatigue, headaches, weakness, twitches, grinding teeth, sweating, chest pain.	*Fatigue*	*N/A*
Cognitive e.g. hypervigilance, changes in memory, lack of concentration, confusion, nightmares, flashbacks, blaming the other person, poor attention.	*Hypervigilance* *Confusion*	*Hypervigilance*
Behavioural e.g. withdrawal, emotional outbursts, change in appetite, pacing, increased drug or alcohol use, change in activity, acting out, change in communication patterns.	*Withdrawal* *Change in appetite*	*Withdrawal*
Spiritual e.g. loss of meaning, loss of trust, questioning meaning of life, questioning spiritual beliefs, questioning God (or Deity).	*Not sure . . .*	*Loss of meaning*
Social e.g. socialising less, avoiding people and social functions, taking time off work, being less engaged at family, work and social events, not answering the phone.	*Less engaged with all my family*	*Less engaged with some of my family members*

2. Reflection on changes over time (including any positive effects)

I first realised I was emotionally estranged from mum when I came back from college and noticed her interactions with her other child (my stepsister). I was really angry and jealous for a while. I now feel sad realising that I NEVER really had that experience with my mother, anyway. She was always absent. Sadness and hurt remain (and a little bit of anger sometimes). I think it is positive that I am learning to forgive others.

EXERCISE 4: REFLECTION ON RESILIENCE

All people draw on strengths, strategies and supports to work through estrangement.

- *Strengths* are the positive personal traits and virtues that people employ in a balanced life, and they can be drawn upon as a guide to, or motivation for, action during times of confusion and distress.
- *Strategies* are the simple and complex plans for action that we develop to bring about positive change, achieve a goal or solve a problem.
- *Supports* are people or things that provide assistance, that buffer or hold some of the weight of negative experiences.

First, reflect on the changes identified in Exercise 2. Then consider the strengths, strategies and supports that positively influenced those changes. Document these in

TABLE 5.4 Resilience inventory

Strengths that I have drawn upon Strengths might include things like open-mindedness, curiosity, integrity, persistence, social intelligence, forgiveness, self-regulation, gratitude, humour, spirituality.	
Strategies that I have used These might include: setting up a more structured routine; planning meals and sitting down to eat regardless of appetite; challenging black-and-white thoughts whenever they arise; taking a friend/partner to difficult social situations; taking up a new activity such as meditation or yoga; and using a diary to let go of, or contain, worry.	
Supports that I have employed These might include: adequate finances; people such as family, friends, neighbours and work colleagues; therapeutic interventions such as counselling; church or social groups; educative supports like documentaries, movies, books and websites; and natural or manmade resources such as beaches, parks, sunsets (and time itself).	
Traits/strengths, strategies and supports that were not useful or became less useful over time	

Table 5.4 'Resilience inventory'. Finally, reflect upon and document any traits/strengths, strategies or potential supports that were not so useful – or became less useful – across the estrangement journey. These might include things like: the strength of independence (which can become problematic if it prevents help-seeking), the trait of stubbornness, or strategies such as social withdrawal and unsupportive influences such as one-way friendships. Note: An example is provided to assist with this process (see Table 5.5).

EXERCISE 5: AREAS FOR ATTENTION

Look back at column (b) in Table 5.2. Identify two to five areas that might require further consideration or attention. Consider the strengths, strategies and supports that you mapped in Table 5.4 and how these might be helpful.

TABLE 5.5 Resilience inventory

Strengths that I have drawn upon Strengths might include things like open-mindedness, curiosity, integrity, persistence, social intelligence, forgiveness, self-regulation, gratitude, humour, spirituality.	*Forgiveness (I am getting there in this process – can't forgive mum but can forgive her stepdaughter and my brother), insight, honesty.*
Strategies that I have used These might include: setting up a more structured routine; planning meals and sitting down to eat regardless of appetite; challenging black-and-white thoughts whenever they arise; taking a friend/partner to difficult social situations; taking up a new activity such as meditation or yoga; and using a diary to let go of, or contain, worry.	*Started yoga and photography. Prepare for family visits so I am calmer.*
Supports that I have employed These might include: adequate finances; people such as family, friends, neighbours and work colleagues; therapeutic interventions such as counselling; church or social groups; educative supports like documentaries, movies, books and websites; and natural or manmade resources such as beaches, parks, sunsets (and time itself).	*My counsellor and my husband. We had a great camping holiday – where I started to think about my life and discuss goals with my husband.*

Traits/strengths, strategies and supports that were not useful or became less useful over time
My brother used to be my support, but he was unable to understand my experience and increasingly distanced himself from me as I bagged out mum. This was unhelpful because through my anger and honesty I lost him too. I didn't consider his feelings about mum and used him as a sounding board a lot. He probably felt caught between us.

Chapter 6 The intergenerational consequences of family estrangement

I'm estranged from my father, mother, their partners, my sister and her family. . . . So my whole blood family, so, big estrangement. . . . It's hard to even say it. I feel like the last person in the world that would have ended up estranged from family.

(Debbie)

Family estrangement is often an historic and intergenerational phenomenon. It is rare for estrangement to exist between two individuals without affecting broader family relationships. It is rare for family estrangement to occur in one generation without affecting the next. Rather, families carry their losses – and particularly the legacy of unresolved losses – across the generations. Historic losses, including relationship dissolutions, become a part of the generational narrative and they influence the expectations, strategies and coping mechanisms of each family member. This chapter explores the labyrinthine issues that establish, maintain and connect estrangement throughout the family tree. It commences with a commentary on three primary types of intergenerational estrangements: (i) the inherited estrangement, where estrangements are passed on from previous generations; (ii) the secondary estrangement, which is instigated when family members take sides after a primary estrangement has occurred; and (iii) the self-protective estrangement, which is enacted by an estranged person in order to further maintain their safety or privacy. The chapter explores the importance of intergenerational connections and the potential losses associated with estrangement. It also examines the potentially risky ways that some families attempt to recreate a sense of family and place after estrangement. Finally, a practice section encourages the reader or client to critically evaluate the effects of estrangement on the intergenerational family.

The transmission of estrangement

I haven't spoken with my brother in a long, long, long time. It's because – well let's say that my mother has done her work thoroughly – that's the person I'm estranged from. My brother, he desperately wanted to have parents – which is understandable. . . . He would use me in order to get her on his side. So he would tell her things about me. . . . I said, I don't want that.

(Tina)

While individuals often portray their estrangement as an aberration, a solitary experience and one that is unique to their immediate family, this is rarely accurate. Studies show that estranged people often report repeated patterns of distancing behaviour, resulting in multiple estrangements across the generations (Agllias, 2011, 2014; Corrigan *et al.*, 2006; Robinson, 2011). One study of adult children who were estranged from their parents revealed that many had grown up with limited intergenerational knowledge and few supportive familial relationships due to their parents' conflictual interactions and estrangements from family (Agllias, 2014). Another study, with older parents who had been estranged by an adult child, suggested that non-estranged familial relationships often became more precarious and tense after an estrangement (Agllias, 2011). The parents said they became more vigilant about the potential recruitment, secrecy and avoidant behaviours of non-estranged family members. Some monitored their own behaviours and made concerted efforts not to undermine or divide familial loyalty. This study showed that unresolved tensions and conflicts, distancing behaviours and estrangement-related losses have the potential to affect the entire intergenerational family system in direct and indirect ways. This section examines the ways that family patterns are repeated and estrangements are created and recreated across time.

Inherited estrangements

> *I don't know half of my family because my mother was thoroughly in divide-and-conquer mode and having a fight with everyone so I never knew most of my family.*

> (Tina)

Children often inherit estrangements from their parents and grandparents when they are born. These estrangements are usually well established before the birth and have nothing to do with the child's existence. However, in some situations estrangements are established at the time of birth to protect the child. This is particularly so if the child is considered at risk of some form of abuse or negative influence from the adult in question. Estrangements of this type can be invisible to the child as they grow up, and little source of distress. Or the existence of the estranged person might emerge across time and become a curiosity to the young person as they ponder the estranged relative's dismissal and any associated secrecy that they detect in familial conversations. In other cases, the 'discovery' of an estranged relative may come as a shock and a disappointment at key developmental periods (e.g. when a child goes to school and realises that other children have grandparents).

In many instances, estrangements are inherited during childhood or adolescence, when a parent or primary caregiver ends a relationship with one or more of the child's family members (e.g. a grandparent, aunt or uncle). Divorce, too, can lead to inherited estrangements, where the custodial or residential parent estranges or limits the child's contact with their ex-partner and their ex-partner's extended family. The middle generation normally serve as 'gatekeepers, mediators and facilitators' between younger children, grandparents and great-grandparents:

> Thus, the quality of parent-child relationships in the two [or more] adult generations is seen as critical for the quality of ties between grandparents and

grandchildren. Here, there is fairly unison agreement in the literature on grandparenthood that the most active, complex grandparent-grandchild ties are found in the maternal line.

(Hagestad, 2006, p. 323)

This, combined with the prevalence of mothers as residential parents, renders paternal ties more vulnerable to some form of estrangement after divorce.

Children often 'witness' (at least some of the) events that lead up to, and eventuate from, the relationship dissolution. They are likely to gather information about the nature of conflictual relationships, and how feelings such as disappointment, hurt and betrayal are dealt with in their intergenerational family. They might experience a range of loss and grief responses, emanating directly from the estrangement with the loved one. Vicarious responses may emanate from witnessing the loss experiences of the estranged party or parties. They might be extremely conflicted and traumatised if they perceive that the estrangement is somehow related to them, or they are to blame.

Interestingly, Agllias's (2014) study found that a number of adult children decided to estrange from their parent when they witnessed behaviour that they perceived to be detrimental to their child, or similar to poor treatment they had experienced in childhood. While these adults were willing to tolerate poor or difficult treatment from their parent, they would not allow it to continue with their own child. In these cases, it is likely that the child is somewhat aware that they are at the centre of the estrangement decision (and probably unaware of the extent of tension, hurt and betrayal that foregrounded the ultimate dissolution). It is also important to recognise that some inherited estrangements are not conflictual as such. Some children grow up with distant and detached relationships from their extended family, rarely knowing, seeing or interacting with these relatives.

Regardless of the origin of inherited estrangements, children usually do not have a choice about the physical estrangements they inherit. Nor do they have a choice about the strained interactions they experience when emotional estrangement exists or access visits occur. Over time, curiosity can develop from a desire to know more about family or family secrecy, which often influences an investigation of or meeting with the estranged party or parties in adolescence or adulthood. This is particularly so if the child becomes estranged from their own parents or siblings. In these instances, their own perceptions of injustice might prompt a reassessment of the family system (as well as the narratives, truths and secrets that maintain it).

Secondary estrangements: Choosing sides

[My daughter] said, 'Mum, I don't know how to tell you this, but there's a party on tomorrow at [aunt] Barbara's place, so the big alienator. It's for me and I know it's tomorrow that . . . [you and I] would see each other.' Well for the first time ever I said to her, 'Boundary, you'll have to make a decision here, but that is so not okay. . . . You go to that party, Tess, and I don't want to see you.' I've never said anything like that before.

(Angela)

Categorisation is the cognitive process that efficiently sorts and groups likes – such as objects, people, ideas or behaviours – to maximise recognition, differentiation and understanding. Unfortunately categories can be imbued with value-laden connotations, and complexity may be overlooked. When family estrangements occur, the action of each party will be swiftly assessed against family values, rules and expectations, as well as the assessor's position in the family, history with the estranged pair, or the version of events that they hear first or believe to be true. Certainly the nature of the intergenerational family makes it a very difficult environment or context in which to remain neutral. As a result, the categorisation of victim and perpetrator can become quickly embedded into the family narrative, requiring lines of loyalty to be established and defended. Studies show that 'choosing sides' is a common phenomenon after family estrangement occurs (Agllias, 2011, 2014; Robinson, 2011; Scharp, 2014).

When family members strongly believe that one party has been seriously wronged during a conflict or estrangement, their decision to also estrange from the offending party usually occurs immediately after this discovery. In some cases, a brief encounter might take place, where the family member confronts the aberrant estranger or estrangee, but generally this occurs when emotions are heightened and accusations are raw, leaving little room for explanation or conciliatory actions. Family members often feel that taking a side is akin to taking a value position, and that their loyalty to the victimised party is a testament to their broader familial commitment.

In some families, any appearance of neutrality can make the non-partisan vulnerable to interest, suspicion, accusations, bullying and attack from one (or both) sides of the estrangement fence. Non-estranged family members might be actively recruited into the estrangement or discreetly enticed over time through false or misleading information, demands of loyalty and significant promises or threats (often related to inheritance or relationship dissolution). As Angela's quote on page 115 illustrates, her daughter, Tess, is caught between two estranged family members: her mother and her aunt. Tess knows that she has promised to spend time with her mother and that her mother has been extremely hurt by her aunt. Declining – or accepting – the invitation is likely to cause one party significant offense.

Triangulation is common when there is a dissatisfaction between two parties – in this case the estranged pair – and the hurt, anxiety and tension is often refocused or projected onto a third party. Initially, the triangulated family member is often used to carrying messages between the estranged pair. However, the 'neutral' third party can become quite vulnerable to projection, with accusations of allegiance developing from unresolved or escalating tension (e.g. 'if you were on my side you would/wouldn't speak to your sister'). Or this might come in the form of recruitment (e.g. 'your sister has always said horrible things about you, but I always stood up for you'). The third party might try to remain neutral or become increasingly drawn into the dispute. Regardless, if this behaviour or position becomes unacceptable to one (or both) of the estranged parties, the third party might be estranged secondarily.

Secondary estrangements often develop subtly over time. Many family members – and particularly those who have strong ties to both parties, or those who are more distantly related – will try to remain in contact with both parties, even if they are not entirely neutral about the cause of the estrangement. They might attempt to intervene by bringing different perspectives to the estranged parties, by encouraging or arranging conciliatory meetings, or delivering messages between the pair. Unfortunately, these acts can be interpreted as judgement or 'taking sides' by the estranger and the estrangee. Estrangers in particular might believe that the instigators of these types of conciliatory interactions underestimate the severity of the hurt, betrayal and distance that has led up to the estrangement, as well as the loss associated with the estrangement decision. Third party contacts that are interpreted as biased, unwanted interference or insufficiently empathic can lead to secondary estrangements. Or the non-estranged member might initiate dissolution if they assess their intervention as unsuccessful or an interaction provides information that compels them to take a 'value position'.

In many families, secondary estrangements develop from discomfort. Initially, most families believe that an estrangement is temporary and they will try to accommodate both parties by maintaining usual levels of contact and care. When special events arise, they might invite both parties but separate their seating and monitor interactions and contact (or they might even conduct separate events). However, relatives who try to cater for both estranged parties often find the burden of this type of care too difficult to maintain in the longer term. The tensions associated with balancing obligations often become frustrating and difficult for non-estranged family members, especially when events become more about the estranged parties than the celebration. Non-estranged members, who rarely understand the depth of angst associated with the estrangement, become less accommodating of a situation they consider to be trivial. The estranged party will become increasingly uncomfortable at family events if they feel the weight of opinion is against them. Non-estranged members might not know what to say or how to approach the estranged party or parties. It is common, then, for one of the estranged parties (most often, but not always, the estranger) to alienate themselves further from these types of events, or for them to be invited less. Over time, this can have an impact on non-estranged relationships too, leading to secondary emotional, physical and mutually disengaged estrangements.

Self-protective estrangements

Then we moved up here and we kept it pretty quiet [so my mother would not know where we were living]. I haven't contacted anyone on her side of the family, uncles or aunties or my grandmother, her mother.

(David)

Maintaining any type of estrangement, as discussed in previous chapters, can take considerable time, effort and emotional energy. When people decide that it is necessary to protect themselves from an estranged family member, they will remain vigilant to any potential threat to the relationship status, and dissolve relationships that cross their self-protection boundaries. Non-estranged family members can be a significant threat to privacy and the maintenance of the estrangement, whether this is deliberate or unintentional. They might provide information about the whereabouts or contact details of the estranged person, or simply breach their confidentiality. Adult children in one study also cited instances where non-estranged relatives took it upon themselves to physically reunite them with the estranged person without consultation or notification (Agllias, 2014). Unwanted attempts at mediation, counselling and 'reasoning' can erode the estranged person's relationship with the non-estranged relative. It is common for estranged people to maintain their safety by temporarily or permanently estranging relatives who might compromise their sense of safety, privacy and trust.

In this schema, there are some relatives who are less likely to be trusted to maintain the estranged person's safety, depending on the pair's previous interactions and experiences. For example, adult children in one study suggested that they were much less likely to trust and maintain contact with siblings who they perceived to be more loved or favoured by the estranged parent (Agllias, 2014). In these instances they perceived the parent's behaviour to be predictive of their sibling's allegiance to the parent, thus determining that they were a threat to the maintenance of the estrangement. As a result, they used emotional and physical distancing from the sibling to maintain the estrangement status with the parent.

Theories of intergenerational transmission

Well anyone that showed me any attention, I just [thought] he just loved me. . . . When I was 17 I joined [an organisation] to get away from home and just the first man I met pretty well, at 17, I said on the first date, I'm going to marry you. . . . It didn't work but we stayed together for 16 years anyway.

(Margaret)

There are a number of theories suggesting that estrangement is generationally recreated through complex biological, relational and social mechanisms that establish the conditions for the inherited, secondary and self-protective estrangements referred to here. Bowen (1982) theorised that when people were less differentiated, they were more emotionally reactive and instinctively attuned to survival, and offered a new way of thinking about the connections between physiology and psychological conditions. Subsequent investigations have concluded that both physical and emotional estrangement might contribute to physiological changes in the individual, such as emotional reactivity, stress and withdrawal responses (Allen, 2003; Friesen, 2003; Harrison, 2003). For example, Allman's thesis about the evolution of the brain suggested that 'the complexity of the human brain evolved with the development of the extended family as a social group' (Friesen, 2003, p. 84). This suggests that species with fewer living generations have a smaller cortex, and those with an increased number and complexity of relational contacts might 'develop more intrinsic ability to discriminate the input from the senses with a wider range of possible associations and behaviours' (ibid., p. 91). As a result, people who are more cut off or estranged from intergenerational contact are likely to respond to stressful situations with less evaluation and more emotional reactivity. Theoretically, this evolutionary adaptation would occur over time, from generation to generation and without intervention, the cut-off of one generation was likely to affect the reactivity of the next.

Bowen's (1982) theory also suggests that unresolved issues in one relationship will be transposed to other relationships and create similar relational patterns. For example, dating or marriage might provide an outlet for an adult child to escape difficult familial relationships, or remedy the emptiness left by an emotional or physical estrangement. However, instinctive responses and behavioural patterns associated with estrangement might mean that 'the dating relationship is guided more by the effort to sustain positive feelings and by reacting to the other than internal principles. The reaction to the other may be over accommodation, distance, conflict or domination' (Klever, 2003, p. 224).

A number of women in Agllias's (2011, 2014) research – also commented on in Chapters 3 and 4 – clearly stated that their initial relationships with men were affected by their detached, emotionally estranged or problematic relationships with their parent(s). (These women were either estranged from their adult child(ren) or their parents at the time of the research.) Some said that the long-term distance or emotional estrangement from their parents contributed to their premature choice of partner or partners who were similarly dismissive or abusive. They speculated that they remained in abusive relationships for long periods due to their intense desire for love and family or the familiarity of the relational experience with the new partner. For example, Laura said, '*The first couple of relationships I had, they treated harshly on me. I just did what Mum did and sucked it up and kept on going.*' Some of the older women believed that their conflictual or abusive marital relationships, and in many cases their subsequent divorce, may have contributed in some way to their estrangements with their own adult children.

In addition to pre-empting early and unsuitable romantic relationships, perceptions of childhood rejection are often linked to:

> patterns of perceived rejection and control in other attachment relationships . . . . [I]ndividuals with a history of perceived rejection from parents and other attachment figures often perceive hostility and rejection from their partners where none is intended, and frequently devalue their own sense of worth – even in the face of contradictory information from their partners or others.
>
> (Rigazio-DiGilio & Rohner, 2015, pp. 477–478)

Bowen (1982) observed that individuals in sustained romantic relationships tended to exhibit similar levels of differentiation. The degree of differentiation between an emotionally immature pair was likely to be similar to or less than the differentiation between each parent and adult child attachment, and behaviours and patterns would be repeated in the romantic relationship (Klever, 2003). For example, recent research with 1,839 couples from the United States found that differentiation of self was an important predictor of the quality of the marital relationship (and that the level of differentiation was carried forward into this relationship at approximately the same level as family of origin) (Holman & Busby, 2011). The anxiety and emotional reactivity brought into, and replicated in, the romantic relationship is likely to be managed through four primary mechanisms, used to varying degrees in most families: 'loss of functioning in a partner, projection to an offspring, emotional distance, and marital conflict' (Murphy, 2003, p. 341). Furthermore, when one or both members of a couple are estranged from family members they will have less support and fewer emotional outlets for any anxiety experienced in crisis periods, thus creating a greater focus and intensified dependence on the other. All of the aforementioned processes have the potential to negatively impact on romantic attachments and marriages, including greater susceptibility to divorce, which is a risk factor for estrangement from children.

Sadly, high levels of anxiety and emotional reactivity might also contribute to, or exacerbate, the abusive elements of relationships. For example, Murphy (2003) suggested that when couples were more estranged from the intergenerational family and relied more heavily on the adaptive mechanism of marital conflict to cope with anxiety and emotional reactivity, this might result in domestic violence. Smith (2003) suggested an interrelationship between the presence of estrangement, isolation from intergenerational support, and child abuse. He posited that aggression and abuse towards children served to decrease anxiety and conflict within the parental dyad. When families were exposed to continual and sustained anxiety, this might progressively result in higher levels of instinctually aggressive and violent behaviour. Clinical observations of families where severe child abuse was occurring commonly included family members with low differentiation, socially isolated families, and families where there was extensive intergenerational estrangement and chronic conflict between the parents (Smith, 2003).

The importance of intergenerational relationships

I was just saying to my doctor the other day that I just have this profound sense of sadness at the moment because my niece has had a baby recently and we didn't know anything about it. We just found out by a third party.

(Rita)

'The family constitutes perhaps the most basic social institution, representing the very first group into which one enters at birth, and these ties remain primary over the life course' (Hoff & Tess-Romer in Lowenstein, 2007, p. 5). It has been well documented that intergenerational bonds have the potential to affect well-being through interacting and often variable, shifting and sometimes contradictory acts of solidarity, including: opportunities for intergenerational interaction and shared activities; reciprocal warmth, affection, trust and respect; consistency of values, attitudes and beliefs; reciprocal financial, physical and emotional exchanges; and, commitment to familial roles and obligations (Bengston & Roberts, 1991; Pillemer & Luscher, 2004). Additionally, there is growing assertion that these ties might have become even more important than in the past (Hagestad, 2006; Lowenstein, 2007). The intergenerational family acts as an important agent of socialisation. It potentially provides a 'continuity of care' through an array of important supportive functions which appear to be mediated through the emotional aspects of the relationship.

Family members occupy a variety of roles across the lifetime, imbued with social and familial expectations about the way they are enacted. Particular relationships and 'roles' have the potential to offer unique benefits. For example, positive early parental interactions have been linked to a range of social, behavioural and psychological outcomes, including better behaviour in children, adjustment outcomes, play competence, conflict resolution, educational attainment and positive self-esteem (Amato, 1999; Cabrera *et al.*, 2007; Carranza *et al.*, 2009; Sarkadi *et al.*, 2008; Stocker, 1994). Parental support has been strongly associated with better mental health, higher academic achievement and less engagement in criminal or antisocial behaviours in adolescents living in socially disadvantaged and stressful environments (Widmer & Weiss, 2000). Warm paternal support has been associated with protective sexual behaviours and reducing delinquency and antisocial behaviour in adolescents (Reeb & Conger, 2011; The Fathering Project, 2013). Sound parenting practices and bonding in childhood provide a protective element against poor mental health in adulthood (Goodwin & Styron, 2012; Morgan *et al.*, 2012).

Parents also provide a range of unique resources to their adult children, the degree to which depends on variables such as socio-economic status, marital status and the number of adult children and grandchildren requiring support (Fingerman *et al.*, 2015). These include the provision of financial, emotional and physical support, and a significant contribution to familial stability through the maintenance and continuance of traditions and cultural knowledge (Connidis, 2010; Fingerman *et al.*, 2015; Goodfellow, 2010).

Grandparents often provide support and advice to adult children in their parental role, childcare for working parents, and some raise grandchildren (COTA [NSW], 2010; Goodfellow, 2010). Research shows that grandparents provide a 'reserve army' for the younger generations; acting as a potential source of emotional support, guidance and practical assistance in times of crisis and need (Goodfellow, 2010; Hagestad, 2006). For example, grandparents have been shown to offer stability and respite for grandchildren during and after a difficult divorce (Ehrenberg & Smith, 2003), which can influence psychological well-being and adjustment in later years (Henderson *et al.*, 2009). They can play a very important secondary carer role when families have children with disabilities (Green, 2001; Mitchell, 2007), or experience a non-normative event like the death of a child (White *et al.*, 2008).

Grandchildren also potentially benefit uniquely from their relationships with grandparents (Attar-Schwartza *et al.*, 2009). For example, grandparents' emotional involvement with grandchildren has been related to pro-social adolescent behaviours and their financial contributions positively related to adolescent school engagement (Yorgason *et al.*, 2011). Cohesive grandparent and grandchild relationships have been linked to decreased depressive symptoms in adolescents and young adults (Ruiz & Silverstein, 2007). Adolescents in one study suggested that 'grandparents are valued primarily because they provide affection, reassurance of worth, and reliable alliance' (Van Ranst *et al.*, 1995, p. 311). It has long been recognised that grandparents potentially occupy a significant 'teaching' role in their grandchildren's lives, but they also gain much from their grandchildren in terms of emotional support, life satisfaction, practical assistance and education (Goodfellow, 2010; Mead, 1970).

The vast majority of physical, emotional and financial support given to people as they grow older comes from family members, and adult children often provide a unique place in care provision (Connidis, 2010). Adult daughters are more likely to provide the hands-on care that older and particularly frail parents require, while sons are more likely to help financially and with household chores and maintenance (Connidis, 2010; Horowitz, 1985; Palo Stoller, 1983). The support provided by adult children is particularly important in crisis or personal situations and when significant decisions need to be made about concerns such as residential care (Neyer & Lang, 2003).

Siblings are also important to emotional, psychological and social well-being across the lifespan. In childhood, siblings positively influence the development of social skills and the negotiation of peer relationships (Downey & Condron, 2004; Downey *et al.*, 2015). Siblings provide a protective buffer through the provision of social support, especially if one of them becomes physically or mentally unwell in adolescence or adulthood (Bowman *et al.*, 2014). Female siblings tend to have a closer attachment in adulthood, and are more likely to help each other with housework and parenting assistance, as well as providing emotional support and advice (Connidis & Campbell, 1995; Voorpostel *et al.*, 2007). Adults who grew up with a sibling with a disability often suggest that this relationship benefited them in terms of the development of empathy, compassion and attention to social justice issues (Hodapp *et al.*, 2010). Additionally, as siblings age, any previous feelings of ambivalence are often overridden by increased affection, and siblings are more likely to become confidants and companions in old age (Connidis, 2010).

It is important to note that relationships are very complex and these claims should be critiqued beyond their broad presentation (which aims to provide a brief overview of some of the potential benefits of unique relationships). The absence of particular relationships should not be viewed as entirely negative, and quality of contact should be considered beyond quantity. Substitute family members can compensate for the absence of a particular relationship and in some cases the absence of a conflictual, abusive or difficult family member has fewer negative effects than the maintenance of that relationship.

Finally, it is clear that individuals can benefit from a range of different family members in their lives. Indeed, functional family interactions can provide a significant advantage to children – and other members – in a range of health and well-being related areas. Conversely, when these resources are limited due to relationship dissolution, family relationships and individual outcomes can be negatively affected. When numerous 'family roles' are left vacant, the remaining family members can be placed under considerable stress to compensate, and the family may become vulnerable to everyday stressors that would normally be buffered by extended family. Crisis periods can be highly deleterious to the isolated family unit.

The experience of intergenerational estrangement

He won't speak to his sister, his brother, anybody in the family at all. His father. He lives near his father. No one. And it's very hurtful, because we have family get-togethers and I've got other grandchildren and they know about their Uncle Curtis and they've never seen him.

(Marguerite)

Intergenerational estrangements – and particularly secondary and self-protective estrangements – usually elicit a range of loss and grief experiences in the individual (see Chapters 3, 4 and 5). Inherited estrangements might vary somewhat, and particularly if the estranged person has never been aware of the person they are estranged from. In these cases, loss responses are often intricately connected to the discovery of family secrets. When family members discover that they have been denied the truth or estranged from another member without consultation, they may start to experience distrust and suspicion. While some might appreciate that they have been 'protected' from the estrangee, or believe that the estrangement was enacted out of necessity, it is likely that the exposure of such a secret will stimulate some curiosity about other familial deceptions. After all, if a family member can be hidden, what else might be secreted away? Similarly, the discovery of information that contradicts the family narrative about the estrangee is likely to evoke feelings of betrayal and subsequent questions and investigations. Loss and grief responses in these circumstances are almost retrospective in nature, where the estranged person mourns potentiality including the loss of relationship, time and experience with the estrangee. They might also mourn a loss of trust in non-estranged relatives who kept the secret and maintained the narrative.

It is also important to consider that estrangements will potentially incur losses that are unique to that particular relational dynamic. For example, the relationship between a grandparent and grandchild is one that has been increasingly raised in social and legal forums, and the rights of grandparents to access their estranged grandchildren has regularly featured. There is some evidence to suggest that when grandparents become non-voluntarily estranged from a grandchild, this can negatively affect their relationships with peers and their sense of life satisfaction and role fulfilment (Agllias, 2011; COTA [NSW], 2010; Jerrome, 1994). Estranged grandparents have reported (often intense) grief responses, and holding fears for their grandchild or grandchildren's safety and well-being (Agllias, 2008; Kruk, 1995). Research that tracked the emotional well-being of grandparents over 15 years concluded that those who had lost contact with at least one set of their grandchildren experienced higher levels of depressive symptoms than other grandparents (Drew & Silverstein, 2007). This section examines the broader losses associated with intergenerational estrangement, including the loss of place and self-understanding.

Losing place and self-understanding

I have no photographs and that really hurts me because I can't show [my children] photos of when I was a child. Because it was that day, get out and that's it. You don't get to have anything.

(Karen)

Human growth consists of autonomy, independence and a future orientation, carefully balanced with a strong bond to the past. Humans are 'driven by a need to form a deep bond with another person, not only to escape the loneliness of the human condition, but also to become, together with another person, part of something that could transcend the ephemeral nature of individual existence' (Almond, 2006, p. 171). Within this schema the intergenerational family becomes the most significant transmitter of important and enduring knowledge, culture, values, rituals and narratives, whether this occurs directly from living relatives or as an historic legacy. While a solitary estrangement includes the possible deprivation of important genetic and historical information, the cumulative losses associated with multiple inter-generational estrangements cannot be underestimated.

The intergenerational family potentially provides humans with a sense of place, belonging and shared identity (Bowen, 1982; Framo, 1976; Lieberman, 1998). These connective elements are understood to form the basis for a sense of self and self-actualisation (Maslow, 1970). Bottero's (2015) review on identity work and family history suggests that a genealogical understanding provides a 'geographical and temporal "place to stand"' (Kramer cited in Bottero, 2015, p. 538), often fulfilling a need 'to create a larger narrative, connect with others in the past and in the present, and to find coherence in one's own life' (Yakel cited in Bottero, 2015, p. 539). Family identity is clearly created through narratives about the past and present family culture as well as conveying expectations about continued membership. However, examin-ations of ostracism suggest that estrangement directly threatens one's fundamental need to belong, while long-term and multiple estrangement might lead to a broader sense of social disconnection (Williams & Zadro, 2001; Zadro, 2010).

Research has demonstrated that a sense of belonging to the family can be a protective factor against a number of negative external influences (Robinson *et al.*, 2011; Stephens Leake, 2007). Conversely, an unfulfilled sense of family belonging, may place family members – and particularly adolescents – at risk of making less healthy affiliations (e.g. subcultures where violence and drug use might be core to identification and membership) (Howell & Egley, 2005; Stephens Leake, 2007). Interestingly, one study conducted in the United States asked adolescents if they knew certain key stories about their family history. It concluded that adolescents with more historical knowledge showed 'higher levels of emotional well-being, and also higher levels of identity achievement, even when controlling for general level of family functioning' (Fivush *et al.*, 2010, p. n/p).

The intergenerational family potentially provides a group of support, where the sheer number of members can increase a long-term sense of being allied with and buttressed against outside forces. When this is fragmented, the sense of being buffered by a *collective strength* can be reduced. For example, one social worker relayed: 'for children and siblings of parents who are palliative, the gap can be so wide that they need to arrange a "roster" system to visit the parent without seeing each other' (Dale, in Agllias, 2013). This type of fragmentation has the potential to affect the patient's sense of collective support and continuity. The support that is gained from inter-personal interactions with others can enhance life satisfaction, increase immunity and decrease the symptoms of some mental health conditions (Cohen, 2004; Haslam *et al.*, 2006; Mistry *et al.*, 2007; Stice *et al.*, 2004). Group support can contribute to a more balanced assessment of risk, increase coping mechanisms and moderate risk-taking behaviours. For the most part, mothers of babies and young children suggest that their most valuable source of support comes from family members (Haslam *et al.*, 2006; Rennie Negron *et al.*, 2013). For example, research shows that parental support reduces post-partum depressive symptoms in new mothers (Haslam *et al.*, 2006). In other words, estrangement not only interferes with actual support, but the feeling of being collectively supported.

The intergenerational family also plays an important 'archival' function through 'the symbolic retention of particular objects, events, and performances which are considered relevant to each member's identity and to the maintenance of the family as a unique existential reality' (Weigert & Hastings, 1977, pp. 1173–1174). Many objects such as photos and awards are displayed as proof of external – and particularly familial – approval, acknowledgement and pride in the individual's and the family's success and cohesion. An absence of archival material, or even the viewing of material that remains, can act as significant reminders of alienation and lost identity. Estrangement often leads to the distortion, fragmentation and loss of important historical and genetic knowledge in subsequent generations, leaving isolated members without a cohesive narrative. It can also increase vulnerability. For example, one study showed that estranged women often felt the absence of maternal childbearing and child-rearing knowledge particularly distressing (Agllias, 2014). So too, genetic information, which is increasingly understood to be a core component of understanding genetic disposition, mitigating disease and maximising health, might be lost in estranged families.

The intergenerational family fashions a frame for individual identity development, and is widely regarded as core to self-understanding (Bottero, 2015; Bowen, 1982; Framo, 1976; Lieberman, 1998). Even though many estrangers suggest that relationship dissolution was core to regaining their self-identity and self-esteem, they usually acknowledge the impact that (often multiple) intergenerational losses incur on their long-term sense of place and identity (Agllias, 2014). This appears to be closely connected to:

> the mental images of family existing in each member's mind. Each member maps or projects his or her 'family' onto the family and lives according to the image. The loss of another member or the destruction of one's 'family' leads to the destruction of identities which were contingent on that image or relationship.
>
> (Weigert & Hastings, 1977, p. 1177)

Estrangement potentially undermines this 'familial image', often replacing it with a 'tainted or stigmatised' version.

Intergenerational estrangement can lead to stigma by association, where a generalised stigma pervades the entire intergenerational narrative. All-encompassing statements about family dysfunction often emerge from within a family that is experiencing multiple relationship breakdowns. These ideas are regularly reinforced by strong, and often internalised, social messages about family functionality. These ideas are regularly encountered by estranged people when they interact with public entities including schools, health care facilities, social, sporting and community groups. Family stigma is characterised by:

> (a) others' negative perceptions, attitudes, emotions, and avoidant behaviors toward a family, because of the unusualness of the family, including the negative situations, events, behaviors, problems or diseases associated with that family, or because of the unordinary characteristics or structures of that family; (b) others' belief that the unusualness of the family is somehow harmful, dangerous, unhealthy, capable of affecting them negatively, or different from general social norms; and (c) others' belief that the family members are directly or indirectly contaminated by the problematic family member, so that every family member is also considered as harmful, dangerous, unhealthy, capable of having a negative effect on others, or different from general social norms.
>
> (Park & Park, 2014, p. 165)

Family estrangement stigma is very similar to that experienced by families who have members with mental illness, addiction, HIV/AIDs and conditions like dementia. In these situations, families often feel blamed for the so-called 'aberrant behaviour', held responsible for its ongoing occurrence and perceived as incompetent due to their inability to contain or correct it (Corrigan *et al.*, 2006; Perlick *et al.*, 2011; van der Sanden *et al.*, 2014). Stigmatised experiences can lead to broader familial secrecy, social withdrawal, reduced health and help-seeking behaviours and psychological distress due to shame, guilt and embarrassment (Corrigan *et al.*, 2006; Perlick *et al.*, 2011; Werner *et al.*, 2012). Families might be excluded from certain social activities and experience problematic engagement with human service and health professionals (Agllias, 2011; van der Sanden *et al.*, 2014; Werner *et al.*, 2012).

Risky endeavors to protect and recreate place

Being a parent, I say to them, you better not – you better talk to me when you're older. I say you've got no reason not to talk to me. I suppose – I hear about people and they've had some little thing and I think God, you're not talking to your parents because of that?

(Karen)

Family estrangement is often described and regarded as a form of psychological trauma where disempowerment and disconnection are core to the loss experience. When people grieve the loss of 'family' they often feel an intense need to protect and recreate core elements such as belongingness, identity and safety in their existing relationships. However, research illustrates that the fear for future generations and the associated anticipatory loss can contribute to some well-intentioned but precarious relational practices, which might actually undermine these relationships, and further risk intergenerational bonds (Agllias, 2011, 2014). The next section, then, discusses the possible effects of family silence, keeping up public appearances and intensely parenting the next generation.

Family silence

My children and I never talk about [my estrangement from their brother]. It's as if it doesn't exist. It's awful.

(Marguerite)

Estrangement is such a stigmatising experience that it is unsurprising that families often remain silent about their estranged status in social situations. However, many families also refrain from discussing estrangement within their familial confines. This might be due to the intense pain it invokes, fear that it will reignite conflict, or the risk that it will alter existing relationships with 'neutral' family members. Older estranged parents in one study claimed that they employed silence as a protective measure to avoid any estrangement-related fallout in their family (Agllias, 2011). While they used silence to protect the entire intergenerational family, they most vehemently employed silence with male partners and non-estranged children. The older parents in this study considered the discussion of estrangement – and particularly their associated grief – to be a burden to their partners and non-estranged children. Some had learned to employ silence because they had experienced anger or been shut down during previous attempts to discuss the estrangement or their estranged adult child. They rarely or never spoke about 'missing' their estranged child for fear this would be interpreted as 'favouritism' by non-estranged children.

Regardless of the intention, when silence is employed to diffuse anxiety and minimise hurt, it usually emerges as a powerful family secret that consumes relational energy. Imber-Black (1998) says that 'living inside a secret may propagate a strange mixture of responsibility, power, anxiety, protectiveness, shame, burden, and fear' (p. 7). Secrets often cast a disproportionately mysterious and shameful shadow over even the most benign conversations and those family members who remain uninformed about the details of the secret – usually children and more distant relatives – are left to imagine the reasons for such tension. 'Living outside a central family secret can shape identity and behavior, generate feelings of self-doubt, distance, and suspicion, and contribute to key decisions that are made without sufficient information' (Imber-Black, 1998, p. 7). Regardless of positioning, rules and expectations are established where future generations learn to use silence to combat anxiety and pain.

Keeping up appearances

Everyone put on a nice face, just be happy. I don't want to be fucking happy. I'm quite happy with my rage actually, just quietly. . . . It's like any family gathering I just expect to hear my name at least eight times. Laura, Laura, don't say that, don't say that.

(Laura)

Most people employ deceptive techniques when they need to protect themselves from harm, social disapproval, and potential relationship loss (Itzhaky & Kissil, 2015; Johnson, 2013). Additionally, 'during social interactions, people often exert significant effort to construct or maintain specific identity-images' (Tyler & Feldman, 2004a, p. 364). For example, human beings employ more deceptive behaviour – such as lies, exaggerations, distortions and omissions – when they want to make a good impression, appear likeable or more competent (Feldman *et al.*, 2002; Tyler & Feldman, 2004a; Weiss & Feldman, 2006). The level and frequency of deception is likely to equate to the importance attributed to the particular audience, as well as the importance of maintaining a particular image in front of them (Tyler & Feldman, 2004a; Tyler & Feldman, 2004b). Additionally, people are more likely to employ deceptive strategies when they feel threatened by comparative information (Tyler & Feldman, 2005).

Given the internalised and external social pressure that families are under to conform to ideals of harmony, unity and cohesion, it is unsurprising that many go to extreme lengths to 'save public face', 'keep up appearances' or 'play happy families', and the 'silence' that is employed – as discussed previously – is often carried into and defended beyond the immediate family. Research with estrangers and estrangees found that many had used deceptive behaviour in social situations for two reasons: (i) to alleviate personal guilt and embarrassment about the estrangement, and (ii) to preserve the broader family image as 'functional' (Agllias, 2011, 2014). Interestingly, several reported employing similar protective measures at intergenerational family gatherings, at celebratory events and everyday interactions with extended family members. Deception included: exaggerating the level and intimacy of contact with estranged relatives; making positive excuses for the estranged person's behaviour; minimising the hurt being experienced from the estrangement; interacting with estranged relatives at an event as if the relationship remained intact; inventing and lying about upcoming family interactions and events; accepting and laughing off any negative comments from the estranged party; and omitting negative details about the relationship.

In some cases, estrangees were unexpectedly invited or pressured into attending a family event to preserve a positive family narrative. For example, Joyce was estranged from a number of her children and had not had contact with her daughter, Mary, for 12 months, when she was suddenly invited to her granddaughter's wedding:

But Mary came, just two days before the wedding . . . the only reason they wanted me to go to the wedding was because I could read at Mass. I'm quite sure, that was all it was. To do a reading – give the impression. Because I'm – haven't spoken to them since. They don't want to speak to me.

Despite suspicions about the motivation for such an invitation, as well as concerns about fraudulent behaviour and possible conflict, most estrangees decide to attend such events in the hope that it will lead to some form of reconciliation, and maintain their family's positive public image.

However, preserving individual and family image might come at a personal and intergenerational cost. First, as mentioned earlier in this book, deception is often incongruent with self-image. Even the smallest of fraudulent activity can contradict personal values, altering one's self perception and feelings of worthiness. Negative perceptions of self-identity can affect the way that people interact with others, even beyond the people they have deceived. Research suggests that when a person detects deception, they are more likely to consider the other person less worthy and reduce closeness, and this is particularly so in ongoing relationships such as familial ones (Johnson, 2013; Tyler *et al.*, 2006). Lying about family harmony can also establish norms of deceptive reciprocity, because it has been shown that people have a greater propensity to lie to those who have deceived them previously (Tyler *et al.*, 2006). Conversely, deception can create considerable acrimony between those members who wish to be honest about the family situation and those who wish to preserve the unity narrative, making the former vulnerable to family exclusion and estrangement.

All of the aforementioned conditions can undermine the quality and quantity of interactions and increase an individual or family's sense of separateness from others. What is most interesting is that families – despite knowing that deception has occurred in the name of self-protection and keeping up appearances – often continue to interact with the deceptive family member or members without drawing attention to, or challenging, this information. Rather, their sense of loyalty to, and protection of, the person and the intergenerational family reputation appears to draw many into ignoring, supporting or promoting the distorted narrative of family unity. In this way, shared systems of meaning – which are also culturally mediated – are developed and maintained beyond the individual narrative. Whole families can take on a contra-dictory narrative that, once established, requires considerable attention and maintenance to avoid public exposure. 'Keeping up appearances' can place enormous stress and tension on the entire family system, making it vulnerable to further relational conflict and dissolution.

Intense parenting

And the kids say a few things to each other, like 'I hate you' and I have to turn around to them and say one day you're going to say I hate you and you'll end up [estranged] like myself. I don't have my brother and sister.

(Lisa)

Estrangement from a parent can create an intense desire to parent the next generation differently, regardless of estrangee or estranger status. Research participants who were estranged from one or both parents in adulthood suggested that estrangement made them more thoughtful, and sometimes vigilant, about their own parenting practices (Agllias, 2014). They were determined to provide a different experience for their children, and this often included 'more love', 'more attention', 'more care', 'more affection' and 'more involvement' in their lives. Several were concerned about their parenting skills, considering that they had limited parental role models and reduced familial support. Many worried about their actual capacity to love their children 'properly' or 'enough', and this was particularly so for parent–child relationships which were structurally similar to their estranged relationship with a parent. For example, Donna believed that her estrangement from her mother impacted on her parenting:

> I struggle with my daughter. I look at my daughter and [wonder if] I'm doing enough – a good enough job. I'm really hard on myself. Then I think it's just so hard to open up to her . . . I shouldn't feel that way. I can't work out why I feel that way. It's like the mother/daughter thing, for me, brings up pain, and I don't want to have her miss out on that . . . I didn't have a mother. It doesn't come easy to you. It's a struggle. It's just harder to say 'I love you' to her. I have to think about it, where the boys I don't. I am working on it.

Estrangement from one's own parent can increase anxiety about parenting, making some more vigilant about their relationship with their child, and highly attentive to any signs that the child might feel rejected or unloved. The desire to 'get it right' often involves parental declarations about activities they will *not* engage in, practices they would *not* enact, and things they would *never* repeat. However, knowing what 'not to do' does not necessarily provide the answers about 'what *to* do', and this negative frame for parenting can leave many without the guidance and support necessary to parent with confidence and consistency. Boundaries, rules and appropriate discipline can be particularly difficult concepts to implement without adequate knowledge, role modelling and emotional support. Additionally, as Tomkinson (2011) warns, there are dangers in parenting after a difficult, abusive or estranged childhood, where the affected generation can inadvertently provide the parent that 'they' wanted or needed, rather than the parent that their 'child' needs at the time.

There appears to be a connection between estrangement and a number of well-intentioned and intense parenting practices in some families (Agllias, 2014). In these families, parenting is often idealised, believed to result in happiness, and fill a void left by estrangement. The desire to protect children from estrangement-related issues or family members, to make up for past intergenerational mistakes, and prevent them from reoccurring, can place enormous pressure on parents (and children). It can contribute to high expectations about closeness and harmony in the relationship, as well as an intense focus on the child's happiness and success. Parents might believe that they need to spend a lot of time with their children, provide more for them than they had, and source substitute family members to make up for estranged relatives. They might feel intensely protective of the child or children, and grapple with how, when and what to tell them about the estrangement.

Additionally, estrangement from one's parent often creates a sense that there is less room for mistakes in parenting the next generation, and the reality is that there are often fewer familial supports and resources. The paradox of parenting after estrangement is that relationship dissolution may reduce the parent's ease with closeness in some circumstances. When this conflicts with their high expectations and intellectual desire for closeness with their child, it can create exaggerated experiences of failure. Research showed that a number of parents possessed a possibly unrealistic desire to be consistently positive with their children, and to 'put on a happy face', even when they were feeling stressed by the estrangement or overwhelmed by the parenting experience (Agllias, 2014). Additionally, the experience of estrangement can make parents highly attuned to the possibility of, and take preventative measures to avoid, estrangement with their own children.

However, research has shown that a commitment to intensive parenting beliefs and practices can have a detrimental effect on a mother's mental health (Rizzo *et al.*, 2013). This is particularly so for mothers who (i) believe that they are the most important source of love and care for the child and that no one else has the skill or commitment to parent the child effectively (an essentialist belief that might derive from a lack of social support, or result in reduced support-seeking), (ii) a belief that parenting is difficult or experiencing parenting as difficult, and (iii) a belief that parents' lives should revolve around their children, and parental needs should be subsumed to those of the child. Additionally, children of over-involved parents are more likely to experience internalising difficulties, such as anxiety and depression (Bayer *et al.*, 2006). Research shows that adults who parent intensely may do so to the neglect of the adolescent or young adult's growing need for autonomy (Padilla-Walker & Nelson, 2012; Schiffrin *et al.*, 2015), which is closely connected to the theories of fusion and differentiation discussed earlier in this chapter.

Conclusion

Theories about intergenerational estrangement have primarily emphasised the notion of fusion and differentiation, where the level of differentiation is recreated in new generations. However, this chapter has made a closer examination of some of the communicative and relational practices, as well as social influences, that also potentially challenge relationship quality and stability. The transmission of estrangement is unique to each generational family, and relational patterns may shift across time, but an historic analysis is an important tool in understanding areas of vulnerability and developing new strategies to reduce the incidence of future estrangement (as described further in Chapter 7).

PRACTICE POINT 5: ASSESSING INTERGENERATIONAL ESTRANGEMENT

This chapter clearly establishes the notion that all estrangements impact on the stability and quality of relationships across and between the generations. Similar to the exploration of family stressors (see Practice Point 1 in Chapter 2), the examination of intergenerational patterns of communication, conflict and relationship dissolution can provide useful insights into the development and maybe even the interruption of future estrangements. The following exercises were developed to situate and encourage reflection upon estrangement in a broad relational context.

Revisiting the Genogram

The genogram was introduced in the practice section of Chapter 2. It can be useful to revisit the original genogram to examine the intergenerational estrangements that have existed and continue to exist beyond those being experienced by the primary person (i.e. the reader or the client).

EXERCISE 1

Employ commonly used or personally meaningful symbols to map and visualise the estrangements and associated communication patterns that exist in the inter-generational family. Figure 6.1 includes the basic symbols that were used in Chapter 2, and new estrangement related symbols for: (i) distant (or emotionally estranged) relationships; (ii) fused relationships; (iii) conflictual relationships; and (iv) relation-ships where contact has never been established (such as some inherited and absent estrangements).

Note: The case example (Jane) that was used in Chapter 2 is developed further to illustrate visual intergenerational patterns. It uncovers additional estrangement-type relationships beyond those that Jane initially documented. It particularly highlights the direct or possible impacts that relationship breakdowns/estrangements have on secondary and inherited estrangements within the family system.

Case example (Jane)

A case example was utilised in Chapter 2 to illustrate a basic genogram and a map of Jane's estranged relationships (see Figure 6.2). This is followed by a more detailed genogram that illustrates the estrangements and related communication patterns in Jane's intergenerational family (see Figure 6.3).

Estrangements in Jane's intergenerational family

Jane's intergenerational family has experienced numerous estrangements across the generations. Her brief four-generation story is as follows: Harold and Katherine married in 1950 and had one daughter, Kat in 1954. Kat always had a difficult relationship with her father, who she considered to be dominant and controlling of her mother, Katherine. Kat left the family home in 1975 to marry Bill, and she had three children, Sam, Jane and Terry. Harold estranged Kat after an argument in 1985 (and Sam, Jane and Terry inherited the estrangement at that time). Neither made an attempt to reconcile before Harold's sudden death in 1988. Kat rarely had contact with her mother, Katherine, while her father was alive, and she physically estranged from her shortly after Bill's death due to a dispute about inheritance and burial. (While Jane and Terry inherited this estrangement at this time, Sam was old enough to visit his grandmother Katherine after school and maintain a connection).

Bill lived in a sole-mother household from the age of 10. He has always had a cordial relationship with his father, Robert, and a sound relationship with his mother, Shirley. Both Robert and Shirley have relatively positive relationships with Bill's wives and his five children. Bill has a conflictual relationship with his son, Terry, who he believes is an entitled person, who uses his ex-wife for money and babysitting.

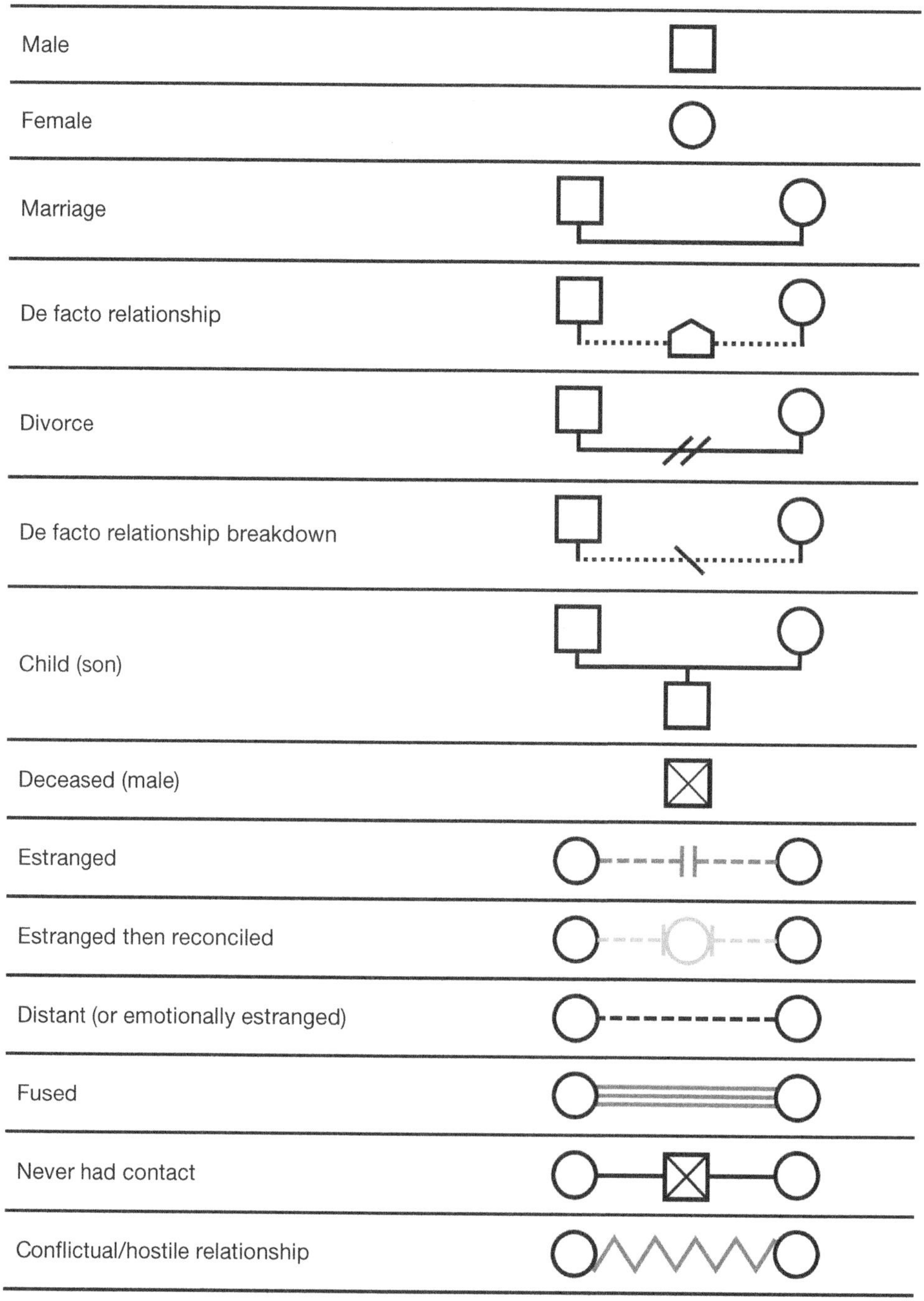

Male	☐
Female	○
Marriage	☐———○
De facto relationship	☐·····⌂·····○
Divorce	☐——//——○
De facto relationship breakdown	☐·······\·······○
Child (son)	☐———○ with ☐ below
Deceased (male)	⊠
Estranged	○---‖---○
Estranged then reconciled	○--◯--○
Distant (or emotionally estranged)	○--------○
Fused	○═══════○
Never had contact	○—⊠—○
Conflictual/hostile relationship	○∧∧∧∧∧○

FIGURE 6.1 Commonly used symbols for estrangement-related genograms

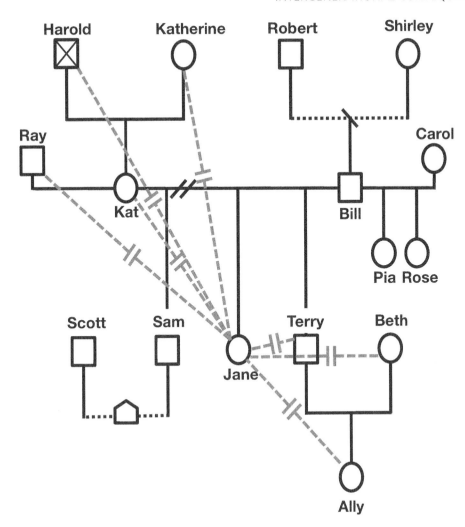

FIGURE 6.2 Jane's estranged relationships

Jane always felt that her mother, Kat, favoured her two male siblings as she grew up, believing that they received more affection and attention and were required to do less chores. She felt that her mother was particularly unfair to her father during their divorce in 1996 and she subsequently lived with her father. Jane – while suggesting she was always emotionally estranged from her mother – made the decision to physically estrange her mother and her partner, Ray, in 2002. This decision was triggered by the discovery that her mother had funded her brother, Terry's, new car. Jane saw this as a significant betrayal of trust and proof of her mother's favouritism: her mother had claimed that she did not have the financial means to offer any support to Jane throughout University. Jane estranged from her brother, Terry, shortly afterwards, believing that his close relationship with her mother made him a risk to her privacy (a protective estrangement). This resulted in a secondary estrangement from Terry's wife Beth (and her niece, Ally, inherited this estrangement when she was born a few years later).

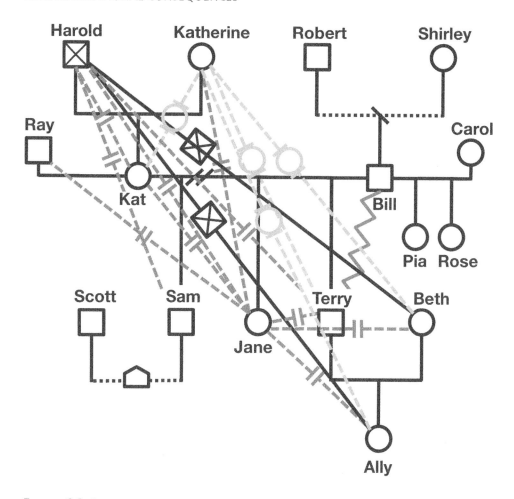

FIGURE 6.3 Estrangements in Jane's intergenerational family

Kat and Katherine gradually recommenced communication in 2009. They have considered their relationship to be reconciled since 2011. While Katherine has also reunified with Terry and his family, she does not wish to have contact with Jane at this time, preferring to show her allegiance to Kat.

EXERCISE 2

Examine the genogram that you have mapped in Exercise 1. Reflect on the types of estrangements (e.g. physical, emotional, mutually disengaged, absent, inherited, secondary and protective) that occur across the generations. What patterns can be observed? Think about the types of relationships that appear to be most affected. For example, are there gendered patterns (e.g. mothers estranging from sons)? Are there patterns in relational positions (e.g. more effects on horizontal relationships such as siblings, than vertical relationships such as parents and children)? What communication patterns might have influenced the estrangement (e.g. favouritism, or excessive closeness)? What are the primary reasons given for estrangement (e.g. financial, abuse, bias, narcissism)? What stressors – as highlighted in Chapter 2 – might have influenced specific estrangements (e.g. mental illness or excessive work due to a family business)? What questions remain and require further investigation and reflection?

Look at the genogram you have mapped and consider the losses that might have occurred across the generations due to conflict and estrangement, as well as the characteristics that have been retained. See Table 6.1 'Important elements of family belonging' for guidance. Then, reflect upon how the losses and retention of certain elements have affected the collective or intergenerational sense of identity and belonging.

Reflect on the following questions in relation to the intergenerational family you have mapped. Try to look beyond the primary estrangement. This can illuminate missing information and instigate curiosity about the broader familial context. Answer as many questions as possible and take note of the questions that need further investigation.

(i) Family silence
- How is estrangement 'generally' acknowledged in the intergenerational family (e.g. spoken about freely, avoided, silenced?)
- Are there people who are exceptions to this 'general rule'? How do they acknowledge the estrangement differently? How are they responded to?
- Are there particular estrangements that are acknowledged or regarded differently (in terms of the way people communicate about them)?
- Consider the way estrangement is acknowledged in the intergenerational family and think about the effects that might result.

(ii) Keeping up appearances
Think about interactions where the intergenerational family come together – or have come together in the past – with people from outside of the family, e.g. a wedding.
- Does the intergenerational family 'generally' acknowledge estrangement to outsiders?
- If estrangement is acknowledged, how does the intergenerational family explain it? Does this explanation minimise, emphasise, or alter certain elements of the estranged relationship?
- Are certain family members cast as problematic, as instigators of the estrangement, as victims of the estrangement, as innocent bystanders, or negative third party influences?
- If estrangement is unacknowledged, how does the intergenerational family keep this from public knowledge? What strategies do members employ to keep up appearances (e.g. silence, avoidance, deflection, deception)?

TABLE 6.1 Important elements of family belonging

	Elements that have been retained	Elements that have been lost, or may be at risk
Knowledge: Facts, information and skills that have been acquired across the generations, e.g. facts about ancestors, cultural information, skills such as bee-keeping.		
Values: The principles or standards of behaviour that help families to prioritise and take action, e.g. trust, affection, dependability. Families might also value particular actions that represent these values, e.g. hard work, education.		
Rituals: An established ceremony, proceeding, rite, service or action that the family adheres to e.g. attending Church on Christmas Eve, burying the dead.		
Archives: Documents or records of family life and achievement, e.g. birth certificates, stamp albums, photos.		
Support: The provision of particular emotional and physical aid, e.g. listening, financial transfers, babysitting.		
Narratives: Stories of events, e.g. how couples met, where children were born and why migration occurred. Stories of character, e.g. stories about courage, collegiality and achievement.		

- Are there exceptions to these 'general rules'? If so, who are the people who offer an alternate story/narrative? How does this differ and how is it received? What affect does it have on others (e.g. they try to silence it, it results in conflict or distancing)?
- Consider the way estrangement is acknowledged outside of the inter-generational family and think about the effects that might result.

(iii) Intense parenting

Think about parenting in the intergenerational family, how this might have changed across the generations, and particularly in the generation after an estrangement has occurred. Focus on your own parenting if this is most relevant.

- What are the 'general' beliefs about the role(s) of parents in the intergener-ational family (e.g. importance of parental role, intensity of involvement in the child's life, responsibility for child's happiness, responsibility for child's success, responsibility for making child feel loved and accepted).
- How are these beliefs practiced in particular families, including your own (e.g. mothers do not work or minimise hours at work, parent's needs subsumed to child's, high expectations about parenting as a source of happiness)?
- What impact might these beliefs have on particular families, including your own? How might parents and children be experiencing these practices?

Chapter 7   Learning, living, growing

It is never as simple as the so called perpetrator being the baddie and the other person [being the] victim and the goodie. Most people are left with a legacy of shame and grief and anger and all of this stuff to deal with.

(Debbie)

As previously highlighted, it is simplistic to view estrangement from a psychological, didactic and relational perspective. Relationship dissolution develops from a complex interplay of socio-economic, historical and cultural factors that intersect with the characteristics – such as personality and genetics – of the parties involved. This chapter examines the principles and strategies that encourage individuals and families to *learn to live with estrangement*. The chapter is relevant regardless of whether reconciliation is considered, attempted or achieved in the future. The focus is on the development of healthy relationships, increased insight, resilience and well-being notwithstanding future intentions and aspirations for the estranged relationship. This is in no way a linear, staged or finite process. Estranged people suggest that learning to live with estrangement is hard work that requires ongoing long-term effort. However, the result can be a liberating experience of self-growth and reconnection. The chapter draws on research and theory to assist people to learn about, and live with, estrangement. These ideas can be adapted and incorporated by estranged people and their families, as well as employed in therapeutic settings, and they are relevant to all types of estrangement. The chapter concludes with a section for professionals which gives a broad overview of the possibilities for therapeutic intervention in this field. Finally, a practice section encourages a strengths-focused assessment of the reader or client's progress towards living with estrangement.

Grieving a significant loss

So you think that you're over it and you think that you've moved on, and it's not there anymore, but I find it is. Sometimes it just comes up. Sometimes you try and push it down. Either way, I think people have to deal with it because if you just ignore it, it affects who you are in a big way.

(Donna)

Most – but not all – people experience estrangement from a family member as a significant loss. The experience and progression of grief will be influenced by a number of factors, including: the type of estrangement; who the person is estranged from and the nature of their attachment; the way the estrangement developed and was realised; the person's experience of previous losses, and particularly other relationship dissolutions; personal variables such as age, sex, reactions to stress and anxiety, and mental health status; social variables such as cultural and religious influences, levels of social connection and support; and concurrent stressors. Some people will feel very little about losing the person, or the estrangement itself – especially those who have never had a close relationship and those who estrange because abuse has occurred – but this does not preclude associated psychological losses (such as loss of innocence, the loss of the symbolic relationship, the loss of dreams), and physical losses (such as safety, financial and practical support).

Research shows that family estrangement often violates people's beliefs about, and ambitions for, family (Agllias, 2011, 2014). It is an uncertain and often traumatic loss with the potential to violate assumptions about life's predictability, spiritual convictions and the goodness and trustworthiness of human beings. Traumatic events shatter one's sense of safety, security and predictability, which can result in a sense of helplessness and hypersensitivity (Wright, 2006). When people experience trauma they often 'feel re-realization (*Is this really happening?*) and depersonalization (*I don't know what I really stand for anymore*)' (ibid., p. 168). These elements make it considerably difficult for estranged people to maintain, or reinstate, narrative coherence in their lives. Additionally, the ambiguity associated with family estrangement, as well as its often disenfranchised status, makes it very difficult for people to move forward, and many struggle with their loss for decades. This section looks at ways of understanding and navigating estrangement-associated loss and grief. It introduces Stroebe and Schut's (1999) *dual process model of coping with bereavement* as a way of conceptualising the processes associated with grieving an estrangement loss, and finally it explores the principles and practices that encourage resilience while learning to live with an ambiguous loss.

Acknowledging the crisis

> [Going] to the shops and feeling incredibly teary a lot of the time. I used to say, I felt like people could just put their hands through me. I felt very fragile and very invisible.

(Debbie)

Estrangers and estrangees often experience a crisis moment when estrangement is declared, and those experiencing other types of estrangements, such as emotional and absent estrangements, might also reach a critical realisation or crisis point. Whether this presents as an event or a realisation, this crisis moment is often experienced as a traumatic and confusing loss that decreases functioning and increases a sense of vulnerability for varying periods of time. Some estrangees find it tempting to get caught in the anger and revenge of an unjust situation during this period, while estrangers may feel undeserving of grief because they instigated the crisis. However, this is an important time and it requires acknowledgement and attention, as well as reassurances about the normality of the physiological and psychological processes that accompany loss (such as numbing, denial, anger, bargaining, disbelief, searching and withdrawal). There are also a number of practical activities and processes that can assist during this period.

It is imperative that life is kept simple during this critical period, and no significant changes are made or risks taken. In fact, the estranged person's world needs to be slowed down considerably and daily activities reduced wherever possible. Estranged people require a safe space, and adequate time, to grieve. A comforting environment is important to this process, whether it is a quiet and isolated place in the home or garden or going surfing. The space should allow a person to cry, to 'talk' to the other person or 'talk' to themselves when required (as well as providing a place to leave some of the grief behind when required). It is important for the estranged person to talk through the initial pain and hurt with trusted others: to express feelings about the loss, protest the actuality of the loss as well as the injustice associated with it, and to express the effects being experienced. Self-soothing methods that have been used successfully in the past – building, music, yoga, getting a massage, or going fishing – should be employed to temporarily distract and comfort. Particular attention should be paid to healthy activities and nutrition during this period as research shows a considerable reduction in immunity – and increased risk of mortality and morbidity – after a significant loss (Buckley *et al.*, 2012).

The dual process model

Stroebe and Schut's (1999) *dual process model of coping with bereavement* offers a way to think about the loss and readjustment processes associated with estrangement, and particularly those discussed in this chapter. The model is influenced by stage and task models, as well as cognitive stress theories. It suggests that grief involves multiple stressors to which people must respond by employing emotional and problem-focused coping strategies (Hansson & Stroebe, 2007; Stroebe & Schut, 1999). The model gives equal recognition to loss and restoration orientations. *Loss orientation* includes processing the experiences and emotions associated with the experience of loss, including yearning and ruminating, revisiting memories and memorabilia of the lost person, going over the circumstances surrounding the loss, and experiencing emotions and behaviours like sadness and crying (Hansson & Stroebe, 2007). *Restoration orientation* refers to responding to secondary sources of stress or attending to the tasks to be completed due to the person's absence, such as taking over tasks previously undertaken by the person, shaping a new identity, and reorganising life without the person (ibid.).

The dual process model is also useful in thinking about the way that men and women *might* grieve – or be expected to grieve – estrangement differently. For example, research suggests that women are *more likely* to be loss oriented or emotionally expressive after loss, whereas men are *more likely* to be restoration oriented, expressing their grief through intellectualisation, actively engaging with, and problem-solving, the practical consequences of the loss (Martin & Doka, 2000; Parkes, 2001; Stroebe & Schut, 2008). In the past, male or restoration-oriented grieving was seen as less adaptive, but studies have increasingly disputed this view in favour of the idea that this type of grieving is different rather than deficient (Doka & Martin, 1998). In the social context, men might be expected to experience grief less intensely and 'get over' family estrangement more quickly than women. These expectations can be problematic for either sex if their way of grieving seems contrary to accepted norms. Therefore, it is important to recognise and accept that people will grieve and express their grief in different and sometimes unexpected ways.

In terms of estrangement, and regardless of a person's natural orientation to grieving a loss, the dual process model suggests that the individual needs to confront and avoid the loss and restoration aspects of grieving at different times in order to live with estrangement. It is important for the estranged person to acknowledge their loss and attend to their grief, while also taking time to rest from this process to reorganise their life. (Physical, absent and mutually disengaged estrangements usually require a reorganisation of life without the other person, while emotional estrangements usually require the reorganisation of life with a changed relationship status). The model suggests that over time, acute experiences of suffering and high levels of distress will subside, and the estranged person will spend more time in restoration (Stroebe & Schut, 2008). While oscillation might continue, the person would gradually move away from both orientations towards adaption (Hansson & Stroebe, 2007). In other words, the system would find a new balance and 'adaptation' would result in 'a new normal' (Corr, 2002).

It is also important to recognise that 'accepting the reality of the loss' is often presumed as core to the grieving process; however, this is a much more difficult proposition when estrangement occurs. Research with parents who had been estranged by an adult child showed that many experienced quite extended periods of loss orientation, although this was shorter for some men (Agllias, 2011). This may be due to the uncertainty surrounding the relationship's finality, and the temptation to postpone the pain originating from acceptance. While an upcoming section discusses the techniques relevant to living with an ambiguous loss, it is important to note here that acceptance of estrangement is more likely when the focus is on acceptance of the *current loss of relationship status*, or *acceptance of the ambiguous nature of the loss*, rather than the *long-term loss of the person* (a condition that cannot be determined in the absence of death).

Acknowledging and attending to chronic and ongoing losses

There's a lot [that] goes on in the subconscious mind that you're not aware of, because every so often I'd see somebody that reminded me of Donna. Once I really got hit in the face with it – like a fish. She was just – profile and everything was just – I stopped in my tracks.

(Yvonne)

An assessment and recognition of cumulative and particularly unresolved losses is essential to understanding and living with estrangement. Davis (2002) acknowledges that 'some estrangements build like beads on a thread, one disappointment at a time ... slowly, inexorably, over the course of many troubled years' (p. 14). Other losses result directly or indirectly from the gradual relationship dissolution, and continue well after an estrangement has been established. The attachment bond, and the nature of intergenerational family interaction, often means that estranged people are regularly exposed to memories, events and unexpected cues that create or recreate loss experiences. While often less dramatic – and less recognisable – than the crisis moment, these losses are no less impactful and no less deserving of attention. It is important to grieve for previous and secondary losses – including those from childhood – because the associated changes and temporary loss of control encourages important long-term personal growth, development, meaning making and life appreciation across the lifespan (Gordon, 2013; Wright, 2006).

An important component of learning to live with estrangement is to evaluate and acknowledge the true long-term effect of the relationship dissolution. A persistent lack of control over external events and the stresses associated with ongoing estrangement losses can be problematic. Few people can live with chronic stress, which leaves them open to a range of stress-related complications. Learning new techniques to address the ongoing effects of the estrangement, such as anxiety and depression, can be warranted, whether this is through books, the Internet, groups or professional sources. For example, the practice of mindfulness, where a person intentionally attends to the present and notices their own thoughts and emotions without judgement, has been shown to effectively reduce emotional reactivity and rumination (Gu *et al.*, 2015). The identification of unhelpful automatic thoughts and behaviours, which are so often related to estrangement losses, can be challenged experientially, and new coping mechanisms developed in response. Boss (1999) also recommends connecting to stable relationships and activities to enhance predictability and mastery, as well as reducing stress. A final strategy to combat the ongoing losses associated with estrangement includes the anticipation of, and planning for, loss triggers (see 'A note on minimising triggers' in this chapter). As each loss is examined and worked through, skills are developed to attend to the next challenge.

Learning to live with ambiguous loss

But then I started to think there is no closure there. Like with my mum it doesn't matter when she dies there'll never be full closure because she's never given me what every child deserves. . . . I don't have to like what's happened or is happening but to accept it.

(Rita)

Pauline Boss's seminal work on ambiguous loss and resiliency will be drawn upon in this section due to its currency and applicability to estrangement, but her specific works should be consulted for a fuller examination of this concept (e.g. Boss, 1999, 2004, 2006a, 2006b; Boss & Couden, 2002; Boss & Yeats, 2014). Ambiguous loss can hinder problem-solving, role and life adjustment because of the uncertainty about the estrangement's finality, as well as who is in and who is out of the family system. Uncertainty can create 'absolutes, either acting as if the person is completely gone, or denying that anything has changed' (Boss, 1999, p. 7). Both of these states can be detrimental to a realistic adjustment because either can be contradicted at any time (through a sighting of the person who is 'gone', or the absence of the person who is 'still there'). The existence of the estranged person, as well as the estranged status, cannot be denied forever. In these situations, the initial aim is not to 'fix' the estrangement, but to encourage resilience in the face of adversity. Resilience is the capacity and flexibility to withstand crisis and stress, followed by a return to normal or greater functioning. Resilience is highly dependent on the individual's capacity to either 'sit – or learn to sit – with ambiguity'. Estranged people often refer to this as 'learning to live with estrangement'.

Learning to live with estrangement – and particularly the ambiguous nature of this relational state – requires the recognition and voicing of conflicting thoughts (such as he'll never return/maybe he will) and conflicting feelings (such as hatred/indifference). In terms of emotional estrangement, the person often needs to fully recognise and voice their resistance to leaving the relationship and their simultaneous desire to end it. Additionally, Boss (1999) says, 'ambiguous loss needs to be validated and labelled as being responsible for the ambivalent feelings ... that under such circumstances mixed feelings are normal' (p. 76). When estranged people realise that their responses to a difficult relational condition are normal, they are more likely to accept change, make decisions and adapt to a different way of being in the family.

Role adjustment is particularly difficult when family members are estranged: 'If I no longer have a child, am I still a father'? Boss (1999) suggests that 'a family is always better off making an educated guess about the status of their loss rather than continuing indefinitely in limbo' (p. 94). This does not mean that one closes the door on other possibilities, just that they continue their life with a greater degree of certainty, direction and eventually less pain. So, an estrangee – making an educated guess that their adult child intends to be permanently estranged – would stop expecting their child to contact on key dates. This 'educated guess' would effectively reduce their previously vigilant activities such as staying home or monitoring the mobile phone, as well as the disappointment associated with a lack of contact. However, it should also be noted that taking such action involves a considerable element of risk and courage early in an estrangement and may require practising the new behaviours with external encouragement and support. Living with estrangement requires new compromises around old expectations.

Research with estranged people suggests that over time many start to *accept* the reality and permanence of estrangement, and some realise that their repeated actions are not changing the relational status (Agllias, 2011, 2014). 'Accepting estrangement' is quite different to 'getting over estrangement', and it generally accompanies conscious decisions and commitments to live again, move on with life, think about estrangement differently, behave differently and focus on self more than the estrangement, as time progresses. These internal shifts often result in increased mobilisation and energy, and more decisive action towards normality and happiness. Indeed, research shows that an important component in recovery from trauma is re-establishing daily routines (Burton *et al.*, 2015). Future actions might include packing up some of the estranged person's belongings, speaking to others about the estrangement, changing conditions of the final will and testament, taking up new sporting and social activities, and creating relational boundaries in the case of an emotional estrangement. These are important steps because they increase mastery and a sense of control that has often been eroded by ambiguity.

Language can also be helpful in living with ambiguous loss. While there are terms for absence and presence, estrangement is somewhere in between, and people often find it difficult to explain it to others. This is especially so if someone is emotionally estranged (where psychological absence and physical presence cannot be explained as easily as physical absence or conflict). Euphemisms for estrangement, such as 'we don't speak', 'he's never around', and 'we don't get along', often mask the extent of the issue, reinforcing denial or confusion about the relational status, and even contributing to a person's sense of powerlessness. Acceptance of the estrangement loss – or confirmation of its reality – is often achieved through the telling of the estrangement story. When something is named, it is brought into 'being'; and it is more likely to be 'heard' and 'recognised' by others. Many people who use the terms *estranged* or *emotionally estranged* in social situations find this an empowering and validating act.

It is generally understood that healing increases when families start to transform or make meaning of a loss that has occurred (Burton *et al.*, 2015; Neimeyer, 2006). When people are able to shift from cause-and-effect thinking, as well as blame, they are more likely to sit comfortably with ambiguity; 'Viewing the world logically, as a fair and just place, can stand in the way of tolerating ambiguous loss' (Boss, 1999, p. 127). It infers that bad things only happen to bad people, creating self-doubt and self-blame, or a projection of blame onto others. When people are able to look at the estrangement event more objectively and engage in examining the external and historical events that have influenced the relational context, they are more likely to find meaning and comfort (discussed further in this chapter). Faith may be a significant source of meaning making for those with a strong religious or spiritual commitment.

Through creativity, flexibility and positive change activities, people can envisage acceptable outcomes, create new rituals and gain hope from the loss. For example, there are a number of estranged people who use their experience to help others through estrangement groups and campaigning to increase understanding about estrangement. Research found that people started to make meaning when they critically examined their intergenerational narrative (Agllias, 2011; 2014). They often found hope and encouragement in their new independence (including role changes and identity shifts), the creation of new family traditions, and their felt capacity to reduce estrangement in future generations. It is important to note that 'sitting with ambiguity' might be easier for people who exhibit or are encouraged to develop healthy and hopeful optimism (Boss, 1999). In terms of estrangement, hopeful optimism relates to a belief that one is entitled to, and will experience, a positive future regardless of the relationship status or likelihood of reconciliation.

Finally, research shows interesting connections between acceptance, hope, gratitude, resilience, well-being and forgiveness (as discussed in the next chapter), where 'increased meaning in life predicted greater forgiveness that predicted greater subjective well-being. More meaning in life, also, predicted increased hope, which then positively influenced subjective well-being' (Yalcin & Malkoc, 2015, p. 923). Similarly, Gupta and Kumar's (2015) research with undergraduates found that acceptance, forgiveness, and gratitude were interrelated predictors of resilience. The processes that encourage and connect acceptance, meaning making, gratitude, hopeful optimism and forgiveness vary between individuals, but the following sections discuss some ways that estranged people can optimise these conditions as they 'learn to live with' relationship dissolution.

A note on minimising triggers

There are lots of triggers. For example, there's a show on BBC television, it's called 'Find My Family'. . . . I find that Christmas [with] my immediate family [only], it proves a little hollow at times.

(Mark)

145

Research shows that grief responses are often reactivated by estrangement-related triggers across the lifespan (Agllias, 2011, 2014). While triggers will never be eradicated entirely, some people find that anticipating and minimising triggers can be a useful way to work through their grief (while being cognisant that one is not *avoiding* grief). Most people will remove or reduce photos and memorabilia that create too much distress. Moving house can be a significant way to create the sense of a new beginning and decrease the temptation to constantly 'look out for' an estranged relative. However, for most people, significant dates and events are the most difficult triggers of all. Planning for birthdays, Mother's Day, Father's Day and Christmas can be very important. When people prepare to do something positive and different – and maybe even incorporate a ritual or small gesture to acknowledge the loss of the family member – they are less likely to experience the depth of pain they might otherwise feel if sitting at home alone, or trying to recreate a ritual where the absence is highlighted. Even thinking differently about memorabilia, possible sightings and events can minimise responses to these triggers.

Time and perspective

> *Way back, and this is where I started to release and separate ... I could start seeing this as a story about somebody else. ... I stopped it being about me.*
>
> (Angela)

Davis (2002) says, 'time usually has to pass before people are able – or willing – to reconsider a relationship that was so painful it had to end' (p. 16). Recent research found that some people became so entrenched in the 'estrangement story', and revisiting the event, the betrayal and the hurt, that they were challenged to move away from this narrative (Agllias, 2008, 2011, 2014). Without clarity or new information, the estrangement story became fixed. Physically estranged people often *imagined* the beliefs, actions and responses of the estranged family member in various fictional scenarios and these interpretations were generally imbued with the pain and hurt of the final encounters (e.g. 'I know that if I bumped into my sister she would bite my head off and make a big scene'). Emotionally estranged people often *imagined* the motives behind the other person's responses when they interacted. When people are hurt, they often focus on any information that confirms their longstanding beliefs about the other person, including their negative behaviours and traits (Dattilo & Nichols, 2011). In some cases, the estrangement becomes a significant component of a victimised identity, where the ingrained view of the other person becomes entirely negative. In these cases, estranged people tend to view time – or the length of the estrangement – as an indicator of the magnitude of the loss.

Interestingly, research showed that those people who reported greater resolution had used time to reconsider and re-story the estrangement event and the relationship status (Agllias, 2008, 2011, 2014). People who appeared less hurt and obligated to the estrangement story seemed more able to: (i) depersonalise the estrangement event, (ii) see patterns in intergenerational relations and the other person's behaviour; (iii) recognise some positive qualities of the other person; and (iv) view the estrangement in context. In these cases, even people who initially claimed that they were completely unaware of the reason for the estrangement started to make *educated guesses* about its origins. This suggests that *time away* from the other person *can* provide an extremely important opportunity to reduce tension and gain perspective about the estrangement (even if this time is due to a physical or emotional distancing). This section examines some constructive ways to examine the estrangement from a less intense and more objective position.

Understanding the intergenerational family

Then two years ago we found another sister who was born after my father died.
... [My mother] doesn't actually know we've found this baby girl.

(Margaret)

Transgenerational theory, which emphasises the communication and acquisition of beliefs, practices and behaviours across generations, suggests that: 'changing a kinship's perceived history should be as powerful a change as directly changing behaviour' (Lieberman, 1998, p. 203). Families regularly have secrets, patterns and myths that are obscured or maintained by ruptured intergenerational relationships. The genogram – as discussed earlier in this book – is a way for people to start exploring these patterns 'on paper'. However, estrangement can offer an opportunity and a new desire or courage to ask questions, to research the family tree, to rethink inherited estrangements and to make contact with relatives who have core information (possibly including distant and estranged intergenerational members). These encounters can bring clarity to the unknown in many instances, and provide insight into the development and maintenance of intergenerational estrangement.

For example, Tina had always carried a memory about a strange family event she attended as a child; primarily she remembered feeling extremely uncomfortable. After estranging from her mother in adulthood, she reconnected with an estranged uncle (an estrangement she inherited from her mother). Her uncle was able to explain that *the strange family event* had happened at his house, and that her mother had not been invited to the particular event and simply turned up to dinner with her children, unannounced. After a few more interactions and connections with her uncle and other – previously estranged – family members, Tina viewed her childhood and patterns in her mother's behaviour with more clarity (and perceived her mother's rejection of her as an adolescent less personally). Additionally, she was able to re-establish some long-term supportive family connections.

Establishing a connection with the intergenerational family may not be a simple task. The estranged person needs to be cognisant of the often disparate, and sometimes polar-opposite views, that two family members might have about the same event or issue. Given the patience to wade through these stories, almost from the position of *detached observer*, clarity will slowly emerge (certainly about the subjective nature of intergenerational relationships if not about the family narrative). Reconnecting to family also encourages the resurrection or re-creation of family traditions and rituals when estrangement has halted, disrupted or soured these. Sometimes even the psychological reconnection to family can create a significant sense of 'belonging', which is essential to growth and healing.

Developing empathy and appreciation for the estranged family member(s)

> *They're fairly loyal sort of kids. I say I always like to think I'm quite loyal. They're being loyal to their mother. They think they're doing the right thing by mum.*
>
> (Gary)

The acute pain of estrangement often results in a stereotyping of the other person's characteristics and behaviours, a focus on the negative and a filtering out of contradictory information. This can be particularly problematic if the negative classification of a certain characteristic trait is one shared by both parties. However, distance and time may diffuse estrangement-related anger enough for the parties to think about each other from a more balanced perspective. Curiosity about the other person can stimulate the gathering of new knowledge and perspectives, and may lead to greater empathy towards them. Empathy is the capacity to put oneself in the position of the other, to understand actions and behaviours from their perspective. It is not about feeling sorry for the other person, accepting or excusing bad behaviours. However, it can increase clarity about long-term estrangement losses, highlight legacies from the relationship (whether these are positive elements or risk factors that should be considered), and lead to more informed decisions about the possibility of relational change and reconciliation. Information can be gathered from archives, from people who know or knew the estranged person, and from a personal revision of historical memory. Emotionally estranged people can also be more conscientious observers of the estranged person and their interactions.

Estranged people often protect their estrangement story, so they are rarely asked to critique their understanding of the other person. Therefore, to engage with this process it is important for them to converse with trusting friends and family – or practitioners – who are willing to gently question strongly held views of the other, point out inconsistencies, and offer contradictory evidence if they have it (in a safe and supportive way). For example, during a research interview, Dale's story of his father was initially one about deliberate neglect and abandonment. When asked to describe his father and the estrangement from his father's perspective, Dale said

> *I think society has bullied him when he was young. That drove him to be business orientated and so he lied to mum I guess. He was going to be the knight in shining armour and he wasn't. He was a knight in shining armour for himself.*

Within one curious conversation, Dale was able to voice how his father's selfish abandonment was tied to his own pain, insecurity, aspirations for his marital relationship and the need for success. He was able to voice the ambiguity in the narrative where his father's good intentions coincided with poor outcomes for the family. Given time and further reflection, Dale might have thought about the positive legacy of his father's drive for success in his own career choices and accomplishments.

Developing empathy and appreciation for an estranged family member can be an important component of living with ambiguity through the continuation of important psychological bonds (especially for estrangees). Grief theorists suggest that the maintenance of 'continuing bonds' – rather than the traditionally held view that one must sever ties in order to establish new attachments – can be a healthy component of grieving an absent person (see Klass *et al.*, 1996 for a full discussion of this concept).

Research with parents who had been estranged by their adult children suggested that they remained proud of aspects of their child including things like appearance, achievements, values (Agllias, 2011). Reminders of these aspects of their child, and particularly their capacity to incorporate these into their family story, assisted meaning making and narrative coherence. For example, Gary (quoted at the beginning of this section) was able to make sense of his children's continued (absent) estrangement as loyalty to their mother. While dissatisfied with the estrangement, he was also able to find meaning in his children's actions and that their shared commitment to loyalty maintained some sort of familial bond between them.

A critical perspective: Understanding the political in the personal

You know [estrangement has] happened always and you know you go back through families and histories there's always been somebody that was cast aside or felt unwanted and dragged themselves aside and wanted to be doing something different.

(Elizabeth)

The deconstruction of personal perceptions and the interrogation of biases are essential to understanding estrangement further. Examining estrangement from a critical perspective can help people to distance from guilt and blame, through a more objective and contextual understanding of relationships. In this section, the term critical perspective is used in its theoretical sense (although critical appraisal and analytical evaluation are also core to this process). A critical perspective is a position that knowledge is socially constructed, that there are multiple realities, and 'that people construct and are constructed by changing structures and relations' (Fook, 2003, p. 18):

> [Critical theory] examines social norms and conditions in order to identify and expose power, control, and oppression in various contexts. . . . One of the cornerstones of critical theory is that knowledge is power. It is assumed that when oppressive forces are identified and understood, the potential exists to enact change which will allow freedom from these forces . . . if we are aware of the factors that influence our perceptions of an experience, we have the opportunity to consciously act and respond with intentionality and purpose.
>
> (Harris, 2009–2010, p. 243)

For example, dominant ideologies about parenting – and particularly motherhood – not only influence the development of estrangement but the way that it is experienced (see 'Case example: Lorna').

An examination of 'family' from a critical perspective – the way it is socially defined, portrayed and critiqued – is also a sound mechanism to address some losses associated with role ambiguity. Role ambiguity can be reduced when people understand and challenge rigid preconceptions of family roles and identities. For example, when a parent rigidly adheres to the idea that their adult child should be the provider of care in old age, they might resist seeking alternative assistance if the child estranges. This can result in additional losses and an unnecessarily exaggerated grief experience in some cases. When these ideas are challenged and resisted, substitute carers might

149

be viewed as more acceptable, and the estrangement-related losses are likely to be reduced.

An examination of the socio-economic and historical context of grieving can also be very important to understand and validate the disenfranchised loss and grief experiences of estranged people. Remennick (2000) suggests that the ability to resist stigmatisation is largely determined by one's capacity to assume a critical stance about

---

Case example: Lorna

Lorna left her job as a seamstress and married at the age of 18. She had two sons during the 1950s. The marriage was an unhappy one, and her husband regularly used emotional and physical violence to keep her isolated in the home, and to reinforce his claims of intellectual superiority. Over time, Lorna's ideas about her own worthiness declined and she left most parenting decisions to her husband. She rarely considered leaving the marriage, and increasingly used distancing practices to keep herself and her sons safe from accusations and violence (e.g., reducing outward affection towards her sons and eating separately from the family). Lorna's two sons physically estranged from her in their late teens after accusing her of weakness, coldness and negligent parenting. Lorna experienced the estrangement as a significant source of shame and self-hatred. She often ruminated: 'If I am no longer a mother, I am nothing'.

If we examine *Lorna's* story of estrangement, from a gendered perspective, it seems to emphasise dominant 1950s ideologies of motherhood as inevitable and all-encompassing, paternal authority, and divorce as unthinkable and economically unviable. We see how these socially derived ideas and conditions are core to Lorna's experience of marriage, parenting and her later experience of estrangement. By examining these issues from a critical theory perspective, Lorna may be encouraged to: (i) establish further curiosity about self, family relationships and dynamics, (ii) take reasonable responsibility for the parenting she provided, and the neglect she allowed, (iii) encourage a more empathic understanding of her son's experiences, iv) externalise and depersonalise her sons' reactions and poor behaviours (i.e. her sons' decisions were more likely to arise from a number of stressors – including inadequate parenting, poor attachment and exposure to violence – than a hatred of their mother), and (v) encouraging self-compassion for injustices experienced and inflicted on others.

Drawing Lorna's sons' attention to the structural and ideological issues that potentially maintained family violence and interfered with Lorna's parenting capacity has the potential to: (i) establish further curiosity about self, family relationships and dynamics, (ii) encourage a more empathic understanding of Lorna and her parenting position, (iii) externalise and depersonalise Lorna's parenting decisions (i.e. Lorna's parenting decisions were more likely to arise from a number of stressors rather than a dislike of her children), (iv) encourage self-compassion for injustices experienced and inflicted on others, and (v) take reasonable responsibility for the destructive ways they expressed their hurt as adults.

---

dominant ideologies and disconnect from the mainstream discourse. Finally, a critical stance on the concept of estrangement is warranted. The notion that all family members will be compatible, trustworthy, of sound mental health and free of addiction, that they will never have conflicting interests and will always care for each other unconditionally, must be examined against the cultural frames that perpetuate such unrealistic expectations. The ideas that 'blood is thicker than water', and 'the home is where the heart is', place undue pressure on families to stay together regardless of the hurts and betrayals they must endure. Distancing and estrangement might be examined in terms of the functions they serve in the intergenerational family, and the benefits they might offer in terms of individual growth.

Self-understanding

I realised that perhaps [estrangement] brings up things in ourselves that we need to work on and it's not always about the person you're estranged from.

(Donna)

The tensions, hurts, disagreements, inner conflicts and myriad losses that surround estrangement – whether overt or unrecognised – can exhaust one's capacity for self-understanding, self-care and personal development. Conflict, abuse and rejection can erode self-concept, self-esteem and more importantly, self-acceptance. It is no wonder that many people suggest that estrangement provides the space to consider their own needs and priorities as well as time to heal and grow. When estrangement is viewed and chosen as the only route to personal growth and healing, the new status can be experienced as a tumultuous mix of grief and relief, where freedom and peace are highly sought and increasingly valued. When estrangement is not chosen, estrangement-related shock and loss can also provide the impetus for self-reflection and a desire to increase health and well-being. This time can also serve as space to review one's actions leading up to the estrangement. Some estranged people suggest that the honest examination of personal responses to certain estrangement-related events, including underlying beliefs, experiences and sensitivities, is important to living with estrangement (Agllias, 2011, 2014). Personal insight can provide important protection against excessive guilt, shame and self-pity, and guide interactions in future relationships.

Know thyself

It really is a pain that I get, or I had. It's certainly resolved through all of the practices that I do today. Meditation, yoga, don't touch alcohol, keep a really good diet. . . . (I also) decided to do a . . . degree.

(Angela)

Our life is storied before we are born and it builds and grows through the merger of an outside story (i.e. external conditions, events and facts) with an inside story (the subjective meaning we attribute to those conditions, events and facts) (Kenyon & Randall, 1997). An important component of learning to live with estrangement is understanding *self*, as an individual, in relational contexts, as a part of an intergenerational family, and as a part of the estrangement narrative. This involves deliberately taking the time to increase awareness about one's personal traits, behaviours, priorities, values and expectations of the self and others. Self-understanding can be increased through personal observation, examining self-talk, self-review, journaling and requesting honest feedback from others. When people acknowledge their areas of strength and those areas that require attention, they are more likely to honour their responses to grief, increase understanding about the development and progression of the estrangement and gain insight into the likelihood of reconciliation.

Sometimes estrangement can alter the view of self and dampen self-awareness. Estranged relationships often become the focus and lens through which individuals view themselves, which can lead to an outright rejection of the traits that are being portrayed or an internalisation of distorted elements. Research showed that, even after estrangement, some estranged people *heard* the disapproval of the estranged relative at particular times (Agllias, 2014). Interestingly, research also showed that most estranged people mentioned a positive and influential relationship with at least one living or deceased relative, often a special aunt, uncle or grandparent (Agllias, 2011, 2014). These more positive relationships – which many people claimed to be fundamental to their current value and belief system – may be core to recreating a new vision of self. By using this often overlooked or underestimated lens, estranged people can start to create an alternative and more accurate vision of the self.

While understanding self can be a dedicated and deliberate process, many people find that estrangement also creates freedom, space and motivation to engage in new activities. Physical and spiritual activities that provide temporary relief from grieving can also be a considerable source of self-understanding and reconnection to forgotten or underdeveloped areas of strength and passion. Some people report that counselling or self-help books, groups and education can be particularly helpful in understanding self as distinct from, but still connected to, the intergenerational family (Agllias, 2011, 2014). These activities can also be very useful in learning to regulate, or let go of, unwanted estrangement-related emotions (such as anger and bitterness).

Self-understanding also requires an examination of previous and existing roles within the nuclear and intergenerational family. A realistic evaluation of one's strengths and weaknesses is important to working through guilt and examining current and anticipated areas of loss. Clarity can also be very important in articulating the boundaries that have been violated leading up to, and in the act of, estrangement, and fortify expectations for both parties if reconciliation is to be considered in the future (see 'Case example: Lesley Part 1').

Examining one's contribution to the estrangement

I had a business and I had to be responsible for that business so I had to forfeit some things. You accept that. Even though you regret it, you accept it.

(John)

Sometimes people deny or minimise their part in the estrangement to avoid guilt, shame and exposure. It is much easier to project blame onto the other person, or a third party, than it is to examine one's own behaviours and reactions. However, an explicit acknowledgement of the errors made can be an important element of compassion and forgiveness of the self and others (as well as a potential route to

---

Case example: Lesley Part 1

Lesley's gregarious intelligence seemed to result in her instatement as *adult problem-solver* in her nuclear family. While this served as a significant source of pride and self-confidence as she grew up, it left her vulnerable to reduced support and high expectations from family members, as well as blame when things went wrong. Through an investigation of her personal strengths and challenges, as well as her family roles, Lesley was able to consider how her sense of ambition and over-responsibility had developed and coincided with her feelings of resentment, jealousy and anger towards her brother (who she later estranged in adulthood). She was able to feel compassion and forgiveness for herself and the adolescent *mistakes* she had internalised.

---

reconciliation if this is desired). It is most effective when compassionately focused, where personal suffering and errors of judgement are regarded with kindness and recognised as core components of the human condition. Higher levels of self-compassion have been associated with psychological health, including elements such as increased life satisfaction, happiness and optimism as well as less depression, anxiety and rumination (Neff & Vonk, 2009).

A potentially problematic position of many estranged people seems to revolve around intentionality, where they believe that a sound intention alleviates them of responsibility for the other person's feelings or reactions. However, it is important to realistically evaluate the ways that personal beliefs, actions and events may have been experienced and interpreted by others, despite intention (see 'Case example: Lesley Part 2'). Equally important when conducting an honest evaluation of one's contribution to the estrangement is the acknowledgement of positive actions and behaviours, despite difficult interactions or situations. Acknowledging the things that were done well can create a more balanced space for self-examination and increase self-compassion. Additionally, there are instances where a person is blameless for the development of an estrangement, and this is particularly important to acknowledge when there is a significant power inequity or abuse of power, such as child abuse, and when an absent or inherited estrangement exists. In these instances, a realistic evaluation of one's capacity to change elements of the estrangement can be most important in relieving unwarranted guilt and shame.

Case example: Lesley Part 2

When Lesley examined her situation – and particularly evaluated the behaviours that developed from parentification – she was able to see how her sense of responsibility and control might have been experienced as interference, superiority and favouritism by her brother (and his partner in later years). He was extremely hurt, despite her sound protective intentions.

Finally, estranged people need to think about their existing behaviours. For example, estrangees are often advised by loved ones, counsellors and support groups, to continue some form of contact with the estranger, and in some cases this might be an appropriate way to keep the door open for reconciliation (see Chapter 8). However, this needs to be considered in terms of the intensity, frequency and impact of these contacts and actions. Estrangees need to remain cognisant of their actions – even those arising from love, care and ideologies perpetuating *a right* to familial contact – and how these might breach the rights of the estranger. It is also important to consider that these actions are likely to be interpreted by the estranger as continued boundary violations and ongoing disrespect. In these instances the estranged person needs to be clear about whether they are putting their needs and wants above the express wishes of the estranger.

Reconnection

I think the big shift over the last year is really appreciating the people who are there as opposed to constantly longing for the people who aren't there. . . . Interestingly, odd people come forward with beautiful love and support. . . . [It's not] downplaying other people's gestures of generosity and hospitality and support, because they are not the people that I think they should be.

(Debbie)

It is increasingly understood that recovery from any traumatic event requires a reconnection to others (Burton *et al.*, 2015; Herman, 1997). Grieving is greatly assisted by the sensitive emotional support and the timely physical support of others. The recreation or re-storying of individual identity involves an understanding of self within the relational context. Reconnection is usually a slow process as people tentatively and bravely risk exposing themselves and their estrangement story to others. Estrangement often erodes the capacity to trust others, and the natural propensity is to minimise further interactions where hurt, embarrassment and shame might occur. However, simple acts of human kindness, acceptance and appreciation often arise naturally during shared activities, so it is important to invest in activities that potentially increase faith in the reliability of others. New associations also offer the estranged person opportunities to try out their new identity, to enact new commitments and to develop supportive networks for the future. While people often experience the dissolution of a family relationship as a highly stigmatised event or condition, they need to gradually establish socially validated accounts of the estrangement in order to live more peacefully. Therefore, it is also important to establish some trusting networks that acknowledge, accept and increasingly understand the consequences of estrangement. Acts of reconnection include reviving previous relationships, developing new ones, joining groups and becoming a part of community activities.

Recognise and improve current relationships

I feel stronger than ever at this point in time because I realise I can love my family without being nasty and without attacking them. . . . I also accept that they're in a different emotional place to me and that I'm a bit more enlightened. . . . I don't feel emotionally tugged to be angry back.

(Donna)

Existing relationships often take a back seat to the estrangement process, and in some cases partners, children, friends and work colleagues may bear the brunt of estrangement-related unhappiness, trauma and grief. When people feel betrayed and rejected, they often find it difficult to recognise *quieter relationships* where trust and warmth still exist. Additionally, research with older estrangees found that they often felt guilty enjoying time with their non-estranged children and grandchildren, and particularly if they were unable to spend time with other grandchildren due to inherited estrangements (Agllias, 2011). Therefore an important component of reconnection is a focused examination of the state of existing relationships. It also involves the recognition of supportive relationships that may have been taken for granted in the chaos, or gestures not appreciated or graciously accepted simply because they were not considered the correct source of support (see Debbie's comment on previous page). It includes a decided effort to enjoy and celebrate existing relationships (despite anger, guilt, hurt or longing for the other). Most estranged people have at least one memorable and supportive relationship with a relative in their past that they can continue, resurrect or draw strength from (even if the person is no longer alive).

Current relationships are important places to invest in new ideas, behaviours and commitments that have arisen through the process of learning to live with estrangement. Efforts to understand family patterns can create a new awareness and commitment to improve difficult or strained relationships. Research also showed that many adults who were estranged from their own parents found that making commitments to different relational patterns with their own children was an important and rewarding step in living with estrangement (Agllias, 2014). The co-creation of new family rituals can be a very important component of reconnection, where the existing family extends compassion and warmth to each other as well as establishing a new sense of unity and strength. Rita spoke of the pain associated with her first Christmas after being estranged by her mother and sisters. For her the process of creating something new with her own children and grandchildren became quite a positive event: '*I love that concept of well what's our new normal? What's our new traditions, what's our new relationships? How do we navigate this life without these people?*'

Some people find that the creation of a new family – often called a family of choice or alternative family – can be an important way to fill emotional and practical voids left from estrangement. New families are often made up of in-laws, like-minded or estranged friends, or they might consist of church friends or the residents and staff at a residential facility. 'Families of choice' have been shown to be very important for potentially stigmatised individuals and groups (Austin *et al.*, 2014), because they are consciously created by people who are not obligated to tolerate and accept each other, but voluntarily wish to do so. Additionally, the inclusion of new or chosen members to fill specific roles can be very rewarding. For example, substitute grandparents are very important in some nuclear families.

Reconnecting with family and friends

You don't tell people that you were called a filthy slut or that you were ugly. ... Anyway, so last Thursday I actually shared with [my childhood friends] a few things – they don't know everything.

(Rita)

Reconnecting with family and friends can be an important route to living with estrangement. As discussed in the earlier section about understanding the inter-generational family, reconnecting to distant relationships and broaching inherited estrangements may be a sound place to commence a new and different relationship with the intergenerational family. Additionally, friendships that have been neglected or simply lost in distance or busyness can be sound sources of reconnection. Estranged people often suggest that the Internet can be a prime, and less-threatening avenue for slowly rebuilding previous relationships. While this process can be very empowering, it is important that it happens incrementally, that trust is developed and earned. While this never fully ensures that the disclosure of estrangement-related experiences are received without judgement, it is a sound way to increase those chances. Despite the risks of disclosure, many people find it extremely important in feeling true to self, engaging authentically in new relationships, and maintaining them (Agllias, 2011, 2014). The disclosure process is likely to become easier as people have more clarity about the estrangement, have the words to explain their situation and feel more competent to create boundaries around their disclosure.

Rejoining community

> I did a lot of voluntary work when I moved into [town]. . . . I joined Bocce in there and I walked every morning. . . . Just to meet people, I would go and have a coffee in the mornings, instead of at home, I'd get out and go and have a coffee. You meet people when you walk.

> (Virginia)

Community involvement – whether online or in person – provides a sense of belonging to something bigger than the individual and the family. People who join together because they have something in common, who communicate and share ideas, often become connected at a more empathic and compassionate level over time. Estranged people can find considerable meaning in community connections and membership, whether this is through their own altruistic involvement or the new supports they develop. When people are more open to others they are more likely to be entrusted with other people's stories of family estrangement. Several estrangees in one study suggested that they often struck up conversations with people on the bus, while walking or in a social group, where the other person disclosed their estrangement status, which could be quite affirming (Agllias, 2011). These opportunities offer the possibility of change, where the humanising of the estrangement condition can help both parties to think about this issue less judgementally. Most importantly, community often allows people to see themselves through the positive eyes of others.

Estrangement groups

There appear to be very few therapeutic estrangement groups that are run by practitioners; however, there seem to be some grass-roots groups that have been developed by people experiencing the phenomenon themselves. There are a number of online estrangement support groups in existence. All of these options can be very useful for people who would like a forum to talk about their estrangement experience with like-minded people. Group affiliation can offer very important and alternative views about the estrangement experience, increase self-acceptance and reduce feelings of isolation and stigmatisation. However, groups should be approached with a healthy scepticism. Some people have reported becoming involved with such a group, only to be estranged by members or rejected from it because they offered a different perspective. Warning signs that these forums may be potentially unhealthy include groups that: take narrow, all-encompassing and causal views of estrangement; take a victim and perpetrator stance; have specific criteria – such as a specific relational dynamic – for entry to the group; and show intolerance towards members who do not agree with, or espouse, the party line. It is important that estranged people investigate groups thoroughly to avoid potentially negative experiences. Professionally run and auspiced therapeutic groups are more likely to espouse a balanced view of estrangement, and these might be preferable dependent on the fit between the group aims and the person's requirement at that time.

Recognising Progress

When friends talked about their family it reminded me that I didn't have a sister, but over time my thinking changed to focus on the family we've created.

(Kent)

Working through estrangement is a gradual and personally nuanced journey where determinants of progress will always be subjective. Most people say that they will never 'get over estrangement', 'forget estrangement', 'forget the other person', or be immune to ongoing estrangement triggers. Some suggest they are never fully 'healed' due to the emotional scars that remain. However, there are some common themes in the narratives of estranged people, who say that they have 'come to terms with estrangement' and made significant progress towards learning to 'live with estrangement', as discussed below.

Progress usually invokes, and is represented by, a greater sense of self as a unique and independent person. This is often accompanied by a sense of pride for estrangement-related progress, increased self-acceptance and less guilt. Many people say that they have discovered – or recognised – new and positive things about themselves. The capacity to see oneself through the positive eyes of others, rather than the estranged person's eyes only, can be regarded as a sign of progress and healing. The capacity to actively challenge negative thought patterns and increasingly regulate estrangement-related feelings and emotions marks progress. People report feeling more emotionally stable as they come to terms with estrangement, and some suggest that they are more cognisant of their estrangement-related feelings and from where they originate.

When people learn to live with estrangement, they often report greater insight into the development of the estrangement, including a more objective understanding of the estrangement from both sides. They are more likely to take reasonable and self-compassionate ownership of their contribution to the estrangement, and feel a degree of compassion or empathy for the other party. They may be able to celebrate, or at least acknowledge, the positive elements of the estranged person that remain and grieve for those that have been lost. Some people are able to forgive the estranged person, while others perform regular symbolic gestures of love, such as lighting a candle for the estranged person. Progress often involves an increased openness about the

157

estrangement, including the capacity to write about it and talk about it with others. This includes greater faith that others will hear their estrangement story without judgement or a belief in one's strength to sit with, or challenge, the misconceptions of others. Estrangement-related humour and irony can be a positive sign for some.

Progress also involves the valuing of existing relationships and the desire to build new ones. This includes the development of a new family story where the estrangement – and the estranged family member(s) – are not forgotten, but feature less. New people are included in the family narrative and there is usually more flexibility in terms of family roles, traditions and expectations. When people feel they are healing from the acute pain of estrangement, they are more likely to focus on 'living' than 'estrangement', and this includes the enjoyment and celebration of activities without thinking about the other person, or feeling guilty about their absence. Some people suggest that they have recognised progress in terms of their overall resilience and capacity to live with the uncertainty of estrangement and other ambiguous conditions. For some, this includes being more comfortable with the possibility of reconciliation, while for others it involves greater sense of peace and life satisfaction. Some people become more thankful for the things they do have, and feel consoled by positive aspects of the estranged person's existence. Sometimes progress is reported as feeling nothing or significantly less about, and for, the estranged person.

Finally, it is worth considering that some estranged people experience what professionals might refer to as *posttraumatic growth*. This concept, originated by Calhoun and Tedeschi (2006), formalises the long-held belief that positive change can develop from considerable adversity. Calhoun and Tedeschi's (2006) work suggests that posttraumatic growth can be signalled by: (i) a changed perception of the self as vulnerable but stronger and with more possibilities for the future; (ii) an increased sense of connectedness with, and compassion for, others (and maybe even a desire and capacity to disclose possibly stigmatised details of their traumatic experience to others); and (iii) a greater appreciation of life, which may include a greater sense of meaning and purpose in life (or spirituality). Interestingly, all of these elements were represented in the estrangement research that supported this chapter (Agllias, 2011, 2014).

Professional intervention

In my experience there is often guilt and shame associated with family estrangement. As a result, clients who are estranged may have a history of being secretive about events/details surrounding the estrangement. Sometimes, the estrangement has not been acknowledged publicly for many years. So it can be challenging.

(Pihu, Social Worker)

While this chapter provides principles and processes that can be utilised in the therapeutic context, it is important to initially consider that estrangement-related grief *does not necessarily require intervention*. Indeed, reviews of the effectiveness of grief therapy continue to find that universal or routine interventions for grieving clients are minimally effective and that a targeted focus on clients experiencing complicated grief produces more effective outcomes (Neimeyer & Currier, 2008; Schut & Stroebe, 2005). Indeed, Schut and Stroebe (2005) suggest that intervention that occurs soon after bereavement 'may interfere with "natural" grieving processes' (p. 140), a sentiment this author would agree with in relation to estrangement. It is suggested that practitioners should be alerted and vigilant when a client describes an estrangement-related loss that they have struggled with for months or years and when their grief reactions include: 'intense and persistent yearning' for the estranged person, 'intrusive and troubling thoughts' about the estrangement, 'emptiness and hopelessness about the future', inability to accept the loss, and problems returning to normal activities (Neimeyer & Currier, 2009, p. 352). These may be indicators that intervention *could be* beneficial.

Interestingly, research with estranged adults suggested that intervention could be perceived as useful or not, primarily depending on the recency of the estrangement crisis and the estranged person's expectations of the interaction (Agllias, 2011, 2014). When estranged individuals went to counselling shortly after the estrangement crisis, and particularly if this was to 'get advice' about estrangement, 'fix' the estrangement, to 'fix' the other party, or to swiftly reconcile with an estranger, they reported finding the experience less than satisfactory. In these cases, most suggested the worker was kind but unhelpful. It appears that when estranged people seek help during a crisis moment or when pain is acute, they usually want immediate relief. Therefore, acknowledging and attending to issues of loss and grief are imperative to developing a trusting therapeutic alliance during that encounter. However, clients would also benefit from practitioners who normalise the estrangement experience, proactively seek and clarify the client's purpose early in the session, clarify the limits and boundaries of intervention, explain the notion of ambiguous loss, and realistically explain the possible benefits that may accrue from a future exploration of the estrangement and its effects (if this is something the client wishes to pursue sometime down the track).

Research also showed that people who attended some time after the estrangement crisis, in order to 'work through' some of their lingering emotional responses to the estrangement, tended to have a much more positive experience (Agllias, 2011, 2014). They suggested that the ïmost effective practitioners normalised the estrangement experience, as well as acknowledging the enormity of the loss in the context of its marginalised or stigmatised status, and acknowledged their existing strengths, resources and progress. Some required assistance with emotion regulation and constructive feedback on their behaviours in the face of challenging estrangement-related encounters.

Additionally, many estranged clients present for different – but often interconnected – issues such as anxiety/depression, self-esteem, marital dissatisfaction, medical complications and childhood abuse or trauma. Research with estranged people found that most practitioners did not specifically enquire about family estrangement, but when this issue was raised and attended to during the intervention, the client experienced this as validating and empowering (Agllias, 2011, 2014). Social workers in palliative settings often suggested that clients were initially protective of their estrangement status or embarrassed upon revealing it:

> Sometimes I work with clients for quite a while before they mention the estranged relative. Patients often feel relieved . . . giving voice to a secret that [they] feel will be judged as unnatural by others.
>
> (Peta, Social Worker, in Agllias, 2013a)

Given shame, stigma, and the capacity to conceal estrangement, there appears to be a need for practitioners to *specifically* include questions about estrangement in their routine assessments and when creating genograms. They need to ask about:

TABLE 7.1 Sample assessment questions about family estrangement

Domain	Example questions and dialogue
Normalising Assessments usually include questions about family members and should, as far as possible, attempt to normalise estrangement where it exists.	I need to take some details about the people in your family. It is quite normal for some families to have family members with whom they find it difficult to interact, or whom they no longer see, but it is useful to include these people in the assessment. Are there people in your family to whom this applies?
Enquiring about estrangement Don't presume clients will necessarily talk about this merely because you have acknowledged and normalised estrangement. Ask directly about estranged members during or after the initial assessment. If appropriate, ask questions to establish whether this is a physical or emotional estrangement, and establish duration and levels of contact.	I am wondering if we have forgotten anyone or whether there were any absent or estranged family members we should include in this assessment? Is there anyone you have not mentioned because you no longer see them? How often do you have contact with Person A? or How long has it been since your last contact with Person A? How do you feel when you are with Person A when you do have contact? What are you most likely to do and discuss when you are with Person A? Does Person A assist or support you in any way? Explore. Do you think you could call upon Person A to support you? Explore.
Assessing impact Explore the impact of the estrangement and client agency.	How does the estrangement affect you emotionally? How does the estrangement affect your other family relationships? How does the estrangement affect your social relationships? How does estrangement affect social activities? How does estrangement affect your daily activities? Are there other ways in which the estrangement affects you? How might estrangement affect or impact on [the presenting issue]? How have these effects changed over time? Who else knows about the estrangement? How do you compensate or make up for the effects of estrangement?
Establishing client requirements Determine whether the client regards estrangement as an issue currently requiring attention (if this is not the presenting issue).	You have described the impact of estrangement on your life: Is this a particular issue you would like to discuss further? Is this an issue that you would like to dedicate some time to during our future meetings and interactions? How important is the estrangement issue in relation to [the presenting issue]? Where would you place estrangement in order of importance? How would you like to proceed?

(i) contact and collegiality with, rather than simply the presence of, family members; (ii) the existence of estranged family members; and (iii) the influence or impact of estranged family members on the family system as well as the presenting issue (see Table 7.1 for sample questions).

Importantly, Boss's (1999) work suggests that practitioners must be cognisant of the symptoms of the estranged person who is experiencing an ambiguous loss, which may appear to be problematic. In these cases, it is important to recognise – and voice – the contextual factors that are interfering with the grieving process quite distinctly from psychological disturbances. While the personal reality of each estrangement narrative should be heard and respected, the possibilities inherent in differing perspectives should not be ignored or underestimated, so the longer-term focus should include an empathic examination of the other side of the story (including intergenerational culture, patterns and myths), a compassionate examination of self, including an acknowledgement of past wrongdoings (where applicable), and a realistic evaluation of the potential for relationship change (all of which are expanded upon in this chapter and the next).

It is also important to note that people have cited negative estrangement-related encounters – including individual, couples and family sessions – with professionals, e.g. police, child protection, family law court, health and mental health services (Agllias, 2011, 2014). During these encounters people perceived professionals to be: making judgements; taking sides; not listening to, or not believing, their side of the story. For example, Dianne recited an encounter with a new doctor:

> *I confided in him about my estrangement and the mental illness of my sons. I thought he sympathised with me, but one day I went to him because I was having particular [physical] problems and he must have thought it was due to stress, and he referred me to a specialist. On the referral, he wrote Dianne has a dysfunctional family. I was so embarrassed and then I really knew what he thought of me, and I couldn't trust him.*
>
> (Dianne)

In other instances, professionals appeared swift to recommend that estranged parents 'forget their adult child' or 'wait it out/leave things alone' in divorce situations where some form of parental alienation appeared to be occurring with a young child or adolescent. In these situations estranged parents felt that the professional did not understand the gravity of such an action. These findings suggest that clients may be wary of estrangement-related conversations, and they remind professionals of the inherent power they can draw upon to enact non-judgemental interactions and self-determination.

This book does not seek to promote one particular theory or therapy in relation to professional practice with people experiencing estrangement, nor would this be appropriate for a multidisciplinary audience in a diverse range of professional contexts. Rather, it acknowledges that practitioners are cognisant with interventions that are relevant and adaptable to the needs of their particular client at any given time. Research with 27 Australian social workers in palliative care suggested that they utilised a number of theories when working with estranged clients at end of life; the vast majority drew on loss and grief, crisis intervention, attachment, lifecycle, systems/family systems, cognitive behavioural and brief solution-focused theories to understand and work with clients, while less than half drew on structural/

critical/feminist theories, and a few drew on conflict resolution models for family meetings (Agllias, 2013a).

As discussed throughout this chapter, there is certainly a role for grief, loss and trauma focused interventions for acute or complicated grief responses. Theories of continuing bonds may support work with some estranged people where acceptance of the estrangement is supported by the creation of a new relationship with the other, rather than an expectation of full detachment. Cognitive behavioural therapy, and particularly motivational interviewing (MI) and acceptance and commitment therapy (ACT) are sound examples of interventions that can promote cognitive changes that reduce stress, anxiety and unhelpful thought patterns, as well as increasing self-awareness and emotional intelligence. MI, ACT and mindfulness techniques are ideal – and maybe even complementary – interventions for working with ambivalence. Narrative-type interventions can assist in interrogating unhelpful and pathologising narratives towards a more self-compassionate understanding. By distancing or extern-alising the estrangement, clients may be able to view it in its socio-political context while working towards an alternative narrative. Systemic, structural and critical per-spectives illuminate individual issues within the relational, social, political and cultural context, which can enhance perspective, contribute to greater personal mastery, and possibly increase compassion and self-compassion. Despite the numerous online advice columns, and a handful of popular books aimed at estranged individuals and families, there are very few scholarly articles or resources that specifically offer advice or models of therapeutic intervention. Exceptions include an article on working with estranged individuals (Framo, 1976), some articles relating to family reunification (e.g., Bowman, 2000; Dattilo & Nichols, 2011; Kabat, 1998), and some that use the therapist's own family to explore routes to reunification (see Eichholz, 2003; Gilbert, 2003; Kelly, 2003; Titelman, 1987, 2003a).

Group work also offers an avenue to redefine and think about the core messages, labels and stigma associated with family estrangement. People often experience relief 'when they meet others who are experiencing life challenges similar to their own. When a group develops some cohesion, isolation is diminished, humour is redis-covered, and a sense of belonging is felt' (Bergart, 2003, p. 39). When people conceal a part of their identity, they might be disinclined to integrate positive feedback about 'self' because they might not view it as a true evaluation, so feedback from group members who are fully aware of the estrangement might be received more readily. Bergart (2003) also suggests that groups with stigmatised populations create a space where members can *see* that others look normal, which increasingly normalises participants' experiences and contributes to a more positive self-evaluation. By hearing others' stories, participants might be able to view their own situation from an observer's perspective, leading to a more objective understanding of the estrangement situation (Lau et al., 2009). Ragins (2008) also suggests that the development of trusting and supportive alliances and relationships might provide the impetus, security and courage needed for people to disclose their stigma – in this case estrangement – outside of the group.

The estrangement continuum: A sound place to start

Individual and group work interventions can benefit from an understanding of the person's position in terms of blame and responsibility for the estrangement. It is important to note that a person's felt responsibility and blame for estrangement is not necessarily connected to their position as estranger or estrangee. However, a client's beliefs about the cause of the estrangement and their attributions of blame and responsibility are important in identifying areas that may be problematic and potential areas for change and growth in the therapeutic setting.

If we position estrangement along an artificial continuum from victim to culprit (Table 7.2), we rarely see anyone identify with extreme positions (a) or (g). Rather, people tend to see themselves as both victims of the other person's behaviour (primarily connected to rejection/hurt/betrayal), and victims of the actual estrangement condition (the negative experiences that result from estrangement). Most people, when questioned in a safe environment, have some notion of their own contribution to the estrangement. Even estrangees who claim that they were never told about the other person's reason for leaving, can make educated guesses about what they might have done or not done, or what personal or situational factors might have contributed. When a person sees oneself as a victim of the other person's behaviour, as in positions (a) and (b), they are unlikely to find compassion for the other or make sense of the estrangement, which can lead to an entrenched sense of victimisation. When a person also sees oneself as a victim of the other person's behaviour and the associated losses (b), they might also view the world as unforgiving and with scepticism. (Note: This is a very different situation if abuse has occurred, where fault lies squarely with the perpetrator and compassion is not a requirement for healing. It is beyond this book to comment on the positioning of, or therapeutic interventions for, survivors of abuse, but it should be acknowledged that this position can be a healthy stance for some survivors, while others find a critical and contextual understanding useful in reducing the internalisation of responsibility for the abuse.)

Many estrangees and estrangers – (c) in the table – claim that they are the primary victim of the other person's behaviour but they are able to acknowledge the contextual factors that might have contributed to the other person's behaviour (e.g. 'my mother was a very neglectful parent, but this was understandable given her age'). Some estrangers and estrangees are able to determine and take responsibility for their own role in the estrangement alongside an empathic understanding of the situational and historic factors that have influenced the other party (d). This is the closest position to acceptance, forgiveness and self-reconciliation, but it does not necessarily mean that reconciliation is sought. Generally, people in this situation are quite clear that positions are immovable, that aberrant behaviours are unacceptable, and that estrangement is the most satisfactory relational position, while some might still believe that reconciliation would be preferable. There *may* be some estrangers and estrangees who openly acknowledge or believe that they are the primary reason for the estrangement and take responsibility for that position. Those who view their culpability in terms of its context are likely to show more compassion towards the other and be more forgiving of self (e). Those who view themselves as solely responsible – (f) and (g) – would appear to be locked in a dogmatic and inflexible position which leaves little room for self-compassion, forgiveness of self, or compassion towards the estrangee. It is likely that people who view themselves as solely responsible for the estrangement and associated losses (f) are likely to experience excessive guilt and remorse. People who see themselves as responsible for the estrangement with little understanding or acknowledgement of the resultant losses (g) are likely to feel little or no guilt and remorse, or empathy towards the other person.

TABLE 7.2 The estrangement continuum

ATTRIBUTIONS OF BLAME AND RESPONSIBILITY						
(a) Views self as innocent victim of the other party (only).	(b) Views self as victim of the other party and the estrangement related losses.	(c) Views self as victim of the other party and the estrangement. Acknowledges the situational or historical factors that influenced the other person's behaviour.	(d) Views both parties as co-contributors to the estrangement. Acknowledges the situational or historic factors that influenced the other person's behaviour and their own contribution to the estrangement.	(e) Views self as responsible for the estrangement and associated losses, but acknowledges the situational or historic factors that contributed to personal actions and reactions.	(f) Views self as solely responsible for the estrangement and associated losses.	(g) Views self as solely responsible for the estrangement (only).

Macro intervention

In terms of macro practice, interventions aimed at improving general family well-being will be effective in combating intergenerational estrangement. When families have access to adequate financial, educational, medical and social resources, they will be better prepared for times of normative and developmental stress. When laws and policies protect family members from discrimination, inequality and violence, and they have access to universal services, they will be better prepared for non-normative stressors. Additionally, practitioners need to be more engaged in social and political consciousness raising, by (i) drawing attention to instances where estrangement from family is indicated as a reasonable and sensible action, (ii) challenging the stigma associated with family estrangement by drawing attention to, and normalising, this phenomenon, and (iii) challenging and deconstructing the 'taken-for-granted' cultural beliefs about 'family'. By naming and educating about the prevalence of family estrangement and the non-resolvability of some estrangements, policy-makers should be encouraged to revise normative policies – including those which assume familial support for ageing populations and those which assume parental support for young people attending tertiary education – and to challenge current assumptions regarding unswerving family allegiance and support.

Conclusion

Regardless of its nature and form, estrangement is often perceived as a senseless condition that brings misery to individuals and families. The processes and long-term losses inherent in estrangement often affect one's sense of self, belonging and meaning. The estrangement crisis or moment of realisation often unleashes unimaginable grief responses that are sharpened and prolonged by their ambiguous nature. Hence, learning to live with estrangement can be extremely difficult and incremental work that requires ongoing long-term attention. When people acknowledge and attend to their grief, make concerted efforts to shift their perceptions of the estrangement and the parties involved through a critical intergenerational lens, they are more likely to experience personal growth and reconnection. This chapter has examined the challenging but often rewarding process of learning to live with estrangement. These foundational processes are core to forgiveness and reconciliation with the other party, if this is considered appropriate, as discussed in the following chapter.

PRACTICE POINT 6: LEARNING TO LIVE WITH FAMILY ESTRANGEMENT

Learning to live with estrangement is a continuous process of readjustment and realignment. Progress is a subjective and conditional state that can change rapidly at any time. There is no one measure of 'progress', nor should there be. However, a reflection on areas related to loss and grief, understanding self and others, and reconnection, can effectively acknowledge progress and highlight areas that might need further attention. The following section provides a reflective exercise that includes a number of indicators that might signal positive shifts towards living with estrangement.

EXERCISE 1: REFLECTING ON PROGRESS

(a) The checklist in Table 7.3 provides some areas to think about your shifting responses to estrangement. There are no right or wrong answers. Rather, this is a tool to reflect upon progress: areas that are going well, areas that are not applicable, and areas that might require attention. (Note: Some people like to measure their progress against a particular time period, so they might reflect on the questions in the following frame, e.g. 'I cry less than I did 2 weeks or 2 years ago'). Take some time to work through the checklist.

(b) Given the use of this tool, and reflection on progress to date, consider the following questions and document if this is useful.
   • Are there areas that stand out?
   • Are there areas of progress that you are particularly proud of?
   • Are there areas that you wish to progress further or concentrate on?
   • Are there strengths, strategies and supports that you can continue to employ or apply to the areas that you wish to work on further?
   • What are the best ways for you to take these ideas and assessments forward? (Think about small, incremental and achievable plans of action).

TABLE **7.3** Living with family estrangement: Reflecting on progress

Potential areas of change	Yes	Not yet	N/A	Comments/Notes/ Reflections
I cry less.				
I feel less angry.				
I feel less sad.				
I feel less hurt.				
I feel less guilty.				
I feel less ashamed.				
I feel less vengeful.				
I ruminate less.				
I revisit the estrangement event less.				
I think less about the estrangement.				
I think less about the estranged person(s).				
I am able to think about the estrangement more objectively.				
I understand the estrangement more.				
I am more able to think about the estranged person more objectively.				
I am able to empathise with the estranged person's situation/life/position more.				
I am able to think about my intergenerational family more objectively.				
I understand my intergenerational family more.				
I am able to think about my areas of strength – including temperament, skills, values, behaviours, knowledge – more objectively.				
I am able to think about the areas I need to work on – including my temperament, skills, values, behaviours, knowledge – more objectively.				

TABLE 7.3 Continued

Potential areas of change	Yes	Not yet	N/A	Comments/Notes/ Reflections
I am able to be more self-compassionate.				
I am able to forgive myself more.				
I am able to see more irony and humour in the estrangement situation.				
I see more positive aspects of my existing family relationships.				
I pay more attention to my existing family relationships.				
I feel more committed to a new life (with or without the estranged person).				
I am more open about the estrangement.				
I am more open about my intergenerational family.				
I am more open to reconnecting with others (friends/family).				
I am reconnecting with others more (friends/family).				
I am more open to connecting/reconnecting with community activities (including groups).				
I am connecting/ reconnecting with community activities more (including groups).				
I am more able to think about the future.				
I am more positive, happy or excited when I think about the future.				
I am more able to see external issues that contribute to estrangement.				

TABLE **7.3** Continued

Potential areas of change	Yes	Not yet	N/A	Comments/Notes/ Reflections
I feel more able to speak about estrangement with receptive family members.				
I feel more able to speak about estrangement with receptive friends.				
I feel more able to speak about estrangement with receptive colleagues.				
I feel more able to speak about estrangement in social situations.				
I speak about estrangement more.				

Chapter 8　Forgiveness and reconciliation

I didn't see [my father] for about a year, and I can remember I was walking up the street, I was working, and he was on the other side of the street. And I kept walking and he crossed the road. He said, 'Dolly, how long is this going to go on for?' . . . I was fine after that.

(Jean)

Reconciliation is often cinematically portrayed as a spontaneous response to an emotive action or event that produces instantaneous forgiveness: in one moment of clarity two parties reprioritise their relationship and sweep away past hurts and feelings of guilt. Reality is significantly different for most estranged family members, where forgiveness and reconciliation are positions or acts that are avoided, pondered, packed away, reconsidered, rehearsed and attempted with various degrees of success across time. Estranged people often have long-term experiences of, and tenuous relationships with, forgiveness and reconciliation. This chapter commences with a brief insight into one person's story of estrangement and reconciliation. Shirley's story emphasises a number of core elements of reconciliation that are discussed throughout the chapter, including: self-awareness and self-healing, patience, persistence, timing, emotional regulation and control, listening, tolerance and acceptance. The following sections examine the current and common definitions, concepts and processes associated with forgiveness and reconciliation, suggesting that they are not definitive states, but ongoing and subjectively determined processes. Forgiveness and reconciliation are considered uniquely in the light of the estrangement experience and ideologies of the perfect family, unconditional love and 'living happily ever after'. The chapter examines areas to consider when working towards reconciliation. It cautions against haste, and offers a discussion of self-reconciliation for those people who are unable or unwilling to reconcile. Finally, a practice section offers a readiness checklist for the reader or client to consider before reconciliation is attempted, in addition to some key resources for estranged family members and the practitioners who work with them.

Shirley's story

Shirley's story of reconciliation is one that highlights how personal growth, persistence, a realignment of expectations and acceptance are core to reconciliation. Shirley said that the reconciliation with her son commenced with her own journey of self-acceptance and spiritual healing (including attendance at a well-being group that assisted her in letting go of hurt). After decades of complete physical estrangement, and an acceptance that she might never see her son again, she gathered enough courage to contact him. Steps included buying a card (which she left in a drawer and never actually sent), and searching for his address in phone books and on the electoral roll. Finally, she found her son's phone number and decided she was strong enough to call:

> Eventually he came on [the phone]. He said, 'Yes, yes.' He went like that and I said, 'Hello Wade, it's your mum here.' And he started screeching, 'I have no mother, I have no father' screaming in the phone. . . . He kept on screaming for a few seconds and eventually he calmed down and I said, 'Well can I ring you again? Is it all right if I ring you again?' I said, 'Would you like my phone number?' He said, 'It's already registered on my mobile phone. I've already got it.' I said, 'Well that's good then, yes okay, lovely to talk to you, take care' and that was that (Shirley).

It was another month before Shirley called again:

> Then about March I got the urge again and I thought well at least he didn't hang up in my ear and he didn't reject me and by doing that workshop it gave me enough confidence, all right then if he rejects me, so what these days. . . . I said, 'Would you like to meet me?' . . . At first he said, 'Yes, that would be nice' (Shirley).

While this first arrangement did not eventuate, Wade agreed to meet his mother at another location on another date, and the meeting proceeded successfully. It is important to note that this research interview was conducted 6 years after that initial meeting. Over that time, Shirley had seen her son on a number of occasions and she continued phone contact with him every couple of months. During their discussions, it became clear that a number of miscommunications had contributed to the estrangement, and Shirley was able to provide important information that her son had been unaware of until their meetings. While the level and type of contact with Wade and his family may not be considered a close relationship by some standards, Shirley was satisfied with the state of the relationship and considered it to be reconciled.

To forgive or not to forgive

I spoke to him on the phone [before he died]. I sent him a picture of Jesus and – it's the power of love to change lives, you know. Because I wanted to change my own life, I didn't want to hang on to any kind of anger and bitterness about it, although believe me I was for quite a while. But I thought if I can forgive and then I can walk away. . . . If I can release it, then I can be free.

(Julie)

Some people find forgiveness to be an important and positive step towards accepting estrangement, reconciling with self and approaching some form of interpersonal reconciliation. McCullough (2008) suggests that revenge is an important and useful instinctual mechanism in humans, but given the right circumstances, forgiveness can be encouraged, developed and enacted as a more helpful long-term response. Indeed, the capacity to forgive is widely heralded by practitioners as an important pathway towards health and well-being, and there is mounting research evidence to support this theory (Enright, 2001; Glaeser, 2008; Lawler *et al.*, 2005; Luskin, 2002; McCullough, 2008). The link between forgiveness, health and well-being appears to be facilitated or mediated by factors such as stress reduction, reduced negative affect, and increased religious or spiritual alignment (Lawler *et al.*, 2005).

Forgiveness is an ongoing process – which starts as a private act – of acknowledging one's hurt at the hands of another, alongside the release of negative feelings towards that person (which is often accompanied by a general reduction in negative affect). It is the compassionate recognition of the other person's humanity and the capacity for benevolence regardless of their deservedness, and without an expectation of restoration or reconciliation. However, some make the distinction between *emotional forgiveness* (where negative, unforgiving and vengeful emotions are replaced with more positive and other oriented ones such as compassion, tolerance and altruism) and *decisional forgiveness* (where a person commits rationally to eliminating revenge) (Lichtenfeld *et al.*, 2015). While there has been limited empirical evidence about the different types of forgiving, recent research has found that people who forgive emotionally are more likely to forget personal characteristics of the offender that were core to the betrayal, compared to people who offer decisional forgiveness, or those who are unable to forgive (ibid.).

There are a number of authors who write about forgiveness processes and models, but it is beyond this chapter to critique these thoroughly. Core elements to emotional forgiveness seem to include:

- being able to identify and articulate feelings associated with the hurtful event(s), especially anger;
- a personal commitment to find inner peace through forgiveness;
- gathering new insights and perspectives about the event(s) and re-storying the event less personally and maybe more empathically (this is not excusing bad behaviour);
- stress management and emotion regulation; and,
- forgiving the other regardless of their contrition or engagement in the forgiveness process (this might involve some form of public announcement or commitment without the other person's presence, sending a letter or engaging in a face-to-face interaction with the other person) (see Enright, 2001; Hargrave, 1994; Luskin, 2002; Malcolm & Greenburg, 2000; Smedes, 1996; Worthington, 1998, 2006).

Enright's (2001) guide also suggests making a gift to the other – a small gesture of time or care – also illustrated in Julie's quote at the beginning of this section. It is important to note that some suggest forgiveness (an individual intrapersonal undertaking) is a separate process to reconciliation (a relational or interpersonal undertaking) (Worthington, 1998). In this schema, forgiveness is viewed as a foundation for potential reconciliation. Others suggest that forgiveness involves some form of reconciliation. For example, Hargrave's (1994) forgiveness process includes the following:

- providing the opportunity for the other to make reparation (i.e. prove their love, trustworthiness, etc.); and
- the overt act of forgiving (where the event is acknowledged, responsibility taken and forgiveness offered in order to make a new start).

Regardless of the theoretical basis for the forgiveness model (e.g. emotional, cognitive, decision-based), originators tend to agree that forgiveness is a long-term process of (often incrementally derived) mastery.

However, forgiveness may not be an important component of learning to live with estrangement or reconciliation for every person. The concept of forgiveness can clash with a person's values and beliefs about responsibility and justice as well as their spiritual and cultural convictions. People and cultures differ in their desire and capacity for forgiveness. For example, research has shown that there are differences in the propensity to forgive across societies that are related to peacefulness, economic conditions and valuing quality of life (see Hanke & Fischer, 2013). Some argue that forgiveness needs to be critiqued as an all-or-none process, citing evidence that we are likely to forgive a transgression differently in a casual relationship compared to a familial one (Worthington, 2006).

External pressure to forgive can be dangerous and detrimental for some people. This is particularly so if the person complies and feigns forgiveness, or offers forgiveness prematurely, because these acts are likely to contradict internalised values of honesty and further compromise one's sense of control during a traumatic period. For example, counsellors in one qualitative study suggested that 'non-forgiveness and feelings of revenge may also play a crucial part in the victim's recovery, as they can help to restore his/her self-respect and rearrange the power balance before the gift of forgiveness can genuinely be granted' (Glaeser, 2008, p. 341). It is important to consider that there may be some people who are able to move from the pain of estrangement and lead fulfilling lives without forgiving the other person. Forgiveness must always be given freely and offer some benefit to the person providing it.

Reconciliation

I think that's all that is required, the courage to actually just face reality. People are capable of huge forgiveness. I would certainly say the same if my family members actually took any responsibility whatsoever and just faced facts. We would be halfway there to beginning that process.

(Debbie)

Estrangement signals the dissolution of trust. Therefore, the creation or restoration of interpersonal – and maybe even intergenerational – trust is central to reconciliation.

Trust is built on a belief that the other person harbours good intentions and has the capacity to implement actions that will ensure these intentions are met (Thomm, n/d). Hence, reconciliation is a long-term process that involves risk and bravery, as attempts at reconciliation may reveal relational patterns that are unable to be changed, or intentions that are unable to be enacted. Even when both parties are determined to reconcile, the process requires considerable commitment, insight and integrity. The following section defines the use of the term *reconciliation* and examines the factors and processes that may increase the likelihood of reconciliation occurring.

Reunification or reconciliation

I have reconciled with my dad. We met at the hospital while visiting [a relative]. We had a good chat. I then saw him and his partner a few times, then they came over to dinner. I am taking things slowly as I know this may not last.

(Rita, diary entry)

The terms *reunification* and *reconciliation* are used interchangeably and variably across disciplines and fields of practice. For example, in the area of child protection and welfare, reconciliation is often viewed as a process of building trust and safety prior to the child being reunified with their parent(s) (i.e. physically relocated from temporary care and back into their parent or parents' care). In other instances, reunification is considered to be more of a 'truce' between parties, whereas reconciliation requires an examination and acknowledgement of the hurt, and a commitment to act differently or make amends. For some, this also requires restoration of trust in the relationship. For the purpose of clarity in this book, and in light of the variety of conciliatory positions involved in estrangement, the term *reconciliation* will be used to describe the reinstatement of a relationship: it will cover a continuum of relational states from the resumption of contact without acknowledgement of previous conflict or dissatisfaction, to the acknowledgement and resolution of previous issues. Most importantly, in acknowledgement of variances in family closeness, contact and affection, it is contended that it is the estranged parties who must define whether they consider themselves to be reconciled or not. In this schema, reconciliation is a state of relational closeness that may not be ideal but it is one that is preferable to the position that was previously experienced as, or considered to be, estrangement.

The reconciliation continuum: Certainty, indecision and obsession

I'd like to sort of repair my relationship with my son. I've tried, you know, on email, even down to just sending him a joke but always making it personal . . . but if I just do that three or four times a week, then I think eventually it will get inside his head or he's going to get so sick of it he's going to say, stop doing it.

(Beth)

The idea of reconciliation is something that most people struggle with at some point in the estrangement process. Positions, which are often opposed in the relational pair, range from certainty about maintaining the estrangement to certainty about the desire to reconcile. Either of these positions can become an obsession with estranged parties, characterised by: (i) using secrecy, physical and emotional barriers to become invisible and untouchable to the other person (usually the actions of an estranger), or (ii) constantly thinking about, contacting and stalking the other person (usually the acts of an estrangee). However, most people, who weigh up what is coveted and what is possible, usually fall somewhere between these extremes, including states such as: (i) undecided or ambivalent about reconciliation (often experienced early in the estrangement when feelings are more raw and variable); (ii) thinking about working towards or preparing for reconciliation; (iii) actively engaged in attempting to reconcile; and (iv) remaining open to reconciliation if events change, or the other person returns or makes contact. It is important to note here that research found that some estrangees – and particularly those who perceived the estrangement to be caused by third party interference – held out hope that shifting external events would prompt the estranger to take conciliatory action (Agllias, 2011). External events included things like the estranger becoming separated or divorced, a change in medications, and becoming an adult or leaving home.

Starting with realistic expectations

> *But I content myself with what I have in my family now because I can still say my family, even though it's at arm's length. There's no close ties there. But my grandkids have their own lives, they get on with them, they're busy. . . . They're all achievers. I can see a lot of myself in them.*

> (Yvonne)

As alluded to in the previous section, decisions about reconciliation can be made from a purely emotional and instinctual place. When the feelings of hurt and betrayal are raw, people might tell themselves that they want to reconcile when in actuality they simply want their side of the story to be heard or to enact revenge on the other party. So it is really important for people to honestly evaluate 'why' they want to reconcile, and whether this is a reasonable and productive reason to attempt contact at that time. The desire to reconcile could include a myriad of interwoven factors including: loneliness; pressure from others (particularly marital partners); fear of failure; guilt; to stop the pain of estrangement; to keep the intergenerational family together or to prevent secondary or inherited estrangements; a key life event that has evoked attachment-related emotions, e.g. pregnancy, loss or marriage; not wanting to die or the other person to die with the estrangement intact; love and affection for the other person; and valuing particular aspects of the relationship with the other person.

Decisions about reconciliation can also be made through an evaluation of the interface between desire, possibility and risk. Desire is a personal yearning for something. In the case of estrangement, where idealised notions of family can be further imbedded by grief and absence, it is important to consider one's desire for reconciliation critically. Sometimes people say, 'I want things to be the way they were before the estrangement'. This is interesting when stated by an estranger because it often contradicts negative depictions of the state of the relationship leading up to dissolution. When stated by an estrangee, it overlooks the aspects of the relationship – often hidden, unspoken or minimised – that contributed to the estrangement in the first place. Hence, reconciliation is best served through an understanding that the reconciled relationship will never be the same as it was before the estrangement. The relationship might be better, or it might be worse, but it will never be the same.

Research shows that reconciliation often requires the realistic evaluation of, and maybe even an adjustment to, the concept of family (Agllias, 2011, 2014). Standing on the outside of other families, especially in the midst of estrangement pain and isolation, can distort reality about the way other families behave and exist. The *normal* family needs to be understood and accepted as an ongoing site of contention, where love and happiness often entwine with jealousy, misunderstanding, favouritism and injustice. The desire for a *perfect* family and a *perfect* relationship with the estranged person – where no one ever disagrees, or feels hurt, offended, misjudged or overlooked – is unrealistic and highly improbable. It is therefore important for estranged people to think about what they *really* want from reconciliation, including the things that they would like, the things they would never accept (elements that cross personal boundaries), and the things that they *could* accept. Consideration must be given to the perceived negative traits of the other person that are likely to carry forward into the new relationship (e.g. behaviours and beliefs that are core to the other person and affect the way that the two parties might interact). Having more realistic expectations of the relationship does not mean giving in to or accepting bad behaviours, rather it means taking the time to examine and consolidate personal values and beliefs about relational boundaries, so that decisions can be made about reconciliation and new roles can be negotiated if this is taken forward.

Once realistic desires are established this must be evaluated against the perceived possibility or probability of those desires being realised. Possibility can be evaluated historically, from current interactions (for people who are emotionally estranged) and from third party information (for people who are physically estranged). For example, was the person respectful, generous or committed to family members in the past? Have they ever shown the capacity to change or repair relationships? Are there indications – from personal observation or third party information – about changes in the person's circumstances, behaviours and attitudes that might indicate a more positive response to conciliatory actions? Reflection on these issues will provide some insights into the likelihood of reconciliation and might also illuminate information that is useful to future conciliatory processes.

Once desire and possibility are considered, the person must also evaluate their tolerance for risk at that point in time. This requires a consideration of things like emotional vulnerability, physical and psychological safety, and other stressors emanating from external sources. People need to evaluate – as best as possible – the risk that they are taking and the potential effects of further rejection (or abuse). When the risks are high, then support might be warranted in the form of close friends, non-estranged family members or professionals. Supporters can provide the space for the person to articulate their thinking process in a non-judgemental forum. They can ask critical questions and provide emotional support regardless of the decision to attempt reconciliation at that time or to delay contact and reconsider at a later point.

It should be acknowledged that if there are valid reasons to terminate a relationship, then there may be valid reasons to maintain an estrangement. Destructive, toxic and abusive people are all born into, and develop within, families. When relationships are based on vast power imbalances that are unlikely to change, and when they are characterised by abuse, manipulation, game playing and purely negative exchanges, it is likely that reconciliation will be detrimental to the less powerful party (and maybe even the intergenerational family). In these instances, a realistic evaluation of desire and possibility may result in a firm decision not to attempt any form of reconciliation. When there is a possibility that the other person *might* change or there are signs of change, then this must be evaluated in terms of personal risk and safety.

It is also important to note that the things that people will accept or not accept in a relationship will vary widely. For example, one mother (estranged from her son) might gratefully agree to visits from her grandchildren and daughter-in-law (while remaining estranged from her son); however, another would never accept such an arrangement. While some people view any form of connection as a small conciliatory gift or step towards a better future, others will regard the same gesture as a symbolic and insulting scrap from the broken relationship. It is important, then, for estranged people to consider *what they would accept* in the short term in order to achieve bigger reconciliation aims. If a person is willing to accept a small gesture from the other – even if it is considered minimal or unsatisfactory in terms of their actual desires for reconciliation – it might form a foundation for, or pathway towards, greater closeness. On the other hand, accepting conditions that are unjust or incompatible with a person's values can create considerable bitterness, thus increasing the likelihood of further conflict and rupture.

Research with people who had reconciled with family members showed a range of experiences and satisfaction levels with the new relationship (Agllias, 2011, 2014). Interestingly, satisfaction and contentment was not necessarily borne of an ideal relationship or conflict resolution. Some people were simply happy to have some connection with the previously estranged person, and felt it unnecessary to broach the cause of the estrangement, to make formal apologies, or declarations of forgiveness. Many successful relationships involve unresolved conflicts, and it appears that some estranged people can reconcile and live happily without addressing the source of the estrangement. However, research with people who remained estranged suggested that many were unable to consider reconciliation unless the other person acknowledged and took responsibility for their actions and the hurt that they caused (Agllias, 2011, 2014). For some, the estrangement conflict, hurt or betrayal is too great to reconcile without acknowledgement from the other person and a commitment to rebuild trust. Reconciliation may mean very different things to the individuals involved, and these expectations must then be negotiated in a relational context charged with negative emotions and hurts. Under these conditions, being clear about one's needs and expectations is a must.

Finally, and most importantly, a realistic evaluation of reconciliation involves the acknowledgement that, while forgiveness can be given without reciprocation, reconciliation clearly involves the cooperation of both parties. If one party does not truly want to reconcile, they will refuse to meet or change (in a physical estrangement), or they will refuse to listen or change (in an emotional estrangement). Some people might commence the process half-heartedly, only to back out quite quickly, or behave and act in ways that will cause the other person to flee. Caught off guard, people might agree to a future meeting which they have no intention of attending.

Readiness is important

I feel like they should make contact with me. I know that's a bit – I know everyone could say that. Oh well they should contact me. No, you should contact them. Then no one contacts each other. . . . The hurt is just, it's so deep, I can't bring myself to. I feel somewhat, a little bit ashamed to say that. Like I feel like I wish I could be magnanimous enough to just pretend nothing happened and just hi, how are you going? But I can't.

(Debbie)

Reconciliation is often stymied because people are simply not ready for such a process, or the parties have mismatched expectations about what the process will entail. However, *learning to live with estrangement* is sound preparation for commencing reconciliation processes. The practices described in the previous chapter are core to self-understanding, self-compassion, managing emotions, and building resilience, as well as developing curiosity about, alternate perspectives of and compassion for the other person and their actions. These skills are foundational to conciliatory preparations and action. The following section examines the factors that should be considered in terms of readiness for reconciliation.

Regardless of the person's role as estranger or estrangee it is highly likely that they have caused the other person some degree of hurt (through the actions that contributed to, and continue to maintain, the estrangement or the act of estrangement itself). One of the most significant barriers to reconciliation appears to be the estranged person's desire to honour the *intent* of an action over the *result* of the action. Often people refuse to recognise, acknowledge or apologise for an action that caused hurt because it came from a place of love, care or sound intent. For example, a man who pays for his father's funeral expenses, rather than splitting the cost with his brother, may do so because he knows his brother is currently out of work. While the man enacts the payment with good intent, the brother may consider the act to be patronising, and be hurt that he was not consulted about an action that prevented him from contributing to his father's final farewell. Another common example is a parent teasing a child about their weight or appearance. While the parent might perceive this as harmless and in good humour, the child might experience this as highly painful and damaging to their self-esteem. Additionally, as time passes, estranged people may forget, minimise or distort behaviours or events that caused hurt. They may claim that they did not do a particular thing or behave a particular way, or suggest that an event did not happen, or happened differently to the other person's version. They will often hold tightly to this defence rather than accepting the other person's account and *experience* of the event. Readiness for reconciliation involves a person's willingness to acknowledge that their words, actions and inactions – regardless of their intentions and regardless of their memory of the event – have hurt the other party.

Another position that is highly contradictory to successful reconciliation concerns the *assumption of knowledge* about wrongdoing, i.e. the other person knows or should know what they have done to upset or hurt. When estrangement is imminent, it is common for one party to ask 'What have I done?' or 'Is there a problem we should discuss?' Quite often this is met with a sentiment resembling: 'If you don't know, I'm not telling you.' The assumption that the other party knows or should know what has caused offence is one that is common, and one that left unchecked, will continue to plague the conciliatory process. Often people have no idea – or they have a distorted idea – about the actions and events that have offended, betrayed or hurt the other. So in order for reconciliation to occur, the parties must be willing to clearly articulate the offending actions, issues and events as well as their effect.

179

Reconciliation is often sought prematurely by estrangees, which may be a very strong and normal grief response, where they continue to reach out for the other person. However, the mismatch between what estrangees often view as acts of love and contrition, and what estrangers perceive as harassment and bullying, is often considerable. In preparing for an attempt at reconciliation estrangees need to assess their actions to date and how these might have been interpreted by the estranger. Important to note is the fact that stalking behaviours rarely go unrecognised by estrangers. So estrangees need to honestly evaluate if their actions have constituted badgering, harassment or stalking, and stop any such behaviours. This assessment is more easily done if the concept of 'family' is taken out of the equation. Estrangees often justify their stalking behaviours by saying '*but* he is my *son*', or '*but* I love my *sister* and I miss her dearly'. So it can be helpful to change the scenario and consider the following: How would you feel if an ex-friend continued to text you twice a week, even after you asked them to stop contacting two months previously? How would you feel if you suddenly found out that a friend – who you stopped contacting six months ago after a disagreement – had been collecting information about you through mutual friends, had secret access to your Facebook page (or viewed your posts through a mutual friend's account), knew all your contact details, regularly looked you up on the Internet, or regularly walked past your workplace in the hope of spotting you?

Many people are encouraged towards reconciliation when they have made changes, or changes have occurred, in their lives. Life events, such as having an adult relationship, having a family, travelling, building a career, experiencing the love and losses of close relationships, and events that highlight one's mortality, can have a profound effect on a person's view of the world. However, people evolve, grow and change at different rates. Therefore the initiator of reconciliation must be cognisant that the other person may have changed dramatically, or they may not have changed at all. The other person may or may not want to reconnect and they may not have developed the same empathy or understanding as the person attempting reconciliation. Additionally, people might have very different ideas about what constitutes reconciliation. For example, one might want to 'start over' without discussion or apology and the other might need a demonstration of insight and acknowledgement of their worth before they can progress. It is impossible to fully predict the position of the other person, or radically change their behaviour on encounter.

Given the aforementioned conditions potentially associated with estrangement, people need to consider a number of readiness factors before they decide to attempt reconciliation. While no one can be *ready* for everything they encounter during the reconciliation process, preparedness and psychological rehearsal can go a long way to controlling emotions and minimising hurt. It is important to consider things like:

- readiness to be rejected by the other person;
- openness to being challenged and confronted about things that may be difficult to hear;
- willingness to own and apologise for actions that caused pain and offense, without defensiveness and unsolicited explanation (and maybe a willingness to ask for forgiveness);

- readiness to deal with core issues (i.e. capacity to be clear about fundamental concerns without needing to revisit or rehash every minor hurt and detail);
- capacity to accept the costs associated with long-term reconciliation (including negative aspects of the previous relationship that are likely to persist in the new one);
- capacity to respond to old issues and communication patterns in new ways.

Additionally, consideration should be given to the skills needed to offer kind words and honest feedback to the other person, as well as clearly articulating personal needs, wants and boundaries. The engagement in such a process requires some level of proficiency in:

- communication (being able to listen, offer empathic responses, be assertive and negotiate new relational roles);
- maintaining boundaries;
- controlling and sitting with strong emotions;
- exiting unsafe situations.

Conciliatory preparation can be enhanced by a sound consideration of the other person's communicative style and preferences (e.g. the types of communication that are interpreted as threatening and those which are more conducive to open discussion). Regardless of whether the person has chosen estrangement or whether they have been estranged, a consideration of the other person's side of the estrangement story – as discussed in Chapter 7 – is important to thinking through the most appropriate way to approach and discuss reconciliation.

Making contact: Breaking the stalemate

She wrote an email ... [saying] let's forget about everything and just start all over again ... well so many things have happened, you can't start over. Things need to be, you need to understand why things are as they are. ... I sent her an email explaining ... everything that had happened, why I had run away and that I would love to have contact with her if only she could give me ten compliments – say ten nice things about me – to be nice to me. I never heard anything.

(Tina)

Sometimes opportunities for reconnection simply arise: key family events might provide the context for a brief and heartfelt connection or an invitation to reconnect afterwards. Sometimes inadvertent or accidental meetings breach the initial silence better than a letter or phone call. Indeed some authors suggest that maintaining connections with the broader intergenerational family is important because key events, such as weddings, illnesses and deaths, might provide unexpected meetings and opportunities for reconnection that could never be orchestrated (Kelly, 2003; Titelman, 2003b). These events most often provide opportunities for the reconciliation of secondary estrangements, which can provide the impetus, experience, and the skills to initiate reconciliation in primary estrangements. However, it is important to be cognisant that in some instances, people might be caught off guard by an unexpected face-to-face encounter, and their automatic fight or flight responses might lead to further conflict or withdrawal. So unplanned encounters are probably most effective when the person who wishes to reconcile makes a brief and genuine statement about their desire for the relationship to be different and an offer of future contact.

Deciding when and how to make a more formal contact can be difficult, and should be guided by knowledge of the other person and the estrangement context. It should be viewed as a potentially long and incremental process. People tend to make (mostly thoughtful) attempts at reaching out to the other person in the hope of a positive response. However, research showed that estrangers and estrangees experienced some contacts as 'too little too late' (Agllias, 2014). This is especially so if the initial contact fails to acknowledge the prime issue or resultant pain (see Tina's quote at the beginning of this section). Most people need some sort of acknowledgement of their pain in order to proceed, but an all-encompassing or generalised apology, an expectation of immediate forgiveness, a rehashing or detailed explanation of the estrangement-related event(s), or the expectation of a deep and meaningful discussion, can be experienced as overwhelming and too confronting by the other party. So offering a genuine 'initial' apology, 'initial' acknowledgment of the other person's hurt, and an opening for the other person to respond with their needs and desires for future contact is likely to be the most effective pathway to reconciliation.

Letters, emails and texts are ways to initiate contact without putting the other person on the spot, and they can offer a genuine apology and a desire for a future meeting, without words becoming confused or misconstrued in high emotion. It is important for those wishing to reconcile to take some time to draft a letter, to consider it from the other person's perspective, and maybe even get feedback from others before sending. The additional risk with face-to-face or phone contact initially is that it can be experienced by the other party as an invasion of privacy or as a confrontational act. Rehearsal is warranted for such an engagement, and a strong capacity to sit with discomfort will be required (as illustrated in Shirley's story). Regardless, the avenue of initial contact must be guided by contextual knowledge of the other person and consider the ways that they might feel about being approached. It should be kept brief, positive and non-confrontational.

If this contact is not acknowledged (in the case of a letter), then a follow-up may be warranted after some time has passed. Generally, this would acknowledge the initial contact, reiterate the desire to meet and make things right, and politely ask the other person if they might have had time to consider the offer. In some instances the initial contact will be acknowledged but a meeting will not eventuate or be desired at that point. If the response has been ambiguous (e.g. I am not sure how I feel about meeting), then it might be appropriate to follow up some time in the future, to see if this position has changed in any way (also illustrated in Shirley's story).

If the other party makes it entirely clear that they do not wish to pursue any further contact, and they do not wish to be contacted again, then this decision should be acknowledged and respected. It is important to end this type of interaction with a positive sentiment – such as 'I truly wish you well' – and an invitation to contact in the eventuality of change. Interestingly, authors and commentators seem to differ in their advice regarding further contact, with some suggesting that being asked not to contact should be the final signal to let go and it should definitely be respected. Others suggest that there are differences across contexts. For example, Coleman (2008) provides guidelines to parents who are estranged from adult children about extending invitations, provisions and contacts dependent on the age or developmental stage of the adult child. He recommends reaching out once a week to children aged between eighteen and thirty years of age, while limiting contact to birthdays and holidays for children over 30 who do not reciprocate contact (see Coleman, 2008, pp. 241–249 for further detail). Other considerations might include mental health status, drug and alcohol use, or the estranged person's vulnerability in particular circumstances. If there are external influences that might be unduly influencing the estranged person's response at that point in time, then the person who desires reconciliation might benefit from a thoughtful and critical discussion with a close friend or a practitioner to develop some guidelines about the appropriateness of further contact (and the frequency of such contact if this is decided upon).

When contact is acknowledged, reciprocal communication offers an opportunity to set boundaries and expectations for both parties, particularly if there is to be a future meeting. These might include conditions such as where the meeting is to be held, who would be in attendance and how long the meeting might be. Public meetings can feel much safer for some people, while others are more comfortable with privacy. A coffee or light meal might provide some distraction, enable informal conversation when there are silences, and diffuse some tension compared to a purely face-to-face sit-down encounter. While some people might need a support person at the meeting, it is important that this information is given to the other party so that they do not feel in any way outnumbered or ambushed. Additionally, a support person should be chosen with consideration of their relationship to the estranged parties, and their role in the meeting clearly defined and agreed upon before the event. (Note: It is not recommended that meetings occur with more than one estranged person at a time unless some sort of mediation is employed, due to factors including power imbalance and multiple agendas). Suggesting a time-limited meeting can be much less confronting for some people and allows the parties a way out if required. Initial meetings should be brief. While all of these details might change by mutual agreement upon meeting, it is important for both parties to have some sort of knowledge about what to expect before meeting the other, and some guidelines to uphold if they are feeling distressed during the meeting.

There are a number of guidelines or rules of engagement that can be applicable to both parties during the first and future encounters. However, the person who has initiated the reconciliation probably has the greatest role to play in setting the tone for proceedings and listening to the other person's experience of the estrangement. The four aims of initial meetings might include (i) to convey the reasons for desiring reconciliation, (ii) to remember and reconnect around areas of commonality and positive past experiences, (iii) to acknowledge and apologise for hurts, and (iv) to commence a dialogue about the origin of hurt, or to develop a trusting space for, and commitment to, future discussion. A discussion about future action and commitments to change may or may not be applicable at this initial meeting.

It is important that the person who initiates reconciliation state the reasons for wanting to reconcile, e.g. that they have missed the other person. They might also like to detail some of the feelings that they have experienced as a result of the estrangement, e.g. sadness and loss (although it is probably not wise to focus on the more controversial emotions that have arisen, e.g. anger and revenge). Rather, at this stage, it might be best to acknowledge the positive things about the person that have been missed since estrangement occurred. However, this needs to be a brief and genuine dialogue, not one aimed at making the other person feel guilty about their absence. Reconciliation attempts should not employ manipulative strategies to draw the other person back into the family. For example, 'we missed you at Christmas' is very different to 'Nan was devastated when you weren't there for Xmas, she can't bear to have it at her house anymore'.

Core communication strategies for such encounters include a focus on listening to the other person and maintaining curiosity about their experience, which demonstrates respect, genuine interest and care. While empathically listening to the other person's experience may be confrontational and emotive, it is important that the other person's version of events are taken seriously. This can be assisted by focusing on the other person's 'experience' or 'feelings' of the event as factual. While versions of events may differ, these are unimportant, and it is the hurt that must remain the focus. When attention is directed towards the hurt instead of the accuracy of the details of the event(s), both parties are less likely to become defensive and reactive. Hurt needs to be acknowledged and validated, and apologies offered where appropriate. Additionally, Coleman (2008) offers some constructive strategies for parents responding to blame and criticism from their adult children that might be relevant to preparing for such encounters (see Coleman, pp. 55–59).

The person who initiates reconciliation needs to be guided by the other party regarding the degree to which estrangement issues and events are confronted at the first meeting. Some people will want to use the meeting to detail all of the hurt and pain they have held from the estrangement, and they may do so and leave the meeting without any intention of further conciliatory attempts. Others will want to use this meeting to determine their desire and capacity to engage in such a conversation. Divulging and discussing hurt can make a person extremely vulnerable, and perceptions of safety will influence this process. Regardless, either end of this continuum can be highly distressing as it can risk leaving both parties feeling traumatised and exhausted or empty and unheard. Ideally, there needs to be a balance between confronting old issues and engaging in polite and positive conversation.

Even if the invited party does not want to confront the issues, and the interaction proceeds without such a discussion, it is important for the person who initiates the meeting to acknowledge that these issues exist and that they are open to discussing these issues when the time is right. While some people report that they never needed to discuss the estrangement cause or related hurt in order to reconcile, evidence would suggest that 'leaving the elephant in the room' maintains a tension that can ultimately result in conflict and further estrangement (Agllias, 2011, 2014). Distance from the original offense and a gradual increase in relational trust may indeed reduce the original pain over time, but if a similar offense is enacted it is likely to exacerbate the hurt immeasurably (and reactions may appear disproportionate to the action or event). Additionally, some people believe that one conversation about the estrangement issue is sufficient to clear the tension and move forward, but this is rarely so. An open invitation to discuss the estrangement and the associated hurt is particularly important in creating and maintaining ongoing honesty and trust. Regardless of the meeting outcome, a positive ending, including acknowledgement of the person's attendance, should be offered.

Professional support can play a significant role in reconciliation, whether this is in the supportive stage of grieving after estrangement, assisting with strategies to learn to live with estrangement, in decision-making about reconciliation, in preparation for reconciliation attempts, and in the facilitation of family meetings. Practitioners can provide the neutral third party that may be necessary in early reconciliation meetings. While families may attempt reconciliation meetings using a family member as the *neutral party* or *mediator*, they often find that these parties have an agenda of their own – hence their reason for volunteering for such a role – and a lot of further pain can result from surprising opinions and 'truths' that emerge in such a context. Practitioners can also play a significant role in debriefing and processing after reconciliation meetings.

Maintaining the connection

Then dad went to counselling and really made amends with me. It took a few years, but he did. He took ownership for his role in things … my relationship with my father is good today because the difference with mum and dad – Dad admitted – look, I haven't been a good father, I'm going to get help and I'm going to make it up to you. [My estranged] mum continued on the same path … she doesn't see she's done anything wrong.

(Donna)

As discussed in Chapter 5, the desire to reconcile with an estranged family member does not always mean that there are enough shared experiences to maintain the relationship to the level that one or both parties desire. It may be difficult to re-establish a connection or move past the hurt in many instances. Conciliatory attempts can also be undermined by different levels of intensity and desire for reconciliation, unrealistic expectations of reconciliation, insufficient recognition of hurt and limited attention to rebuilding trust within the relationship. Sometimes one or both parties simply do not have the capabilities to fulfil their desire or intention to reconcile.

Even positive and useful reconciliation meetings can leave participants exhausted and with a significant amount of information and emotion to process, so it is important that discussions are kept open and ongoing until both parties feel satisfied in their own resolution. Too often one party wants to 'get on with' the relationship and leave difficult discussions behind before the other is ready to do so. Additionally, one party may be more invested in the reconciliation or more enthusiastic about it than the other, which can create anxiety and tension. If one party pursues too intensely – even if the pursuit consists of seemingly positive elements such as invitations, gifts or contacts – there is a risk that the other party will feel suffocated, pressured or overwhelmed by the attention. For example, Frances said she thought her relationship with her previously estranged daughter (and grandson) was improving until she decided to make a surprise visit to her grandson's school: '*One afternoon I went and waited for her to pick him up and I went to see him and she roused on me big time*' (diary entry). Reconciliation faltered at this point and estrangement quickly ensued. Making an effort to do something meaningful or selfless for the other person is a sound way of developing trust. Once again, however, the person who initiates reconciliation needs to be guided by the other party, and try to balance offering too much and offering too little. Cards, notes and texts are minimally invasive ways of letting the other person know that they are cared for, or that their attendance at a meeting was appreciated.

Both parties also need to be aware that unexpected triggers for pain can occur in future meetings. This is particularly so for people who have been distanced from a number of family members or for a long period of time. In these instances the introduction of new information, and revelations about things that they may have missed during the estrangement period, may heighten their perception of being an outsider. New information can be experienced as a significant retrospective loss and may make retreat seem like a more viable option than reconciliation. People often underestimate the length of the readjustment period after initial reconciliation attempts are made. Additionally, hopes for reconciliation can be threatened by other parties who have been involved in or connected to the primary estrangement (particularly in the case of third party alienation or secondary estrangement). In these instances, other parties may have an investment in maintaining the estrangement status quo and try to stop or undermine any sort of reconciliation, so it is important to openly discuss these tensions and how they might be approached.

Finally, reconciliation requires considerable ongoing commitment, compromise and effort. The acknowledgement of transgression may ease some of the associated hurt, but it may never dissipate entirely, so an ongoing effort may be required to build and maintain trust. In many cases expectations for the relationship may need to be reduced or renegotiated intra- or interpersonally, as discussed earlier in this chapter. While tolerance and acceptance are important components of any ongoing relationship, it is important that reconciliation does not involve tolerating unacceptable behaviour in an effort to avoid what may be viewed as a secondary relational failure at any cost. Similarly, it can be tempting to dampen emerging conflict after reconciliation, and while letting go of small issues can be productive, addressing ongoing and divisive issues is important to ongoing personal and relational growth.

Emotional estrangement

Reconciling from an emotional estrangement is complicated by the unspoken elements of the relationship. In a physical estrangement, contact is generally a signal that reconciliation is being considered or attempted. In an emotionally estranged relationship, the person who is considering reconciliation can choose to: (i) broach the subject of the emotional distancing and ask the other party to work on improving the relationship, (ii) attempt to mend the relationship through their own conciliatory actions and modelling only, or (iii) attempt to mend the relationship though their own conciliatory actions and modelling up to a point where acknowledgement of the emotional distancing is made and a reconciliation conversation is broached. Regardless of timing, it is recommended that both parties make some acknowledgement of the emotional distancing (including the losses each party has experienced and the contributions each party has made to the estrangement), and some verbal commitment to improve the situation. While some people choose never to acknowledge the past, and the relationship improves regardless, they risk a backlash from unresolved tensions and unacknowledged hurts that can bubble up again in the future. The processes described in this chapter and the previous one can be remarkably useful in attempting emotional as well as physical reconciliation.

Holding out hope

He brought all his clothes and everything . . . and knocked on the door and said, 'Mum can I come and live with you?' And fell into my arms, 'I can't do it anymore.'

(Lois)

Some estranged people find it important to hold onto some hope that the other person might return, even when all avenues of reconciliation appear to have been exhausted, and when they have accepted that the likelihood is miniscule. There is some evidence that adult estrangers are more motivated to attempt reconciliation at times of significant change, when they have received new information that challenges their previous perceptions of the relationship, and during periods of personal growth (Agllias, 2011, 2013a, 2014). This coincides with Darnall and Steinberg's (2008a, 2008b) research with children aged between 4 and 17 years who made spontaneous requests for reunification with alienated parents. Research with older people who were estranged from their adult children found that many held out hope that they would one day be reconciled with their estranged grandchildren and in some cases, grandchildren did initiate contact with grandparents as they became more independent and curious about the absent relative (Agllias, 2011).

So, holding out realistic hope that an estranged relative might reconsider the relationship is not always unreasonable, and particularly if that position can be incorporated into the process of learning to live with estrangement. The afore-mentioned crisis or change periods might provide key opportunities for reconciliation, particularly if both parties are receptive and prepared at that time. However, these contacts are also fraught with risk if one person returns with particular expectations or in order to fulfil an immediate or particular need. Estranged people sometimes return or seek reconciliation when they are in significant need or distress; they might need financial support or harbour a deep desire to provide their new baby with a grandparent (Agllias, 2008, 2011, 2014). If the requirement is unable to be fulfilled at that point in time, and particularly if the relationship falters as a result, the person who has been holding out hope is likely to feel resentful and maybe even used by the returnee. The returnee is likely to feel justified in their initial estrangement decision.

Reconciliation with self

Both are actually left with a lot of dark stuff to wade through. Even if the two parties are not able to come anywhere near each other, it's just too hard, I still think there are ways to begin that healing process on your own.

(Debbie)

In many instances the estranged person or pair cannot change to the degree necessary for reconciliation to occur. The task at this point is to accept the reality of life without the other person or to accept the reality of a different relationship with the other person. While the other person's possible return will always remain ambiguous, self-reconciliation is core to preparing for either eventuality. Reconciliation with self is founded on self-compassion and self-acceptance. This is not about self-esteem, nor is it about deriving value and worth from external actions and input. Reconciliation with self is an intrinsic unconditional acceptance of one's humanity, including the dark and hidden elements.

In its most general sense, *reconciliation* is a term that refers to the restoration of compatible and harmonious relations that have previously been destroyed or halted by a lack of understanding, intolerance and disrespect. It involves a long-term process of reinstating trust, truth, justice and healing through forgiveness and reparation. Estrangement is a process that often damages a person's relationship with self. It has the significant potential to alter one's sense of truth, trust and justice, and it can easily change the capacity to forgive others and the self. *Reconciling with self*, then, involves the provision of care and forgiveness in the same way it would be extended to others in a conciliatory process. It involves a deliberate shift from approval-seeking behaviours and a realignment of, and commitment to, personal values and goals. A contextual investigation of past behaviours is incorporated in a decided effort to understand and pardon transgressions, as well as preventing their recurrence and letting go of unhelpful guilt and blame. It also involves the contextual investigation of the other person's behaviour in order to depersonalise transgression and betrayal. Reconciliation with self involves the nurturance of a generalised appreciation for life and its manifest opportunities, and a commitment to living a good life.

Conclusion

This book has portrayed estrangement as a complex and multifaceted process where individual, interpersonal, intergenerational and historical stressors can maintain secrets, exacerbate tensions, and distort truths to the point where they culminate in actions or perceptions of ultimate betrayal. Estrangement can be one of the most significant and painful interruptions across the life cycle. However, this chapter and the previous one have also illustrated estrangement as a prime site for personal, relational and intergenerational growth (and a number of relevant resources are supplied in the practice point). This book has promoted and encouraged trust in one's own personal experience, history and instincts throughout the estrangement journey. Indeed, this chapter commenced with Shirley's story of self-growth, healing and reconciliation. It seems fitting, then, that her thoughts be used to close this chapter and the book. After discussing the series of events that led to her estrangement from her son, and the decades of estrangement that ensued, I asked Shirley why she had decided to contact her son after such a long period apart. Shirley said:

> I felt – I wanted something off him and then [later] he called me 'mother' and I cried and cried and cried. So I wanted to be acknowledged I think ... and the way he said it, something clicked in me and I thought, God, all this drama and all this pain just to be acknowledged.

PRACTICE POINT 7: RECONCILIATION CHECKLIST AND ADDITIONAL RESOURCES

This Practice Point provides a checklist to consider reconciliation readiness, as well as a number of additional resources for readers who wish to investigate particular topics in more depth.

EXERCISE 1: RECONCILIATION READINESS

A checklist is provided in Table 8.1. Please use it as a guide to assess readiness for reconciliation and as a tool for reflecting upon areas that have changed across time and those that may require further attention.

TABLE 8.1 Reconciliation readiness checklist

1. Honestly reflect on and document the reasons that you want to reconcile at this time. 2. What are my realistic desires for reconciliation? 3. What is the possibility or probability of these desires being realised? 4. What risks might be associated with reconciliation at this time?				
Potential areas of readiness	**Yes**	**No**	**Un-sure**	**Comments/Notes/ Reflections**
Have I considered that I might be rejected by the other person?				
Do I have the strength and resources to work through rejection if it occurs?				
Am I open to being challenged and confronted about things that may be difficult to hear?				
Do I have the strength and resources to work through things that are difficult to hear?				
Am I willing and able to own and apologise for actions that caused pain and offense, without defensiveness and unsolicited explanation?				
Am I willing to ask for forgiveness?				
Am I prepared to clearly voice my core issues and concerns (without revisiting minor hurts and details)?				

TABLE 8.1 Continued

Potential areas of readiness	Yes	No	Un-sure	Comments/Notes/ Reflections
Am I prepared to work through mutual issues and concerns?				
Have I made an effort to prepare and rehearse for this meeting?				
Have I over prepared and over rehearsed for this meeting?				
Do I have the desire or capacity to live with the negative aspects of reconciliation?				
Do I have the capacity to respond to old issues and communication patterns in new ways?				
Am I ready to listen and offer empathic responses?				
Am I ready to be assertive and negotiate new relational roles?				
Am I ready to maintain appropriate boundaries between myself and the other person?				
Am I ready to control and sit with strong emotions?				
Am I able to exit an unsafe situation?				
Have I considered the other person's communicative style and preferences?				
Have I considered that the other person may have changed dramatically?				
Have I considered that the other person may not have changed at all?				

Additional resources

Estrangement self-help

Coleman, J. (2008). *When parents hurt: Compassionate strategies when you and your grown child don't get along.* New York: HarperCollins.

Davis, L. (2002). *I thought we'd never speak again: The road from estrangement to reconciliation.* New York: Quill.

Imber-Black, E. (1998). *The secret life of families: Making decisions about secrets: When secrets can harm you, when keeping secrets can help you – and how to know the difference.* New York: Bantam Books.

LeBey, B. (2001). *Family estrangements: How they begin, how to mend them, how to cope with them.* Atlanta: Longstreet Press.

McGoldrick, M. (1995). *You can go home again: Reconnecting with your family.* New York: W.W. Norton & Company, Inc.

Richards, N. (2008). *Heal and forgive II: The journey from abuse and estrangement to reconciliation.* Nevada City: Blue Dolphin Publishing.

Sichel, M. (2004). *Healing from family rifts: Ten steps to finding peace after being cut off from a family member.* New York: McGraw Hill.

Sucov, E. B. (2006). *Fragmented families: Patterns of estrangement and reconciliation.* Jerusalem: Southern Hills Press.

Forgiveness and reconciliation

Enright, R. (2001). *Forgiveness is a choice.* Washington DC: American Psychological Association.

Hahn, T. N. (2010). *Reconciliation: Healing the inner child.* California: Parallax Press.

Hargrave, T. D. (1994). *Families and forgiveness: Healing wounds in the intergenerational family.* New York: Bunner/Mazel Publishers.

Luskin, F. (2002). *Forgive for good: A proven prescription for health and happiness.* New York: HarperCollins Publishers Inc.

McCullough, M. E. (2008). *Beyond revenge: The evolution of the forgiveness instinct.* San Francisco: Jossey Bass.

Smedes, L. B. (1996). *Forgive and forget: Healing the hurts we don't deserve.* New York: Harper Collins.

Worthington, E. L. (2006). *Forgiveness and reconciliation: Theory and application.* New York: Routledge.

Genograms

McGoldrick, M. (1995). *You can go home again: Reconnecting with your family.* New York: W.W. Norton & Company, Inc.

McGoldrick, M., Gerson, R., & Petri, S. (2008). *Genograms: Assessment and intervention* (3rd ed.). New York: W.W. Norton & Company, Inc.

Grief, loss and trauma recovery

Boss, P. (1999). *Ambiguous loss: Learning to live with unresolved grief.* Cambridge, MA: Harvard University Press.

Boss, P. (2006). *Loss, trauma and resilience: Therapeutic work with ambiguous loss.* New York: W.W. Norton & Company Inc.

Calhoun, L. G., & Tedeschi, R. G. (Eds.). (2006). *Handbook of posttraumatic growth: Research and practice*. New York: Taylor and Francis.

Doka, K. J. (Ed.). (2002). *Disenfranchised grief: New directions, challenges and strategies for practice*. Illinois: Research Press.

Herman, J. L. (1997). *Trauma and recovery: The aftermath of violence – from domestic abuse to political terror*. New York: Basic Books.

Klass, D., Silverman, P. R., & Nickman, S. (Eds.). (1996). *Continuing bonds: New understandings of grief*. New York: Routledge.

Parental alienation

Baker, A. J. L. (2007). *Adult children of parental alienation syndrome: Breaking the ties that bind*. New York: W.W. Norton & Company Inc.

Baker, A. J. L., & Fine, P. R. (2014). *Surviving parental alienation: A journey of hope and healing*. Maryland: Rowman and Littlefield.

Glossary of terms

Absent estrangement: When an estrangement has developed from parental absence in childhood and has continued into, or been re-established in the child's adulthood.

Abuse: Intentional or unintentional behaviours that risk or cause physical or emotional harm, including physical abuse, emotional abuse, sexual abuse, online abuse, exposure to domestic violence and neglect.

Addiction: A physical or psychological dependency on a substance or activity such as alcohol, drugs, sexual activity and gambling.

Alienation: See third party or parental alienation.

Ambiguous loss: A specific type of stressful condition where there is confusion about the absence or presence of another. For example, the person might be physically present but psychologically absent, such as a person with dementia or an emotionally estranged person. Or the person might be physically absent but still psychologically present in the mind of the person experiencing the loss of the other, such as a missing or physically estranged person.

Ambivalence: The experience of conflicted feelings, beliefs or reactions to a person or object, including both positive and negative elements.

Anticipatory grief: A grief reaction that occurs prior to an expected or impending loss.

Attachment: A strong and enduring emotional bond connecting one person to another.

Bowen Family Systems Theory: A theory developed by Dr Murray Bowen suggesting that each family is a complex emotional unit that has evolved across generations. Family members are intricately connected, interdependent and influenced by the emotional system or reactivity of other members.

Compassion: The quality of empathically understanding the circumstances of others.

Complicated grief: When grief reactions are so severe and enduring that they affect the acceptance of the loss and the resumption of normal activities.

Cutoff: A *Bowen Family Systems Theory* term used to describe the reduction or cessation of contact with a family member due to unresolved emotional issues. It is most likely to occur when the parties have a fused (or less differentiated) relationship, resulting in higher levels of emotional reactivity in anxiety-provoking situations.

Cyclical estrangement: When a relationship moves between physical estrangement, emotional estrangement and/or periods of reconciliation across a number of cycles.

Differentiation of self: The ability to discern between feelings and thoughts, manage anxiety and respond with logic instead of emotion in times of anxiety and stress. It also involves the capacity to have and voice thoughts and feelings that are different from others (including family, friends and peers).

Disenfranchised grief/loss: Grief and loss that is not recognised, acknowledged or accepted by society.

Emotional estrangement: When family members have limited, uncomfortable and emotionally absent or strained contact, and exchanges of support are usually perfunctory or obligatory.

Estranged person: A person who has no, or limited, emotional and or physical interactions with one or more family members, regardless of how this developed, and feels dissatisfied with this arrangement.

Estrangee: A person who has been physically or emotionally estranged, disowned, or cut off by a family member or members. An estrangee does not choose the relationship dissolution.

Estranger: A person who chooses to dissolve a family relationship, or emotionally distance themselves from a family member or members. They may declare this position to the other party, stop contact without an announcement or use emotional withdrawal to maintain distance.

Family estrangement: The condition of being physically and/or emotionally distanced from one or more family members, either by choice or at the request or decision of the other. It is generally enacted to reduce implicit or explicit conflict, anxiety or tension between the parties. It is characterised by a lack of trust and emotional intimacy, disparate values and a belief that resolution is highly unlikely, unnecessary or impossible. It involves some level of dissatisfaction by at least one party.

Forgiveness: The process of acknowledging one's hurt at the hands of another, compassionately recognising the other person's humanity and releasing negative feelings towards them.

Fusion: A *Bowen Family System Theory* concept that relates to a lack of differentiation, where a person's intense dependence on other family members is marked by emotional reactivity and responsiveness rather than thought and logic.

Grief: This is the natural and expected response to a *loss* and it can encompasses emotional, physical and psychological dimensions (also see loss).

Hypervigilance: A state of heightened sensory sensitivity where people are constantly tense, on guard and inspecting the environment for threats.

Inherited estrangement: When an estrangement is passed from one generation to the next (usually a child inherits their parent or parents' estrangements).

Intensive parenting: An attitude to parenting including the beliefs that: mothers are essential; parenting is difficult, but fulfilling; and parents' lives should revolve around their children and keeping them stimulated and engaged in activities.

Intergenerational family: The term *intergenerational family* is used to describe an extended family form consisting of two or more generations or demographic cohorts, who may or may not reside together.

Loss: A loss is a negative perception of an event or change of circumstances. Losses include events like: the death of a loved one or pet; the termination of a job or relationship; or a new way of life, way of being or way of feeling. This change often results in a grief response (see Grief).

Meaning-making: In the context of grief, this term refers to the process of making sense of a loss and finding meaning – or even benefits – in the loss.

Mutually disengaged estrangement: Occurs when relationships dissipate over time and shared experiences are minimal or non-existent. While often dissatisfied with the situation, neither party appears to have the desire to continue the relationship.

Parental alienation: Refers to specific behaviours and strategies used by one parent to encourage or manipulate their child to unjustly reject the other (targeted) parent. Behaviours and strategies include portraying the other parent as bad or dangerous, undermining the other parent and limiting communication between the targeted parent and child.

Phenomenological research: Research that primarily examines a person's lived experience of an event or phenomenon and how they perceive, interpret or make meaning of that experience.

Physical estrangement: When physical contact, affection and support is dramatically reduced or ceased between family members.

Reconciliation: The reinstatement of a relationship covering a continuum of relational states from the resumption of contact without acknowledgement of previous conflict or dissatisfaction, to the acknowledgement and resolution of previous issues.

Reconciliation with self: The state of being on good terms with oneself, including self-compassion and acceptance of one's humanity.

Relational evaluation: The extent to which a person perceives that a relational partner values them.

Resilience: The capacity and flexibility to withstand crisis and stress, followed by a return to normal or greater functioning.

Role ambiguity: A lack of clarity about a particular role. When a family member is absent this ambiguity often revolves around the reorganisation of family roles, i.e. whether to fill the role or leave it vacant.

Rumination: The tendency to overly and repetitively focus one's attention on a difficult situation or traumatic experience, including the events that led up to it.

Secondary estrangement: This develops from a primary estrangement, when a third party takes sides with one of the estranged pair, or they may be drawn, or enticed, into an estrangement by one of the parties.

Self-protective estrangements: Estrangements that are enacted by an estranged person who tries to protect their privacy or safety from the other estranged party, by cutting off a third person (who might pass on information).

Self compassion: The quality of empathically understanding and acknowledging one's own humanity, especially in times of perceived inadequacy or failure. Being warm, caring and kind to the self.

Self reconciliation: See Reconciliation with self.

Stigma: When a person or group of people possess an attribute (such as a disfigurement or being estranged) that is discredited and labelled by society, thus setting them apart from others and making them susceptible to discrimination and stereotyping.

Third party alienation: Refers to specific behaviours and strategies used by one person to encourage or manipulate another to unjustly reject a third targeted person.

Trauma: A natural response to a significantly threatening and deeply distressing event that involves a threat to one's physical or psychological integrity, invoking considerable fear and helplessness, which overwhelms a person's capacity to cope with everyday living.

Trigger: An event, vision or thought that reminds a person of a previous difficult or traumatic event, often invoking a range of loss-associated responses.

References

Agllias, K. (2008). *Every family: The experience of family estrangement in later life.* University of Newcastle. Unpublished data.

Agllias, K. (2011). *Every family: Intergenerational estrangement between older parents and their adult children.* (PhD Social Work), University of Newcastle, Newcastle, Australia.

Agllias, K. (2013a). Family estrangement in palliative care. University of Newcastle: Unpublished raw data.

Agllias, K. (2013b). The gendered experience of family estrangement in later life. *Affilia: Journal of Women and Social Work, 28*(3), 309–321.

Agllias, K. (2014). *Report on the adult child's experience of estrangement from at least one parent.* Unpublished report. University of Newcastle.

Agllias, K. (2015a). Difference, choice and punishment: Parental beliefs and understandings about adult child estrangement. *Australian Social Work, 68*(1), 115–129.

Agllias, K. (2015b). Disconnection and decision-making: Adult children explain their reasons for estranging from parents. *Australian Social Work, Online First.* doi: 10.1080/0312407X. 2015.1004355

Allen, P. R. (2003). Depression: A symptom of cutoff in relationship processes. In P. Titelman (Ed.), *Emotional cutoff: Bowen family systems theory perspectives* (pp. 315–336). New York: The Haworth Clinical Practice Press.

Almond, B. (2006). *The fragmenting family.* New York: Oxford University Press.

Amato, P. R. (1999). Paternal involvement and children's behavior problems. *Journal of Marriage and Family, 61*(2), 375–384.

Anda, R. F., Brown, D. W., Dube, S. R., Bremner, J. D., Felitti, V. J., & Giles, W. H. (2008). Adverse childhood experiences and chronic obstructive pulmonary disease in adults. *American Journal of Preventive Medicine, 34*(5), 396–403.

Arshad, A., & Naz, F. (2014). Inter-parental conflict, parental rejection and personality maladjustment in university students. *Journal of Behavioural Sciences, 24*(2), 83–99.

Attar-Schwartza, S., Tanb, P., & Buchananc, A. (2009). Adolescents' perspectives on relationships with grandparents: The contribution of adolescent, grandparent, and parent–grandparent relationship variables. *Children and Youth Services Review, 31*(9), 1057–1066.

Austin, E. L., Lindley, L. L., Mena, L. A., Crosby, R. A., & Muzny, C. A. (2014). Families of choice and noncollegiate sororities and fraternities among lesbian and bisexual African-American women in a southern community: Implications for sexual and reproductive health research. *Sexual Health, 11*, 24–30.

Baker, A. J. L. (2007). *Adult children of parental alienation syndrome: Breaking the ties that bind.* New York: W.W. Norton & Company Inc.

Baker, A. J. L., & Darnall, D. (2006). Behaviours and strategies employed in parental alienation: A survey of parental experiences. *Journal of Divorce and Remarriage, 45*(1/2), 97–123.

197

Baker, A. J. L., & Chambers, J. (2011). Adult recall of childhood exposure to parental conflict: Unpacking the black box of parental alienation. *Journal of Divorce and Remarriage, 52*(1), 55–76.

Baker, A. J. L., & Fine, P. R. (2014). *Surviving parental alienation: A journey of hope and healing.* Lanham, Maryland: Rowman and Littlefield.

Barrera, A. M., Bloomer, L. M. C., & Soenksen, S. H. (2011). Revisiting adolescent separation-individuation in the contexts of enmeshment and allocentrism. *The New School Psychology Bulletin, 8*(2), 70–82.

Bastian, B., Jetten, J., & Ferris, L. J. (2014). Pain as social glue: Shared pain increases cooperation. *Psychological Science, 25*(11), 2079–2085.

Baum, A., & Polsusnzy, D. (1999). Health psychology: Mapping biobehavioral contributions to health and illness. *Annual Review of Psychology, 50*(1), 137–163.

Baumeister, R. F., & Leary, M. R. (1995). The need to belong: Desire for interpersonal attachments as a fundamental human motivation. *Psychological Bulletin, 117*(3), 497–529.

Bayer, J. K., Sanson, A. V., & Hemphill, S. A. (2006). Parent influences on early childhood internalizing difficulties. *Journal of Applied Developmental Psychology, 27*(6), 542–559.

Beaton, J. M., Norris, J. E., & Pratt, M. W. (2003). Unresolved issues in adult children's marital relationships involving intergenerational problems. *Family Relations, 52*(2), 143–153.

Beckwith, L., Cohen, S. E., & Hamilton, C. E. (1999). Maternal sensitivity during infancy and subsequent life events relate to attachment representation at early adulthood. *Developmental Psychology, 35*(3), 693–700.

Bedford, V. H., & Blieszner, R. (1997). Personal relationships in later-life families. In S. Duck (Ed.), *Handbook of personal relationships* (pp. 523–540). Chichester, West Sussex: John Wiley & Sons Ltd.

Beck, A. T., Emery, G., & Greenberg, R. L. (2005). *Anxiety disorders and phobias: A cognitive perspective.* New York: Basic Books.

Bengston, V. L., & Roberts, R. E. L. (1991). Intergenerational solidarity in aging families: An example of formal theory construction. *Journal of Marriage and the Family, 53*(4), 856–870.

Bengston, V. L., & Oyama, P. S. (2007). Intergenerational solidarity: Strengthening economic and social ties. United Nations Headquarters, New York: Department of Economic and Social Affairs Division for Social Policy and Development.

Bergart, A. M. (2003). Group work as an antidote to the isolation of bearing an invisible stigma. *Social Work with Groups, 26*(3), 33–43.

Boothby, E. J., Clark, M. S., & Bargh, J. A. (2014). Shared experiences are amplified. *Psychological Science, 25*(12), 2209–2216.

Boss, P. (1999). *Ambiguous loss: Learning to live with unresolved grief.* Cambridge, MA: Harvard University Press.

Boss, P. (2004). Ambiguous loss. In F. Walsh & M. McGoldrick (Eds.), *Living beyond loss: Death in the family* (pp. 164–175). New York: W.W. Norton & Company Inc.

Boss, P. (2006a). *Loss, trauma and resilience: Therapeutic work with ambiguous loss.* New York: W.W. Norton & Company Inc.

Boss, P. (2006b). Resilience and health. *Grief Matters: The Australian Journal of Grief and Bereavement, 9*(3), 52–57.

Boss, P., & Couden, B. A. (2002). Ambiguous loss from chronic illness: Clinical interventions with individuals, couples, and families. *JCLP/In Session: Psychotherapy in Practice, 58*(11), 1351–1360.

Boss, P., & Yeats, J. R. (2014). Ambiguous loss: A complicated type of grief when loved ones disappear. *Bereavement Care, 32*(2), 63–69.

Bottero, W. (2015). Practising family history: 'Identity' as a category of social practice. *The British Journal of Sociology, 66*(3), 534–556.

Bowen, M. (1982). *Family therapy in clinical practice* (2nd ed.). New York: Jason Aronson.

Bowlby, J. (1979). *The making and breaking of affectional bonds.* London: Tavistock.

Bowman, K. (2000). A daughter estranged from her dying father. *American Family Physician,* 62(11), 2543–2545.

Bowman, S., Alvarez-Jimenez, M., Wade, D., McGorry, P., & Howie, L. (2014). Forgotten family members: The importance of siblings in early psychosis. *Early Intervention in Psychiatry,* 8(1), 269–275.

Bretherton, I. (1995). The origins of attachment theory: John Bowlby and Mary Ainsworth. In S. Goldberg, R. Muir & J. Kerr (Eds.), *Attachment theory: Social, developmental and clinical perspectives* (pp. 45–84). Hillsdale, NJ: The Analytic Press.

Buchanan, F. (2008). Mother and infant attachment theory and domestic violence: Crossing the divide, Stakeholder paper 5. 1–15: Australian Domestic and Family Violence Clearinghouse.

Buckley, T., Sunari, D., Marshall, A., Bartrop, R., McKinley, S., & Tofler, G. (2012). Physiological correlates of bereavement and the impact of bereavement interventions. *Dialogues in clinical neuroscience,* 14(2), 129–139.

Bulduc, J. L., Caron, S. L., & Logue, M. E. (2007). The effects of parental divorce on college students. *Journal of Divorce and Remarriage,* 46(3/4), 83–104.

Burton, M. S., Cooper, A. A., Feeny, N. C., & Zoellner, N. A. (2015). The enhancement of natural resilience in trauma interventions. *Journal of Contemporary Psychotherapy,* 45, 193–204.

Cabrera, N. J., Shannon, J. D., & Tamis-LeMonda, C. (2007). Fathers' influence on their children's cognitive and emotional development: From toddlers to pre-K. *Applied Development Science,* 11(4), 208–213.

Cahall Young, J., & Spatz Widom, C. (2014). Long-term effects of child abuse and neglect on emotion processing in adulthood. *Child Abuse & Neglect,* 38(8), 1369–1381.

Calhoun, L. G., & Tedeschi, R. G. (Eds.). (2006). *Handbook of posttraumatic growth: Research and practice.* New York: Taylor and Francis.

Carr, K., Holman, A., Stephenson-Abetz, J. J., Koenig Kellas, J., & Vagnoni, E. (2015). Giving voice to the silence of family estrangement: Comparing reasons of estranged parents and adult children in a non-matched sample. *Journal of Family Communication,* 15(2), 130–140.

Carranza, L. V., Kilmann, P. R., & Vendemia, J. M. C. (2009). Links between parent characteristics and attachment variables for college students of parental divorce. *Adolesence,* 44(174), 253–271.

Cartwright, C., Farnsworth, V., & Mobley, V. (2009). Relationships with step-parents in the life stories of young adults of divorce. *Australian Institute of Family Studies,* No 82, 30–37.

Charles-Edwards, D. (2007). Neimeyer and the construction of loss. *Therapy Today,* 18(5), 15–17.

Cisler, J. M., & Koster, E. H. W. (2010). Mechanisms of attentional biases towards threat in anxiety disorders: An integrative review. *Clinical Psychology Review,* 30(2), 203–216.

Cohen, S. (2004). The Pittsburgh common cold studies: Psychosocial predictors of susceptibility to respiratory infectious illness. *International Journal of Behavioral Medicine,* 12(3), 123–131.

Coleman, J. (2008). *When parents hurt: Compassionate strategies when you and your grown child don't get along.* New York: HarperCollins.

Comijs, H. C., Jonker, C., van Tilburg, W., & Smit, J. H. (1999). Hostility and coping capacity as risk factors of elder mistreatment. *Social Psychiatry and Psychiatric Epidemiology,* 34(1), 48–52.

Compas, B. E., Banez, G. A., Malcarne, V., & Worsham, N. (1991). Perceived control and coping with stress: A developmental perspective. *Journal of Social Issues,* 47(4), 23–34.

Connidis, I. A. (2010). *Family ties and aging* (2nd ed.). Thousand Oaks, CA: SAGE Publications Inc.

Connidis, I. A., & Campbell, L. D. (1995). Closeness, confiding, and contact among siblings in middle and late adulthood. *Journal of Family Issues, 16*(6), 722–745.

Connidis, I. A., & Walker, A. J. (2009). (Re)visioning gender, age, and aging in families. In S. A. Lloyd, A. L. Few & K. R. Allen (Eds.), *Handbook of feminist family studies* (pp. 147–159). Los Angeles: Sage.

Corr, C. A. (2002). Revisiting the concept of disenfranchised grief. In K. J. Doka (Ed.), *Disenfranchised Grief: New directions, challenges, and strategies for practice* (pp. 39–60). Champaign, IL: Research Press.

Corrigan, P. W., Watson, A. C., & Miller, F. E. (2006). Blame, shame, and contamination: The impact of mental illness and drug dependence stigma on family members. *Journal of Family Psychology, 20*(2), 239–246.

COTA (NSW). (2010). *Listening to grandparents.* Sydney: NSW Ministerial Advisory Committee on Ageing.

Culpin, I., Heron, J., Araya, R., Melotti, R., & Joinson, C. (2013). Father absence and depressive symptoms in adolescence: Findings from a UK cohort. *Psychological Medicine, 43*(12), 2615–2626.

Culpin, I., Heron, J., Araya, R., & Joinson, C. (2015). Early childhood father absence and depressive symptoms in adolescent girls from a UK cohort: The mediating role of early menarche. *Journal of Abnormal Child Psychology, 43*(5), 921–931.

Cummings, E. M., Goeke-Morey, M. C., Papp, L. M., & Dukewich, T. L. (2002). Children's responses to mothers' and fathers' emotionality and tactics in marital conflcit in the home. *Journal of Family Psychology, 16*(4), 478–492.

Daniels, J. A. (1990). Adolescent separation-individuation and family transitions. *Adolescence, 25*(97), 105–116.

Darnall, D., & Steinberg, B. F. (2008a). Motivational models for spontaneous reunification with the alienated child: Part I. *The American Journal of Family Therapy, 36,* 107–116.

Darnall, D., & Steinberg, B. F. (2008b). Motivational models for spontaneous reunification with the alienated child: Part II. *The American Journal of Family Therapy, 36,* 253–261.

Dattilo, F. M., & Nichols, M. P. (2011). Reuniting estranged family members: A cognitive-behavioral-systemic perspective. *The American Journal of Family Therapy, 39,* 88–99.

Davis, L. (2002). *I thought we'd never speak again: The road from estrangement to reconciliation.* New York: Quill.

Doka, K. J. (Ed.). (2002). *Disenfranchised grief: New directions, challenges and strategies for practice.* Champaign, IL: Research Press.

Doka, K. J., & Martin, T. (1998). Masculine responses to loss: Clinical implications. *Journal of Family Studies, 4*(2), 143–158.

Doka, K. J., & Aber, R. A. (2002). Psychosocial loss and grief. In K. J. Doka (Ed.), *Disenfranchised grief: New directions, challenges, and strategies for practice* (pp. 217–231). Champaign, IL: Research Press.

Downey, D. B., & Condron, D. J. (2004). Playing well with others in kindergarten: The benefit of siblings at home. *Journal of Marriage and Family, 66*(2), 333–350.

Downey, D. B., Condron, D. J., & Yucel, D. (2015). Number of siblings and social skills revisited among American fifth graders. *Journal of Family Issues, 36*(2), 273–296.

Downey, G., & Feldman, S. I. (1996). Implications of rejection sensitivity for intimate relationships. *Journal of Personality and Social Psychology, 70*(6), 1327–1343.

Downey, G., Mougios, V., Ayduk, O., London, B., & Shoda, Y. (2004). Rejection sensitivity and the defensive motivational system. Insights from the startle response to rejection cues. *Psychological Science, 15*(10), 668–673.

Drew, L. M., & Silverstein, M. (2007). Grandparents' psychological well-being after loss of contact with their grandchildren. *Journal of Family Psychology, 21*(3), 372–379.

Duck, S. (1982). A topography of relationship disengagement and dissolution. In S. Duck (Ed.), *Personal relationships. 4: Dissolving personal relationships* (pp. 1–30). London: Academic Press.

Dykstra, P. A., & Fokkema, T. (2011). Relationships between parents and their adult children: A West European typology of late-life families. *Ageing and Society*, 31(4), 545–569.

Ehrenberg, M. F., & Smith, T. L. (2003). Grandmother–grandchild contacts before and after an adult daughter's divorce. *Journal of Divorce & Remarriage*, 39(1), 27–43.

Eichholz, A. (2003). Managing cutoff through family research. In P. Titelman (Ed.), *Emotional cutoff: Bowen family systems theory perspectives*. New York: The Haworth Clinical Practice Press.

El-Shiekh, M., & Erath, M. A. (2011). Family conflict, autonomic nervous system functioning, and child adaptation: State of the science and future directions. *Development and Psychopathology*, 23(2), 703–721.

Enright, R. (2001). *Forgiveness is a choice*. Washington, DC: American Psychological Association.

The Fathering Project. (2013). How fathers and father figures can shape child health and wellbeing. Retrieved May 15, 2015, from http://thefatheringproject.org/wp-content/uploads/2013/08/How-fathers-and-father-figures-can-shape-child-health-and-wellbeing-Wood-Lambin-UWA-2013.pdf.

Feldman, R. S., Forrest, J. A., & Happ, B. R. (2002). Self-presentation and verbal deception: Do self-presenters lie more? *Basic and Applied Social Psychology*, 24(2), 163–170.

Field, N. (2006). Unresolved grief and continuing bonds: An attachment perspective. *Death Studies*, 30(8), 739–756.

Fingerman, K. L., Hay, E. L., & Birditt, K. S. (2004). The best of ties, the worst of ties: Close, problematic and ambivalent social relationships. *Journal of Marriage and Family*, 66(3), 792–808.

Fingerman, K. L., Chen, P., Hay, E., Cichy, K. E., & Lefkowitz, E. S. (2006). Ambivalent reactions in the parent and offspring relationship. *The Journals of Gerontology: Series B* 61B(3), 152–161.

Fingerman, K. L., Pitzer, L., Lefkowitz, E. S., Birditt, K. S., & Mroczek, D. (2008). Ambivalent relationship qualities between adults and their parents: Implications for well-being of both parties. *The Journals of Gerontology: Series B*, 63(6), 362–371.

Fingerman, K. L., Kim, K., Davis, E. M., Furstenberg, F. F., Birditt, K. S., & Zarit, S. H. (2015). 'I'll give you the world': Socioeconomic differences in parental support of adult children. *Journal of Marriage and Family*, 77(4), 844–865.

Fiori, K. L., Consedine, N. S., & Magal, C. (2009). Late life attachment in context: Patterns of relating among men and women from seven ethnic groups. *Journal of Cross Cultural Gerontology*, 24(2), 121–141.

Fivush, R., Duke, M., & Bohanek, J. G. (2010). 'Do you know . . .' The power of family history in adolescent identity and well-being. Retrieved September 3, 2015, from http://publichistorycommons.org/wp-content/uploads/2013/12/The-power-of-family-history-in-adolescent-identity.pdf.

Floyd, K., Mikkelson, A. C., & Judd, J. (2006). Defining the family through relationships. In L. H. Turner & R. West (Eds.), *The family communication sourcebook* (pp. 21–39). Thousand Oaks, CA: Sage Publications, Inc.

Fook, J. (2003). *Social work: Critical theory and practice*. London: Sage.

Ford, M. B., & Collins, N. L. (2013). Self-esteem moderates the effects of daily rejection on health and well-being. *Self and Identity*, 12(1), 16–38.

Formoso, D., Gonzales, N. A., & Aiken, L. S. (2000). Family conflict and children's internalizing and externalizing behavior: Protective factors. *American Journal of Community Psychology*, 28(2), 175–199.

Fraley, R. C., & Brumbaugh, C. C. (2007). Adult attachment and preemptive defenses: Converging evidence on the role of defensive exclusion at the level of encoding. *Journal of Personality, 75*(5), 1033–1050.

Framo, J. (1976). Family of origin as a therapeutic resource for adults in marital and family therapy: You can and should go home again. *Family Process, 15*(2), 193–210.

Friesen, P. J. (2003). Emotional cutoff and the brain. In P. Titelman (Ed.), *Emotional cutoff: Bowen family systems theory perspectives* (pp. 83–107). New York: The Haworth Clinical Practice Press.

Gabriel, Z., & Bowling, A. (2004). Quality of life from the perspectives of older people. *Ageing and Society, 24*(5), 675–691.

Galvin, K. M., Bylund, C. L., & Brommel, B. J. (2008). *Family communication: Cohesion and change* (7th ed.). Boston: Pearson Education Inc.

Gardner, R. A. (2001). Denial of the parental alienation syndrome also harms women. *The American Journal of Family Therapy, 30*(3), 191–202.

Gilbert, R. M. (2003). Bridging cutoff with divorced relationships and with family. In P. Titelman (Ed.), *Emotional cutoff: Bowen family systems theory perspectives*. New York: The Haworth Clinical Practice Press.

Glaeser, M. (2008). What does it take to let go? An investigation into the facilitating and obstructing factors of forgiveness – the therapist's perspective. *Counselling Psychology Quarterly, 21*(4), 337–348.

Goffman, E. (1963). *Stigma: Notes on the management of spoiled identity*. Englewood Cliffs, NJ: Prentice-Hall.

Goodfellow, J. (2010). *Grandparents and family separation: Literature review*. The University of Newcastle: Interrelate Family Centres & The Family Action Centre.

Goodwin, R. D., & Styron, T. H. (2012). Perceived quality of early paternal relationships and mental health in adulthood. *The Journal of Nervous and Mental Disease, 200*(9), 791–795.

Gordon, T. A. (2013). Good grief: Exploring the dimensionality of grief experiences and social work support. *Journal of Social Work in End-Of-Life & Palliative Care, 9*(1), 27–42.

Green, S. E. (2001). Grandma's hands: Parental perceptions of the importance of grandparents as secondary caregivers in families of children with disabilities. *International Journal of Aging and Human Development, 53*(1), 11–33.

Gu, J., Strauss, C., Bond, R., & Cavanagh, K. (2015). How do mindfulness-based cognitive therapy and mindfulness-based stress reduction improve mental health and wellbeing? A systematic review and meta-analysis of mediation studies. *Clinical Psychology Review, 37*, 1–12.

Gupta, N., & Kumar, S. (2015). Significant predictors for resilience among a sample of undergraduate students: Acceptance, forgiveness and gratitude. *Indian Journal of Health and Wellbeing, 6*(2), 188–191.

Ha, J., & Ingersoll-Dayton, B. (2008). The effect of widowhood on intergenerational ambivalence. *The Journals of Gerontology: Series B, 63*(1), 49–58.

Hagestad, G. O. (2006). Transfers between grandparents and grandchildren: The importance of taking a three-generation perspective. *Zeitschrift für Familienforschung, 18*(3), 315–332.

Hahn, T. N. (2010). *Reconciliation: Healing the inner child*. Berkeley, CA: Parallax Press.

Hanke, K., & Fischer, R. (2013). Socioeconomical and sociopolitical correlates of interpersonal forgiveness: A three-level meta-analysis of the Enright Forgiveness Inventory across 13 societies. *International Journal of Psychology, 48*(4), 514–526.

Hansson, R. O., & Stroebe, M. S. (2007). *Bereavement in later life: Coping, adaption, and developmental influences*. Washington, DC: American Psychological Association.

Hargrave, T. D. (1994). *Families and forgiveness: Healing wounds in the intergenerational family*. New York: Bunner/Mazel Publishers.

Hargrave, T. D., & Anderson, W. T. (1992). *Finishing well: Aging and reparation in the intergenerational family*. New York: Brunner/Mazel Inc.

Hargrave, T. D., & Anderson, W. T. (1997). Finishing well: A contextual family therapy approach to the aging family. In T. D. Hargrave & S. M. Hanna (Eds.), *The aging family: New visions in theory, practice, and reality* (pp. 61–80). New York: Brunner/Mazel.

Harris, D. (2009–2010). Oppression of the bereaved: A critical analysis of grief in Western society. *OMEGA, 60*(3), 241–253.

Harrison, V. (2003). Reproduction and emotional cutoff. In P. Titelman (Ed.), *Emotional cutoff: Bowen family systems theory perspectives* (pp. 245–269). New York: The Haworth Clinical Practice Press.

Harvey, J. H., Weber, A. L., Yarkin, K. L., & Stewart, B. E. (1982). An attributional approach to relationship breakdown and dissolution. In S. Duck (Ed.), *Personal relationships. 4: Dissolving personal relationships* (pp. 107–126). London: Academic Press.

Haslam, D. M., Pakenham, K. I., & Smith, A. (2006). Social support and postpartum depressive symptomatology: The mediating role of maternal self-efficacy. *Infant Mental Health Journal, 27*(3), 276–291.

Henderson, C. E., Hayslip, B., Sanders, L. M., & Loudon, L. (2009). Grandmother grandchild relationship quality predicts psychological adjustment among youth from divorced families. *Journal of Family Issues, 30*(9), 1245–1264.

Herman, J. L. (1997). *Trauma and recovery: The aftermath of violence – from domestic abuse to political terror*. New York: Basic Books.

Hill, R. (1947). *Families under stress: Adjustment to the crises of war separation and reunion*. New York: Harper.

Hill, R. (1957). Social stresses on the family: Generic features of families under stress. *Social Casework, 39*(2–3), 139–150.

Hodapp, R. M., Urbano, R. C., & Burke, M. M. (2010). Adult female and male siblings of persons with disabilities: Findings from a national survey. *Intellectual and Developmental Disabilities, 48*(1), 52–62.

Hoerning, E. M. (1985). Upward mobility and family estrangement among females: What happens when the 'same old girl' becomes the 'new professional women?'. *International Journal of Oral History, 6*(2), 104–117.

Holman, T. B., & Busby, D. M. (2011). Family-of-origin, differentiation of self and partner, and adult romantic relationship quality. *Journal of Couple & Relationship Therapy, 10*(1), 3–19.

Holt-Lunstad, J., Uchino, B. N., Smith, T. W., & Hicks, A. (2007). On the importance of relationship quality: The impact of ambivalence in friendships on cardiovascular functioning. *Annals of Behavioural Medicine, 33*(3), 278–290.

Horowitz, A. (1985). Sons and daughters as caregivers to older parents: Differences in role performance and consequences. *The Gerontologist, 25*(6), 612–617.

Howell, J. C., & Egley, A. (2005). Moving risk factors into developmental theories of gang membership. *Youth Violence and Juvenile Justice, 3*(4), 334–354.

Imber-Black, E. (1998). *The secret life of families: Making decisions about secrets: When secrets can harm you, when keeping secrets can help you – and how to know the difference*. New York: Bantam Books.

Ingersoll-Dayton, B., Dunkle, R. E., Chadiha, L., Lawrence-Jacobson, A., Li, L., Weir, E., & Satorius, J. (2011). Intergenerational ambivalence: Aging mothers whose adult daughters are mentally ill. *Families in Society, 92*(1), 114–119.

IpsosMORI. (2014). Family estrangement survey for Stand Alone. Retrieved October 28, 2014, from https://www.ipsos-mori.com/researchpublications/researcharchive/3456/Family-estrangement-survey-for-Stand-Alone.aspx

Itzhaky, H., & Kissil, K. (2015). It's a horrible sin. If they find out, I will not be able to stay: Orthodox Jewish gay men's experiences living in secrecy. *Journal of Homosexuality*, *62*(5), 621–643.

Jerrome, D. (1994). Family estrangement: Parents and children who 'lose touch'. *The Association for Family Therapy*, *16*(3), 241–258.

Johnson, M. P. (1982). Social and cognitive features of the dissolution of commitment to relationships. In S. Duck (Ed.), *Personal relationships. 4: Dissolving personal relationships* (pp. 51–74). London: Academic Press.

Johnson, W. F. (2013). Deceiving others after being deceived: Lying as a function of descriptive norms. *Psychology Honors Project, Paper 30*.

Juvonen, J., & Gross, E. F. (2005). The rejected and the bullied. In K. D. Williams, J. P. Forgas & W. Von Hippel (Eds.), *The social outcast: Ostracism, social exclusion, rejection and bullying*. New York: Psychology Press.

Kabat, R. (1998). The conjoint session as a tool for the resolution of separation-individuation in the adult mother–daughter relationship. *Clinical Social Work Journal*, *26*(1), 73–88.

Kaufman, G., & Uhlenberg, P. (1998). Effects of life course transitions on the quality of relationships between adult children and their parents. *Journal of Marriage and the Family*, *60*(4), 924–938.

Kelly, B. J. (2003). Toward undoing cutoff: A twenty-five-year perspective. In P. Titelman (Ed.), *Emotional cutoff: Bowen family systems theory perspectives*. New York: The Haworth Clinical Practice Press.

Kenyon, G. M., & Randall, W. L. (1997). *Restorying our lives: Personal growth through autobiographical reflection*. Westport, CT: Praeger.

Khaleque, A., & Rohner, R. P. (2002). Perceived parental acceptance-rejection and psychological adjustment: A meta-analysis of cross cultural and intracultural studies. *Journal of Marriage and Family*, *64*(1), 54–64.

Klass, D., Silverman, P. R., & Nickman, S. (Eds.). (1996). *Continuing bonds: New understandings of grief*. New York: Routledge.

Klever, P. (2003). Marital functioning and multigenerational fusion and cutoff. In P. Titelman (Ed.), *Emotional cutoff: Bowen family systems theory perspectives* (pp. 219–242). New York: The Haworth Clinical Practice Press.

Koken, J. A., Bimbi, D. S., & Parsons, J. T. (2009). Experiences of familial acceptance-rejection among transwomen of colour. *Journal of Family Psychology*, *23*(6), 853–860.

Kowal, A. K., Krull, J. L., & Kramer, L. (2004). How the differential treatment of siblings is linked with parent–child relationship quality. *Journal of Family Psychology*, *18*(4), 658–665.

Krause, N., & Rook, K. S. (2003). Negative interaction in late life: Issues in the stability and generalizability of conflict across relationships. *Journal of Gerontology*, *58B*(2), 88–99.

Kruk, E. (1995). Grandparent–grandchild contact loss: Findings from a study of 'grandparents rights' members. *Canadian Journal of Aging*, *14*(3), 737–754.

Kurdek, L. A., & Berg, B. (1987). Children's beliefs about parental divorce scale: Psychometric characteristics and concurrent validity. *Journal of Consulting and Clinical Psychology*, *55*(5), 712–718.

Lau, G., Moulds, M. L., & Richardson, R. (2009). Ostracism: How much it hurts depends on how you remember it. *Emotion*, *9*(3), 430–434.

Lawler, K. A., Younger, J. W., Piferi, R. L., Jobe, R. L., Edmondson, K. A., & Jones, W. H. (2005). The unique effects of forgiveness on health: An exploration of pathways. *Journal of Behavioural Medicine*, *28*(2), 157–167.

Leary, M. R. (2005). Varieties of interpersonal rejection. In K. D. Williams, J. P. Forgas & W. Von Hippel (Eds.), *The social outcast: Ostracism, social exclusion, rejection and bullying* (pp. 35–52). New York: Psychology Press.

Leary, M. R., Springer, C., Negel, L., Ansell, E., & Evans, K. (1998). The causes, phenomenology, and consequences of hurt feelings. *Journal of Personality and Social Psychology*, 74(5), 1225–1237.

Leary, M. R., Koch, E. J., & Hechenbleikner, N. R. (2001). Emotional responses to interpersonal rejection. In M. R. Leary (Ed.), *Interpersonal rejection* (pp. 145–166). Oxford: Oxford University Press.

LeBey, B. (2001). *Family estrangements: How they begin, how to mend them, how to cope with them*. Atlanta: Longstreet Press.

Lichtenfeld, S., Buechner, V. L., Maier, M. A., & Fernández-Capo, M. (2015). Forgive and forget: Differences between decisional and emotional forgiveness. *PLoS ONE*, 10(5), 1–11.

Lieberman, S. (1998). History-containing systems. *Journal of Family Therapy*, 20(2), 195–206.

Link, B. G., & Phelan, J. C. (2001). Conceptualizing stigma. *Annual Review of Sociology*, 27(1), 363–385.

Lobb, E. A., Kristjanson, L. J., Aoun, S. M., Monterosso, L., Halkett, G. K. B., & Davies, A. (2010). Predictors of complicated grief: A systematic review of empirical studies. *Death Studies*, 34(8), 673–698.

Lowenstein, A. (2007). *Intergenerational solidarity: Strengthening economic and social ties*. New York: Retrieved from www.un.org/esa/socdev/unyin/documents/egm_unhq_oct07_lowenstein.pdf.

Luecken, L. J., Kraft, A., & Hagan, M. J. (2009). Negative relationships in the family-of-origin predict attenuated cortisol in emerging adults. *Hormones and Behavior*, 55(3), 412–417.

Luo, J., Wang, L. G., & Gao, W. B. (2012). The influence of the absence of fathers and the timing of separation on anxiety and self-esteem of adolescents: A cross-sectional survey. *Child Care, Health and Development*, 38(5), 723–731.

Luskin, F. (2002). *Forgive for good: A proven prescription for health and happiness*. New York: HarperCollins Publishers Inc.

McCullough, M. E. (2008). *Beyond revenge: The evolution of the forgiveness instinct*. San Francisco: Jossey Bass.

MacDonald, G., Kingsbury, R., & Shaw, S. (2005). Adding insult to injury: Social pain theory and response to social exclusion. In K. D. Williams, J. P. Forgas & W. Von Hippel (Eds.), *The social outcast: Ostracism, social exclusion, rejection and bullying* (pp. 77–90). New York: Psychology Press.

McEwen, B. S. (2007). Physiology and neurobiology of stress and adaptation: Central role of the brain. *Physiological Reviews*, 87(3), 873–904.

McEwen, B. S., & Wingfield, J. C. (2003). The concept of allostasis in biology and biomedicine. *Hormones and Behavior*, 42(1), 2–15.

McGoldrick, M. (1995). *You can go home again: Reconnecting with your family*. New York: W.W. Norton & Company, Inc.

McGoldrick, M., Gerson, R., & Petri, S. (2008). *Genograms: Assessment and intervention* (3rd ed.). New York: W.W. Norton & Company, Inc.

McLanahan, S., Tach, L., & Schneider, D. (2013). The causal effects of father absence. *The Annual Review of Sociology*, 39, 399–427.

Major, B., & Eccleston, C. P. (2005). Stigma and social exclusion. In D. Abrams, M. A. Hogg & J. M. Marques (Eds.), *The social psychology of inclusions and exclusion* (pp. 63–87). New York: Psychology Press.

Malcolm, W. M., & Greenburg, L. S. (2000). Forgiveness as a process of change in individual psychotherapy. In M. E. McCullough, K. I. Pargament & C. E. Thoresen (Eds.), *Forgiveness: Theory, research, and practice* (pp. 179–202). New York: Guillford Press.

Martin, T. L., & Doka, K. J. (2000). *Men don't cry … women do: Transcending gender stereotypes of grief*. Philadelphia, PA: Brunner/Mazel.

Maslow, A. (1970). *Motivation and personality* (2nd ed.). New York: Harper and Row.

Mead, M. (1970). *Culture and commitment: A study of the generation gap*. Garden City, NJ: National History Press.

Meier, J. S. (2009). A historical perspective on parental alienation syndrome and parental alienation. *Journal of Child Custody*, 6(3/4), 232–257.

Miller, C. T., & Kaiser, C. R. (2001). Implications of mental models of self and others for the targets of stigmatization. In M. R. Leary (Ed.), *Interpersonal rejection* (pp. 189–212). Oxford: Oxford University Press.

Miller, G. R., & Parks, M. R. (1982). Communication in dissolving relationships. In S. Duck (Ed.), *Personal relationships. 4: Dissolving personal relationships* London: Academic Press.

Minuchin, S. (1974). *Families and family therapy*. London: Tavistock.

Mistry, R., Stevens, G. D., Sareen, H., De Vogli, R., & Halfon, N. (2007). Parenting-related stressors and self-reported mental health of mothers with young children. *American Journal of Public Health*, 97(7), 1261–1268.

Mitchell, W. (2007). Research review: The role of grandparents in intergenerational support for families with disabled children: A review of the literature. *Child & Family Social Work*, 12(1), 94–101.

Morgan, Z., Brugha, T., Stewart-Brown, S., & Fryers, T. (2012). The effects of parent–child relationships on later life mental health status in two national birth cohorts. *Social Psychiatry and Psychiatry Epidemiology*, 47(11), 1707–1715.

Murphy, D. C. (2003). Emotional cutoff and domestic violence. In P. Titelman (Ed.), *Emotional cutoff: Bowen family systems theory perspectives* (pp. 337–350). New York: The Haworth Clinical Practice Press.

National Union of Students. (2008). Evaluating estrangement: A report into the estrangement application process in higher education student finance. Retrieved February 12, 2015, from www.nus.org.uk/PageFiles/12238/Estrangement_report_web.pdf.

Neff, K. D., & Vonk, R. (2009). Self-compassion versus global self-esteem: Two different ways of relating to oneself. *Journal of Personality*, 77(1), 23–50.

Neimeyer, R. A. (2006). Making meaning in the midst of loss. *Grief Matters: The Australian Journal of Grief and Bereavement*, 9(3), 62–65.

Neimeyer, R. A., & Currier, J. M. (2008). Bereavement interventions: Present status and future horizons. *Grief Matters: The Australian Journal of Grief and Bereavement*, 11(1), 18–22.

Neimeyer, R. A., & Currier, J. M. (2009). Grief therapy: Evidence of efficacy and emerging directions. *Current Directions in Psychological Science*, 18(6), 352–356.

Netedu, A., & Chimilevschi, A. (2012). Migration and intergenerational relationships. *Scientific Annals of the 'Al. I. Cuza' University*, 5(1), 208–218.

Newsom, J. T., Nishishiba, M., Morgan, D. L., & Rook, K. S. (2003). The relative importance of three domains of positive and negative social exchanges: A longitudinal model with comparable measures. *Psychology and Aging*, 18(4), 746–754.

Newsom, J. T., Mahan, T., Rook, K. S., & Krause, N. (2008). Stable negative social exchanges and health. *Health Psychology*, 27(1), 78–86.

Neyer, F. J., & Lang, F. R. (2003). Blood is thicker than water: Kinship orientation across adulthood. *Journal of Personality and Social Psychology*, 84(2), 310–321.

O'Grady, M. A., & Meinecke, L. (2015). Silence: Because what's missing is too absent to ignore. *Journal of Societal and Cultural Research*, 1(1), 1–25.

Ouwerkerk, J. W., Kerr, N. L., Gallucci, M., & Van Lange, P. A. M. (2005). Avoiding the death penalty: Osctracism and cooperation in social dilemmas. In K. D. Williams, J. P. Forgas & W. Von Hippel (Eds.), *The social outcast: Ostracism, social exclusion, rejection and bullying* (pp. 321–332). New York: Psychology Press.

Oxford Dictionaries. (2015). Ambivalence. Retrieved September 11, 2015, from www.oxforddictionaries.com/definition/english/ambivalence.

Oxford Dictionaries. (2014). Estrange. Retrieved October 21, 2014, from www.oxford dictionaries.com/definition/english/estrange.

Pachankis, J. E., Goldfried, M. R., & Ramrattan, M. (2008). Extension of the rejections sensitivity construct to the interpersonal functioning of gay men. *Journal of Consulting and Clinical Psychology*, 76(2), 306–317.

Padilla-Walker, L. M., & Nelson, L. J. (2012). Black hawk down? Establishing helicopter parenting as a distinct construct from other forms of parental control during emerging adulthood. *Journal of Adolescence*, 35(5), 1177–1190.

Palo Stoller, E. (1983). Parental caregiving by adult children. *Journal of Marriage and Family*, 45(4), 851–858.

Park, S., & Park, K. S. (2014). Family stigma: A concept analysis. *Asian Nursing Research*, 8(3), 165–171.

Parkes, C. M. (2001). A historical overview of the scientific study of bereavement. In M. S. Stroebe (Ed.), *Handbook of bereavement research: Consequences, coping and care*. Washington, DC: American Psychological Society.

Peisah, C., Brodaty, H., & Quadrio, C. (2006). Family conflict in dementia: Prodigal sons and black sheep. *International Journal of Geriatric Psychiatry*, 21(5), 485–492.

Perlick, D. A., Nelson, A. H., Mattias, K., Selzer, J., Kalvin, C., Wilber, C. H., Huntington, B., Holman, C. S., & Corrigan, P. W. (2011). In our own voice-family companion: Reducing self-stigma of family members of persons with serious mental illness. *Psychiatric Services*, 62(12), 1456–1462.

Peters, C. L., Hooker, K., & Zvonkovic, A. M. (2006). Older parents' perceptions of ambivalence in relationships with their children. *Family Relations*, 55(5), 539–551.

Pillemer, K., & Suitor, J. J. (2002). Explaining mothers' ambivalence toward their adult children. *Journal of Marriage and Family*, 64(3), 602–613.

Pillemer, K., & Luscher, K. (Eds.). (2004). *Intergenerational ambivalences: New perspectives on parent–child relations in later life*. Amsterdam: Elsevier.

Pillemer, K., Suitor, J. J., Mock, S. E., Sabir, M., Pardo, T. B., & Sechrist, J. (2007). Capturing the complexity of intergenerational relations: Exploring ambivalence within later life families. *Journal of Social Issues*, 63(4), 775–791.

Pompili, M., Mancinelli, I., Girardi, P., & Tatarelli, R. (2004). Making sense of the nurses' role in the prevention of suicide in schizophrenia. *Issues in Mental Health Nursing*, 25, 5–7.

Price Tangney, J., Stuewig, J., & Mashek, D. J. (2007). Moral emotions and moral behavior. *Annual Review of Psychology*, 58, 345–372.

Quirk, S. W., Wier, D., Martin, S. M., & Christian, A. (2015). The influence of parental rejection on the development of maladaptive schemas, rumination, and motivations for self-injury. *Journal of Psychopathology and Behavioral Assessment*, 37(2), 283–295.

Ragins, B. R. (2008). Disclosure disconnects: Antecedents and consequences of disclosing invisible stigmas across life domains. *Academy of Management Review*, 33(1), 194–215.

Rando, T. A. (1986). *Loss and anticipatory grief*. Lexington, MA: Lexington Books.

Reeb, B. T., & Conger, K. J. (2011). Mental health service utilization in a community sample of rural adolescents: The role of father–offspring relations. *Journal of Pediatric Psychology*, 36(6), 661–668.

Remennick, L. (2000). Childless in the land of imperative motherhood: Stigma and coping among infertile Israeli women. *Sex Roles*, 43(11/12), 821–842.

Rennie Negron, R., Martin, A., Almog, M., Balbierz, A., & Howell, E. A. (2013). Social support during the postpartum period: Mothers' views on needs, expectations, and mobilization of support. *Maternal Health Journal*, 17(4), 616–623.

Reynolds, L., & Botha, D. (2006). Anticipatory grief: Its nature, impact, and reasons for contradictory findings. *Counselling, Psychotherapy, and Health*, 2(2), 15–26.

Richards, N. (2008). *Heal and forgive II: The journey from abuse and estrangement to reconciliation*. Nevada City, CA: Blue Dolphin Publishing.

Rigazio-DiGilio, S. A., & Rohner, R. P. (2015). Interpersonal acceptance-rejection theory and clinical applications. In E. Kourkoutas, A. Hart & A. Mouzaki (Eds.), *Innovative practices and interventions for children and adolescents with psychosocial difficulties and disorders* (pp. 476–515). Newcastle Upon Tyne, UK: Cambridge Scholars Publications.

Rizzo, K. M., Schiffrin, H. H., & Liss, M. (2013). Insight into the parenthood paradox: Mental health outcomes of intensive mothering. *Journal of Child and Family Studies*, 22(5), 614–620.

Robinson, E., Power, L., & Allan, D. (2011). What works with adolescents? Family connections and involvement in interventions for adolescent problem behaviours. *Family Matters*, 88, 57–64.

Robinson, J. L. (2011). *'Everything in motion, motion in everything': The experience and process of negotiating developmental transitions*. (Doctor of Psychology), City University, London, Unpublished.

Rolland, J. S. (1990). Anticipatory loss: A family systems developmental framework. *Family Process*, 29(3), 229–244.

Roloff, M. E., & Waite Miller, C. (2006). Mulling about family conflict and communication: What we know and what we need to know. In L. H. Turner & R. West (Eds.), *The family communication sourcebook* (pp. 143–164). Thousand Oaks, CA: Sage.

Rook, K. S., Luong, G., Sorkin, D. H., Newsom, J. T., & Krause, N. (2012). Ambivalent versus problematic social ties: Implications for psychological health, functional health, and interpersonal coping. *Psychology and Aging*, 27(4), 912–923.

Ruiz, S. A., & Silverstein, M. (2007). Relationships with grandparents and the emotional well-being of late adolescent and young adult grandchildren. *Journal of Social Issues*, 63(4), 793–808.

Russell, A., Bergeman, C. S., & Scott, S. B. (2012). Daily social exchanges and affect in middle and later adulthood: The impact of loneliness and age. *International Journal of Aging & Human Development*, 74(4), 299–239.

Sarkadi, A., Kristiansson, R., Oberklaid, F., & Bremberg, S. (2008). Fathers' involvement and children's developmental outcomes: A systematic review of longitudinal studies. *Acta Pædiatrica*, 97(2), 153–158.

Scharp, K. M. (2014). *(De)constructing family: Exploring communicative practices in accomplishing and maintaining estrangement between adult children and their parents*. (PhD Communication Studies), The University of Iowa, Iowa City, IA.

Scharp, K. M., Paxman, C. G., & Thomas, L. J. (2014). 'It was the straw that broke the camel's back': The estrangement backstories adult children tell about distancing themselves from their parents. *In Press*.

Schiffrin, H. H., Liss, M., Godfrey, H., & Erchull, M. J. (2015). Intensive parenting: Does it have the desired impact on child outcomes? *Journal of Child and Family Studies*, 24(8), 2322–2331.

Schut, H., & Stroebe, M. S. (2005). Interventions to enhance adaptation to bereavement. *Journal of Palliative Medicine*, 8(S1), S140–147.

Segrin, C., & Flora, J. (2005). *Family communication*. Mahwah, NJ: Lawrence Erlbaum Associates.

Shapiro, A. (2003). Later-life divorce and parent–adult child contact and proximity: A longitudinal analysis. *Journal of Family Issues*, 24(2), 264–285.

Shaver, P., Mikulincer, M., Lavy, S., & Cassidy, J. (2009). Understanding and altering hurt feelings: An attachment-theoretical perspective on the generation and regulation of emotions. In J. P. Vangelisti (Ed.), *Feeling hurt in close relationships* (pp. 92–120). Cambridge: Cambridge University Press.

Shaver, P. R., & Tancredy, C. M. (2001). Emotion, attachment and bereavement: A conceptual commentary. In M. S. Stroebe (Ed.), *Handbook of bereavement research: Consequences, coping and care* (pp. 63–88). Washington, DC: American Psychological Society.

Shear, M. K. (2015). Complicated grief. *The New England Journal of Medicine, 372*(2), 153–160.

Sheets, E. S., & Craighead, W. E. (2014). Comparing chronic interpersonal and noninterpersonal stress domains as predictors of depression recurrence in emerging adults. *Behaviour Research and Therapy, 63*, 36–42.

Short, P. (1996, November 26–29). *No-one to turn to: Estrangement and need in kinship economies.* Paper presented at the 5th Australian Family Research Conference, Brisbane, Australia.

Sichel, M. (2004). *Healing from family rifts: Ten steps to finding peace after being cut off from a family member.* New York: McGraw Hill.

Silverstein, M., & Bengston, V. L. (1997). Intergenerational solidarity and the structure of adult child–parent relationships in American families. *American Journal of Sociology, 103*(2), 429–460.

Sims, M., & Rofail, M. (2013). The experiences of grandparents who have limited or no contact with their grandchildren. *Journal of Aging Studies, 27*(4), 377–386.

Smart, C. (2011). Families, secrets and memories. *Sociology, 45*(4), 539–553.

Smart Richman, L., & Leary, M. R. (2009). Reactions to discrimination, stigmatization, ostracism, and other forms of interpersonal rejection: A multimotive model. *Psychological Review, 116*(2), 365–383.

Smedes, L. B. (1996). *Forgive and forget: Healing the hurts we don't deserve.* New York: Harper Collins.

Smith, J. B. (1998). The use of Bowen theory in clinical practice with the elderly. In P. Titelman (Ed.), *Clinical applications of Bowen family systems theory.* New York: The Haworth Press.

Smith, W. H. (2003). Emotional cutoff and family stability: Child abuse in family emotional process. In P. Titelman (Ed.), *Emotional cutoff: Bowen family systems theory perspectives* (pp. 351–378). New York: The Haworth Clinical Practice Press.

Spitzberg, B. H. (2009). Agression, hurt and violence in close relationships. In J. P. Vangelisti (Ed.), *Feeling hurt in close relationships* (pp. 209–232). Cambridge: Cambridge University Press.

Sprecher, S. (1992). Social exchange perspectives on the dissolution of close relationships. In T. L. Orbuch (Ed.), *Close relationship loss: Theoretical approaches.* New York: Springer-Verlag.

Stephens Leake, V. (2007). Personal, familial, and systemic factors associated with family belonging for stepfamily adolescents. *Journal of Divorce & Remarriage, 47*(1/2), 135–155.

Stewart, P. (2015). You moved up, did you forget us?: The influence of African American intra-familial social mobility on extended family relationships. *Journal of African American Studies, 19*(2), 214–232.

Stice, E., Ragan, J., & Randall, P. (2004). Prospective relations between social support and depression: Differential direction of effects for parent and peer support? *Journal of Abnormal Psychology, 113*(1), 155–159.

Stocker, C. M. (1994). Children's perceptions of relationships with siblings, friends, and mothers: Compensatory processes and links with adjustment. *Journal of Child Psychology and Psychiatry, 35*(8), 1447–1459.

Stroebe, M. S., & Schut, H. (1999). The dual process model of coping with bereavement: Rationale and description. *Death Studies, 23*(3), 197–224.

Stroebe, M. S., & Schut, H. (2008). The dual process model of coping with bereavement: Overview and update. *Grief Matters: The Australian Journal of Grief and Bereavement, 11*(1), 4–10.

Sucov, E. B. (2006). *Fragmented families: Patterns of estrangement and reconciliation.* Jerusalem: Southern Hills Press.

Sun, H., Tan, Q., Fan, G., & Tsui, Q. (2014). Different effects of rumination on depression: Key role of hope. *International Journal of Mental Health Systems*, 8(1), 53–58.

Sun, R., & Matthews, S. H. (2012). Lineage depth and family solidarity: Is there a link between them? *Journal of Intergenerational Relationships*, 10, 64–79.

Swendeman, D., Rotheram-Borus, M. J., Comulada, S., Weiss, R., & Ramos, M. E. (2006). Predictors of HIV related stigma among young people living with HIV. *Health Psychology*, 25(4), 501–509.

Szydlik, M. (2008). Intergenerational solidarity and conflict. *Journal of Comparative Family Studies*, 39(1), 97–118.

Thomm, K. (n/d). Enabling forgiveness and reconciliation in family therapy. Retrieved November 20, 2015, from www.familytherapy.org/documents/enabling_forgivess_ktom.pdf.

Titelman, P. (1987). The therapist's own family. In P. Titelman (Ed.), *The therapist's own family: toward the differentiation of self*. Northvale, NJ: Jason Aronson Inc.

Titelman, P. (2003a). Efforts to bridge secondary emotional cutoff. In P. Titelman (Ed.), *Emotional cutoff: Bowen family systems theory perspectives* (pp. 111–137). New York: The Haworth Clinical Practice Press.

Titelman, P. (2003b). Emotional cutoff in Bowen family systems theory: An overview. In P. Titelman (Ed.), *Emotional cutoff: Bowen family systems theory perspectives* (pp. 9–65). New York: The Haworth Clinical Practice Press.

Tomkinson, I. (2011). *Not like my mother: Becoming a sane parent after growing up in a crazy family*. Bloomington, IN: AuthorHouse (TM).

Tyler, J. M., & Feldman, R. S. (2004a). Cognitive demand and self-presentation efforts: The influence of situational importance and interaction goal. *Self and Identity*, 3(4), 364–377.

Tyler, J. M., & Feldman, R. S. (2004b). Truth, lies, and self-presentation: How gender and anticipated future interaction relate to deceptive behavior. *Journal of Applied Social Psychology*, 34(12), 2602–2615.

Tyler, J. M., & Feldman, R. S. (2005). Deflecting threat to one's image: Dissembling personal information as a self-presentation strategy. *Basic and Applied Social Psychology*, 27(4), 371–378.

Tyler, J. M., Feldman, R. S., & Reichert, A. (2006). The price of deceptive behavior: Disliking and lying to people who lie to us. *Journal of Experimental Social Psychology*, 42(1), 61–77.

Uchino, B. N., Cawthon, R. M., Smith, T. W., Light, K. C., McKenzie, J., Carlisle, M., Gunn, H., Birmingham, W., & Bowen, K. (2012). Social relationships and health: Is feeling positive, negative, or both (ambivalent) about your social ties related to telomeres? *Health Psychology*, 31(6), 789–796.

Uphold-Carrier, H., & Utz, R. (2012). Parental divorce among young and adult children: A long-term quantitative analysis of mental health and family solidarity. *Journal of Divorce & Remarriage*, 53(4), 247–266.

van der Sanden, R. L. M., Stutterheim, S. E., Pryor, J. B., Kok, G., & Bos, A. E. R. (2014). Coping with stigma by association and family burden among family members of people with mental illness. *The Journal of Nervous and Mental Disease*, 202(10), 710–717.

Vandevelde, L., & Miyahara, M. (2005). Impact of group rejections from a physical activity on physical self-esteem among university students. *Social Psychology of Education*, 8(1), 65–81.

Van Gaalen, R. I., & Dykstra, P. A. (2006). Solidarity and conflict between adult children and parents: A latent class analysis. *Journal of Marriage and Family*, 68(4), 947–960.

Van Ranst, N., Verschueren, K., & Marcoen, A. (1995). The meaning of grandparents as viewed by adolescent grandchildren: An empirical study in Belgium. *International Journal of Aging & Human Development*, 41(4), 311–324.

Voorpostel, M., van der Lippe, T., Dykstra, P. A., & Flap, H. (2007). Similar or different? The importance of similarities and differences for support between siblings. *Journal of Family Issues, 28*(8), 1026–1053.

Walen, H. R., & Lachman, M. E. (2000). Social support and strain from partner, family, and friends: Costs and benefits for men and women in adulthood. *Journal of Social and Personal Relationships, 17*(1), 5–30.

Walter, C. A., & McCoyd, J. L. M. (2009). *Grief and loss across the lifespan: A biopsychosocial perspective.* New York: Springer Publishing Company.

Watson, J. B. (2014). Bisexuality and family: Narratives of silence, solace, and strength. *Journal of GLBT Family Studies, 10*, 101–123.

Weigert, A. J., & Hastings, R. (1977). Identity loss, family, and social change. *American Journal of Sociology, 82*(6), 1171–1185.

Weinfield, N. S., Sroufe, L., & Egeland, B. (2000). Attachment from infancy to early adulthood in a high-risk sample: Continuity, discontinuity, and their correlates. *Child Development, 71*(3), 695–702.

Weiss, B., & Feldman, R. S. (2006). Looking good and lying to do it: Deception as an impression management strategy in job interviews. *Journal of Applied Social Psychology, 36*(4), 1070–1086.

Weiss, R. S. (2001). Grief, bonds, and relationships. In M. S. Stroebe (Ed.), *Handbook of bereavement research: Consequences, coping and care* (pp. 47–62). Washington, DC: American Psychological Society.

Werner, P., Mittleman, M. S., Goldstein, D., & Heinik, J. (2012). Family stigma and caregiver burden in Alzheimer's disease. *The Gerontologist, 52*(1), 89–97.

West, S. G., & Hatters Friedman, S. (2008). These boots are made for stalking: Characteristics of female stalkers. *Psychiatry, 5*(8), 37–42.

White, D. L., Walker, A. J., & Richards, L. N. (2008). Intergenerational family support following infant death. *International Journal of Aging Human Development, 67*(3), 187–208.

Widmer, E. D., & Weiss, C. C. (2000). Do older siblings make a difference? The effects of older sibling support and older sibling adjustment on the adjustment of socially disadvantaged adolescents. *Journal of Research on Adolescence, 10*(1), 1–27.

Williams, D., & Zadro, L. (2001). Ostracism: On being ignored, excluded and rejected. In M. R. Leary (Ed.), *Interpersonal rejection.* Oxford: Oxford University Press.

Williams, K. D., Forgas, J. P., Von Hippel, W., & Zadro, L. (2005). The social outcast: An overview. In K. D. Williams, J. P. Forgas & W. Von Hippel (Eds.), *The social outcast: Ostracism, social exclusion, rejection and bullying* (pp. 1–16). New York: Psychology Press.

Winters, K. C., Stinchfield, R. D., Lee, S., & Latimer, W. W. (2008). Interplay of psychosocial factors and the long-term course of adolescents with a substance use disorder. *Substance Abuse, 29*(2), 107–119.

Worthington, E. L. (Ed.). (1998). *Dimensions of forgiveness: Psychological research and theological perspectives.* Philadelphia: Templeton Foundation Press.

Worthington, E. L. (2006). *Forgiveness and reconciliation: Theory and application.* New York: Routledge.

Wright, H. N. (2006). *Recovering from losses in life.* Grand Rapids, MI: Revell.

Yalcin, I., & Malkoc, A. (2015). The relationship between meaning in life and subjective well-being: Forgiveness and hope as mediators. *Journal of Happiness Studies, 16*(4), 915–929.

Yoo, G., Park, G. H., & Jun, H. J. (2014). Early maladaptive schemas as predictors of interpersonal orientation and peer connectedness in university students. *Social Behaviour and Personality, 42*(8), 1377–1394.

Yorgason, J. B., Padilla-Walker, L., & Jackson, J. (2011). Nonresidential grandparents' emotional and financial involvement in relation to early adolescent grandchild outcomes. *Journal of Research on Adolescence, 21*(3), 552–558.

REFERENCES

Zadro, L. (2010). Silent rage: When being excluded and ignored leads to acts of aggression, vengeance, and/or self-harm. Retrieved September 3, 2015, from www.sydneysymposium. unsw.edu.au/2010/chapters/ZadroSSSP2010.pdf.

Zadro, L., Williams, K. D., & Richardson, R. (2005). Riding the 'O' train: Comparing the effects of ostracism and verbal dispute on targets and sources. *Group Processes and Intergroup Relations*, 8(2), 125–143.

Zhang, W. (2012). Negative social exchanges, acculturation-related factors, and mental health among Asian Americans. *Medical Sociology*, 6(2), 12–29.abandonment *see* absent estrangement

Index

Taylor & Francis eBooks

Helping you to choose the right eBooks for your Library

Add Routledge titles to your library's digital collection today. Taylor and Francis ebooks contains over 50,000 titles in the Humanities, Social Sciences, Behavioural Sciences, Built Environment and Law.

Choose from a range of subject packages or create your own!

Benefits for you

>> Free MARC records
>> COUNTER-compliant usage statistics
>> Flexible purchase and pricing options
>> All titles DRM-free.

Benefits for your user

>> Off-site, anytime access via Athens or referring URL
>> Print or copy pages or chapters
>> Full content search
>> Bookmark, highlight and annotate text
>> Access to thousands of pages of quality research at the click of a button.

eCollections – Choose from over 30 subject eCollections, including:

Archaeology	Language Learning
Architecture	Law
Asian Studies	Literature
Business & Management	Media & Communication
Classical Studies	Middle East Studies
Construction	Music
Creative & Media Arts	Philosophy
Criminology & Criminal Justice	Planning
Economics	Politics
Education	Psychology & Mental Health
Energy	Religion
Engineering	Security
English Language & Linguistics	Social Work
Environment & Sustainability	Sociology
Geography	Sport
Health Studies	Theatre & Performance
History	Tourism, Hospitality & Events

For more information, pricing enquiries or to order a free trial, please contact your local sales team: www.tandfebooks.com/page/sales